TESTAMENTS TO BALLYHOO! BACKSTAGE BIG TOP
What they're saying about Warren Nelson's new book.

W P Nelson proves again there's a sucker in every bookstore.
P.T. Barnum

Nelson raises the English language to new balconies. All the tent's his stage. Oh Warren Warren where art thou been?
Bill Shakespeare, best-selling author of *Romeo and Juliet, Hamlet,* etc...

Mr.Nelson distribulutes epiphanically, unleashiating his memorables very wary toungingly.
Danny Webster, author of *Webster's Dictionary*

I loved layin' back, smokin' some Leaves of Grass and reading this book.
Walt Whitman

I was wearing my blue suede shoes when I met Warren Nelson twice in Las Vegas in 1969 at the International Hotel while I was singing in the theatre next to his. I was hoping he'd remember me and so I'm more than a little bummed I never made it in the book. Maybe the next one.
Elvis Presley

When I polished off the Fifth, I passed out gently while reading this book.
L. van Beethoven, composer

From the moment I picked up your book until I laid it down, I was convulsed with laughter. Someday I intend to read it.
Groucho Marx

Warren Nelson and I have a common story. We both became real men while growing moustaches and chasing buffalo in the badlands of North Dakota. We're look-a-likes. This is a bully book! Bully bully! Wooly bully!
Teddy Roosevelt, 26th President of the United States

To Betty —

thank you!!

Ballyhoo!
BACKSTAGE BIG TOP

Tent Show *"Memorywars"*
of the Song and Chance Man

WARREN NELSON

SONG FARM PRESS

Washburn WI 54891

SONG FARM PRESS
PO Box 97
Washburn, WI 54891

This book is a work of memoirs. Any resemblance to actual persons, living or dead, events, or locales is entirely non-coincidental.

Library of Congress Cataloging-in Publication Data is Available
ISBN 978-0-615-48753-3

Publication of this book has been generously assisted by:
Pat and Judy Sebranek
Mary Rice

This publication is supported in part by a grant from the Chequamegon Bay Arts Council and the Wisconsin Arts Board with funds from the State of Wisconsin.

First Edition June 2011
Book design: Christine Engfer, Carolyn Sneed, Warren Nelson

Printed and bound in the U.S.A by
Worzalla Publishing
Stevens Point, Wisconsin 54481

WORKS OF WARREN NELSON

Warren Nelson Shows
   A Martin County Hornpipe
   Old Minnesota - Song of the North Star
   *Centennial Green: The Over and Understory of the U.S. Forest
      Service*
   The Yo Ho Buffalo Hour

Nelson-Ferris Concert Company Shows (Warren Nelson & Betty Ferris)
   Souvenir Views   *Riding the Wind*
   Whistle Comin' In   *Keeper of the Light*
   On the Velvet   *30th Star*

Museum Installations (Warren Nelson & Betty Ferris)
   Over to Old LaPointe
   Under the Upper Lake

Shows led by Warren in collaboration with other artists
   Dance of the Seasons   *Take It To The Lake*
   Wild River   *Earth to Wendell*
   Riverpants   *Showpants*

Recordings .. CD's and tapes
   Nellie's Folk   *A Martin County Hornpipe*
   Souvenir Views   *Riding the Wind*
   Take It To The Lake   *Whistle Comin' In*
   Keeper of the Light   *Green Room to Run*
   Live At Patsy's (2 volumes)   *30th Star*
   Song In Your Hat

DVD
   *Centennial Green with Milwaukee Public Television
      and the US Forest Service*

Television Shows
   Old Minnesota with Twin Cities Public Television

Books
   Ditch of Witches (with Karlyn Holman)
   Ballyhoo! Backstage Bigtop

UNDER OVER BESIDE AND AROUND THIS BOOK

My immeasurable thanks to my editors Carolyn Sneed and Christine Engfer who not only put their eagle eyes to the pages in grammar and content but pushed me along all the way, to Christine for formatting the script into book form, to Ruth Goetz for partnering in Warren Nelson Presents and sticking with me, to Betty Ferris for the great years in the joys and struggles of digging up new shows and for being at the center start and all along the evolution of BTC, to Mary Rice and her late great parents Bill and Betty Hulings for their confidence and long wide support, to the Blue Canvas Orchestra, Singers and Actors–Jack Gunderson, Bruce Burnside, Bruce Bowers, Sally Kessler, Tom Mitchell, Phil Anich, Ed Willet, Cheryl Leah, Severin Behnen, Randy Sabien, Liz Woodworth, Lisa McGinley, Mary Bondeson, Cal Aultman, Andy Dee and all the others I performed with–for the pleasure of standing stages with you from the Big Top to the touring halls and for all the laughs during rehearsals, to Mark McGinley, Andy Noyes and Andy Okey for long houred soundchecks and sending the noise out professionally under the canvas, to the late Noel Meyer for keeping the light first, to all the tech and backstage crews, especially Lisa Sandholm for roping me in (you will always be my stage manager), to Jerry Phillips for staging Gilbert and Sullivan and to Mary with love, to all BTC's Board of Directors, to the Board of Directors of Minnesota Shows, Inc. of Fairmont, to all the volunteers who worked the tent dream for free making it possible, to Paul Buckles and Jonathan Falconer, expert canvasmen, to Jerry and Carol Carlson for their partnering and friendship, to the concessions workers and bartenders working the hill, especially Kevin Smith and Deb Rusch (put it on my tab) to Corey Carlson for being the hippie, to Terry Meyer for knowing there's no business like show business, to Therene Gazdik for the years and years of hard work helping it all, to Mark and Elaine Frankart for friendship and dedication to the Big Top, to Kathy Moore for roping volunteers, to Patsy and Wayne Avery and all the gang down at Patsy's Bar for the years of stuffing brochures and putting up with me, to the Sons of Bunyan for their manly volunteerism, to Les and Oma Ferris for care-taking Medora and Rowan in the busy summers, to Dick and Ramona Thearin and their family for the soul saving getaway they offered me at Northland Lodge, to Don Funk for his support and sincere brotherhood, to Pat and Judy Sebranek for coming aboard and becoming close friends, to Norbert Blei for his brothership and writing inspiration, to Mason Williams, The Kingston Trio, John Stewart, John Hartford, The Smothers Brothers, The Chad Mitchell Trio, Tom Paxton, Glenn Yarbrough, Bob Gibson, Robert Bly, The Nitty Gritty Dirt Band for the pleasure of your company and for showing me the way, to Potts of Potts Inn, birthplace of Lost Nation, to Lake Superior, the greatest of the great Great Lakes, to David Obey, Wisconsin Congressional Representative, for the great support provided for our mission, to Bob Jauch our State Representative for understanding our dream, to State Representative Barb Linton for support and all the Madison good times, to Dominic Papatola for spreading the word, to Tony Judge for partnering with us in radio and touring, to Ernie and Myra Bliss my favorite house managers, to Don and Marlena Putnam, Ron and Ann Matta, Joe and Char Lambert for being there, to Gerry DePerry for spirit you've shared, to Kelly Randolph for visuals work in the early years, to Tom Rosen for the gifts of support, to Woody Woodward for keeping track, to Hank Cole for the early tent days and the Prairie Queen, to Jan Moran for your designing talent, to Don Albrecht for friendship and photos, to George Eggers for the same, to Bob Sneed for going along with the big doings, to Dennis McCann for inspiration, to Beth Hoff (Elizabeth Berg) for reading a few chapters and telling me I sound like me, to the BTC office staff for minding the store, to Christine Engfer for personal unending faith in me and formatting this book, to all the names I have forgotten here to thank, a standing ovation to you the audiences who gave and give us the reason to sing, to my late parents Alvin and Clestle Nelson, Dad who loved the hub bub of the Fairs and Mom the storyteller, to my children Medora and Rowan Nelson-Ferris who top the list.

And with a heavy heart to the late great Don Pavel, my sidekick music man for 38 unbelievable years before and during Chautauqua, and to the late Mark "Pete" Nelson who was not only my brother but the truest of pals and the nicest man I ever met.

And again and again to Carolyn Sneed who stood the pilothouse with me on the great ship Lake Superior Big Top Chautauqua for 23 years.

WPN

Lake Superior

BIG TOP
CHAUTAUQUA

1986 SUMMER SEASON

to the Tent

to my editors Carolyn Sneed and Christine Engfer

BALLYHOO BACKSTAGE BIGTOP

Table of Contents

FORWARD by Carolyn Sneed

My first introduction to Warren Nelson was in 1983, when he invited the Barbershop Octette I was singing in to perform in *Souvenir Views*, the historical musical he and Betty Ferris were creating about Washburn, Wisconsin, the small town we all call home. It was not long before I realized that Warren is a man of many ideas and they are all BIG. Big show, big cast, big idea, BIG TENT!

Over the next few years, we became friends and he began talking about his newest idea, a Chautauqua. For a while I wondered, "What is he talking about?" When I understood that he was imagining a big tent to be located at the foot of Mount Ashwabay, a ski hill about 3 miles from the city of Bayfield and its 600 people, where he and his cast of superb musicians would perform shows about the area, I said I would like to be part of it. At the time I was an elected supervisor on the Bayfield County Board, treasurer of the League of Women Voters, on the boards of several local performing arts organizations, and so, with my interests and experience in mind, I suggested that we might form a nonprofit organization of which I could be treasurer.

Then, in March of 1986, I met Betty Ferris at the Nelson-Ferris home and we drove to a County Unified Services meeting. When we returned, Warren met us, saying, "I went to Tom Lindsey's law office today where we drew up the papers for the corporation, Big Lake Chautauqua. Betty, you're president; Carolyn, you're secretary/treasurer; and Tom said he would be vice-president since a corporation must have three officers." From Warren's imagination, firm determination and leadership, the canvas tent show circus soon to be renamed Big Top Chautauqua, was born.

There was no prototype for what we were doing. In any forms we filled out, our category was always "other." We had many meetings where the topic of discussion centered around how to do this "big dang deal," as Warren called it. One thing that was always a great priority was support for the performers, to get more work and better pay for these extraordinary troupers. And, we were sure that this outdoor entertainment venue would be very good for our area, economically as well as spiritually. In the beginning, we received a few letters addressed simply to "The Magic" and the Post Office delivered them, correctly, to Big Top Chautauqua.

It was very satisfying that the educational value of the Nelson-Ferris historical musicals was widely recognized. To have history, environmental awareness and respect for all cultures presented with music, visuals and humor made the shows entertaining; and children and adults all expressed great enthusiasm for this avenue of learning. Schools across the region wanted the Big Top to come to them with these shows but few could afford what it cost to book our large ensemble. We all are indebted to our Congressman, Dave Obey, for grants that made those tours possible. State Senator Bob Jauch has also been a supporter from the earliest days, as were Governors Tommy Thompson and Jim Doyle.

We never doubted that the magic would continue, under canvas, at the base of the ski hill near Lake Superior. One of our guest artists remarked, on first seeing the tent and observing our operation, "This is genius." Warren's genius and intuition mixed with humor, energy and boundless work were the ingredients that led to this Wisconsin Treasure.

We gratefully acknowledge everyone who has played a role in the continuity of this magical community under canvas: performers, volunteers, staff, boards of directors, donors, businesses, audience members ...Thank you.

PREFACE

For 23 years I was the centerpole of the greatest venue in the history of the Universe, Lake Superior Big Top Chautauqua, being host of the stage shows and *Tent Show Radio*, creator and co-creator of the original musicals and resident writer "Man Of The Cloth." But the story of its founding in 1986 and the dream is much older than that.

As a young lad I ran county fairs in southern Minnesota thanks to my late great dad, Alvin Nelson, who as a dairy equipment salesman helped set up the dairy barns for the week-run fairs. Those were the Martin County Free Gate Fair, the Faribault County Fair and the Jackson County Fair. In the summer glory we'd arrive on setup day at dawn and stay the week. While he dealt in his friendly manner with the farmers and fairgoers, I would pass out brochures for him and he'd give me pocket money to wander the days and nights in the bright carny lights from morning to closing time.

It was then and there in those years that I learned to love the bright lights of fun and the smell of canvas and sawdust. It was a yearly visit we also paid to the Minnesota State Fair, the grandest of all delights.

Those transfusions of pure joy never left my blood in the years after, planting the promise that one day I would have a tent show or run away with a carnival or the circus. I woke up as a teenager to the gift of being born a songwriter/ entertainer, quit college and ran away with show groups I led in the 60s and early 70s, traveling the U.S.

As for learning the art of entertaining and storytelling, I give my mom, Clestle Lorraine Gillespie Nelson, the tip of the hat of my career. She was a natural.

In the years of my kidhood, Gillespie's Beauty Shop in Fairmont, Minnesota was a henhouse of chatter and laughter. It was a family business with my grandmother, Effie, my aunt Velma and mom cackling away all day. It was a school of comedy for me. Little wonder I love the stage.

It was a music circus I was given the opportunity to raise in the air on Mt. Ashwabay south of Bayfield, Wisconsin. Reading of the great tradition of tent shows, I came across the story of Chautauquas, a grand idea founded in New York in 1874 as a summer gathering place for adult education. The idea led to the founding of regional Chautauquas. They inspired the birth of circuit chautauquas which spread all across America from 1905 into the 1920s, bringing "Culture Under Canvas" to rural people. Theodore Roosevelt called Chautauqua "The most American thing in America."

This is my personal scrapbook/portrait/history of Big Top Chautauqua from backstage and backrooms. It's rare for anyone to be given the chance to raise a personal dream on such a scale. It started big and got bigger. BTC is now known near and far as a very rare, special venue. From the first night it's been a daring magical journey, with struggles in joy and all it takes to raise a dream. I'm taking the high road in this book of memorywars leaving the hard times and trouble in the dust.

This effort is the second half of a longer work—an autobiography to be entitled *Song and Chance Man, The Memorywars of Warren Nelson*. My story as a writer and entertainer began in 19 B.C. (Before Chautauqua). Many tales from those years are told of lightly herein.

The launching and sailing of the good ship Big Top Chautauqua has taken an enormous crew from staff to board to performers to volunteers to keep it afloat. To all my partners over the years in every aspect of putting on the show, I give a standing ovation. To every audience member who has ever attended and come to love the tent, I say BALLYHOO!

For my time at the captain's wheel in the pilothouse and on stage as MC, I am forever unspeakably grateful. Ladies and Gentlemen, Wide Awake Citizens, welcome to Lake Superior Big Top Chautauqua, The Carnegie Hall of Tent Shows. And welcome backstage.

Warren Nelson
Sioux River Song Farm
November 26, 2010

B. C.
Before
Chautauqua

(Big Top Chautauqua...that is)

It is to a poet a thing of awe
to find that his story is true.
Isak Dinesen *The Diver*

THE HARBOR THEATRE

I tell this story here, which is outside the Big Top ring, because it's a Bayfield tale and if things had worked out, in the end perhaps there never would have been a Big Top Chautauqua. In fact, I'm certain of it.

The year is 1982 and The Lost Nation String Band is gigging summer Sunday nights at Bate's Bar. Those were the days live music had only a few homes on the peninsula and in Bayfield, Bates Bar quickly became a hot spot. This classy bar was jumping every week. Mary Rice remodeled it, setting it up with a stage and dance floor.

It's Sunday night after the gig; Don Pavel, Jack Gunderson and I finish packing up. We are walking down Rittenhouse Avenue with the two bartenders and a couple employees to Goldman's Cafe. Unbelievably, it's open 24 hours, a musician's dream. It is now well past 2:00 a.m.

We pass the Harbor Theatre which was built in 1942 as a movie house, one-floor seating of around a hundred. On the billboard out front is notice that *Song Of The South*, the Uncle Remus animated Walt Disney movie, is now playing—two shows Friday and Saturday, 7 and 9. "Zip-a-Dee-Doo-Dah" I'm thinking as I'm walking across the street, "I'd love to see that again." We are more than a little beered up and put in our order, Don as always asking for gravy on his French fries.

"Hey" I ask, "who owns the theatre? I want to see the movie now." One of the employees answers, "Grub Wachsmuth owns it and he loves to make a buck." Hence the nickname, I guess. I put a twenty-dollar bill on the table. "Who's in? Maybe he'll do it." It is now a little past 3 a.m. The bills start piling at the center of the table. I throw in 10 more. We're up to 78 dollars and now eighty, now 84. Laughter abounds.

"Where's he live?" "He lives two blocks up just half a block from Bates." "I'll call him, where's the nearest phone?" "There's a phone booth down by the bank."

So six or seven of us are parading down the middle of the street singing "Zippity Do Dah...Zippity Aye...my oh my what a wonderful day." I scan down to the W's and find Wachsmuth, Larry. "That's him." I drop the 35 cents in. It's now twenty to 4. A woman answers in half a voice, "Hello." "Hello, this is Warren Nelson, is Grub there?" "You mean Brub?" Uh oh. "Yes, Brub." "Just a minute." Why in this world didn't she hang up?

Thirty seconds travels by, I'm fearless. "Hello." "Brub, this is Warren Nelson; this is not a crank call, let me cut to the quick." A couple unawake sighs breathe into the phone. "Brub, I have a small crowd here who wants to see *Song Of The South*." Silence. "Mr. Wachsmuth, I know this sounds insane but we would like to see it now." Silence. "We have 84 dollars and would love if you'd open the theatre and play the movie. Brub, you know it's Bayfield's 125th anniversary as a town and something like this happens only every 125 years or so." Silence. "Now?" "Now. We really want to see it." Longer silence. "Give me fifteen minutes." "Thanks Brub, I really mean that."

To make a short story longer, Brub tells us to meet him at the corner where he lives. We need beer. One of the bartenders opens Bates and we take a case of bottles in hand walking towards the corner of Brub's house. Not a car on the street, houses up and down the hill are all dark, the streetlights swirling with insects. Zippity Doo Dah.

Fifteen minutes later Brub Wachsmuth, a tall lanky man I instantly like, walks out his front door and crosses the street to meet us. "Brub, I'm Warren, this is stupendous." He is not smiling, not frowning as he looks at me and says, "no popcorn." We follow him to the theatre respectfully grinning.

A click of the key and the door opens into the small lobby. Brub turns on the lights, shakes his head, and gives a little laugh. I hand him the 84 in cash. He takes the stairs to the projection booth and we stagger a bit down the aisle to the front row, reaching for beers. One of the highlights of my life is here, I'm thinking, one of those once-in-a-lifetimes. A grand spontaneous idea coming to immediate life.

Brub is loading the movie, I see him through the little window up above. "Thanks Brub," I yell from the front row. We spread out in the seats for our private showing. A sudden light swirls the room, the flashlight probe from Bayfield's woman police officer. She asks sharply from the back of the house, "What's going on here?" I turn and lift a beer towards her. "We're waiting for the feature!" Pause. "Brub, are you up there?" "Yeah." "You're welcome to stay officer," I say. She leaves.

It's now precisely 4 a.m. The lights dim and the sound of the 35-millimeter film rolls from on high. Cartoons and all. I love this movie, not having seen it for years. No popcorn.

It's now 6 a.m. The show is over and we walk out to the new Bayfield morning after effusively thanking Brub. One car in sight. The sun is rising over Madeline Island, the birds are whistling, a mist lifting off the lake. We walk to the end of the city dock, stand silently a minute, say so longs and walk to our cars.

This story hangs both the happy and sad masks of theatre on the walls of my memory. The punch line herein is a couple years away.

Before the next Applefest, I call Brub and inquire about renting the theatre for Saturday and Sunday. We, The Lost Nation String Band, had the idea to do a vaudeville schedule of shows all day, 30 minutes each, four bucks a ticket, a dollar per man. We were out on the street barking before the shows, me doing my grandstand ballyhooing. In the two days we had a total of 13 customers adding up to 52 bucks, 13 bucks apiece. We laughed and played music while outside 20,000 people strolled the streets to eat. They would pack around us while we played a tune or two on the sidewalk and then not follow us in.

I kept in touch with Brub over the next couple years. He said the place was for sale as he would be retiring as an insurance salesman and moving to California. Immediately I remembered the look of the theatre. It was the style of the forties, the movie houses I grew up with. The seats hadn't been changed. The old time movie lobby lit up with the popcorn machine, the glass counter full of Red Hots, Snicker's bars, Milk Duds. "I wish I wish I could buy it Brub." He believed, "We could do it on a land contract." "I want this to happen Brub. I've always wanted my own theatre/concert hall. Talk to you later."

This was before *Riding The Wind*, before Chautauqua. No moola lying around to even make the down payment. What would I tell the bank? "I'm making squat playing in a band here and there, but I know it'll work, will you lend me a large cup of money?"

It wasn't long after that my friend, the very talented artist Diana Randolph, came up with the idea of a multimedia show to be called *Dance of the Seasons*. She called Sally Kessler and me and thanks to an Arts Board grant it was a go to create and play. We chose the Harbor Theatre for the venue. The spring equinox was opening night. A perfect snowfall whitened Bayfield. Our cast included Lost Nation, Steve and Jeff Eckels, and a circle of local talented dancers and singers.

Rehearsals ran for several nights before the two-night stand and in that time I fell head over dreams in love with the Harbor. I began to feel at home.

A very lively acquaintance of mine, Bayfielder Susan Soucheray, took note of the possibilities of what the Harbor could be and began a campaign to save it. Susan, bless her memory, was a pistol. She enthusiastically sprayed the idea around the Bayfield peninsula. The buttons sold to start the funding effort read "Keep The Harbor Lights Lit." Susan and her husband, Dr. Phil, hosted a kickoff party, all this lighting my eyes toward the possibility. I wish now I had chased that dream and roped it. Why in the year 1984 I didn't sell house and home to make it happen is one of the great regrets, one of the unanswerable questions of my life. No moola.

It was a gallant effort. A few concerts were booked to show the showplace. They were well attended but eventually, with not enough dedicated financial support, the candle went out.

What totally took my attention away from the Harbor, beginning in January 1985, was the commission given to Betty Ferris and me to create *Riding The Wind*.

It was a Thursday night in spring; I got a call out of the blue from Brub who had made his move to California. "Warren, I've had an offer on the Harbor Theatre." I could tell in his voice this was his last call. He wanted me to have it. It would stay a theatre. He must have been thinking of his father who had built it 40 years before. He must have been remembering all. "Warren, I've been offered $42,000 for it." Pause. Long pause. His voice was breaking. "Warren, I'd sell it to you for 30,000 on a land contract. Maybe 28." Pause. Longer pause. My heart was breaking. Pause. It was like getting word that a family member who wasn't yet born had just died. Pause. I couldn't get my tongue to say it. Pause.

"Brub, I can't do it." Brub was sniffling as he said, " OK." He understood all I was feeling. He wished me well. "Take care, Warren." "Thank you Brub." "I hope I see you again sometime." "So long." "So long."

At least I didn't cry. I wept.

LOST NATION—SURVIVORS OF THE NORTH

The history of the band's founding and moving up north is told in this book in the portraits of the members: Don Pavel, Cal Aultman, Jack Gunderson, Bruce Burnside, Tom Mitchell and yours truly. Cal, Jack and Tom are still active in Chautauqua. Don, Cal and I are the originals. Jack replaced Cal. Tom replaced me.

Gradually after moving up north in the fall of 1979, we began to find more gigs, especially in the summers—lots of bars, clubs and resorts, private parties and a few theatre concerts. I was a full time member for seven and a half years. Those were great years for me, great friendships, a million laughs, and a repertoire of songs that we knew so well, allowing us to play on the fly. I miss the four-hour bar gigs. Many nights we were just getting warmed up when it was time to quit. We made new friends being out and about making music. Many of those new friends continued to follow the band at the Big Top and elsewhere. From the times I stood behind the mic, my memory still swallows shots of Lost Nation moments, gigs, jokes, travel, good times.

Ladies and gentlemen, friends and neighbors, here are some side trips and odd hours from the side-winding history of The Lost Nation String Band, from the days I traveled with them.

The Lost Nation String Band LP

Back before iPods, back before CDs, back before cassettes, back when Lost Nation recorded an LP in 1981. We were playing regularly and feeling great about our music when we decided to record an album. Burnside knew of Marv Nonn, a Wisconsin Public Radio engineer, who had a studio in Cross Plains, Wisconsin. We rehearsed with unusual attention, bought new strings and headed down with the feeling we were ready to have fun making a record.

Marv Nonn was an extremely nice guy, with an extreme amount of engineering talent, with an extreme sense of efficiency and order, and with an extremely antiseptic beautiful studio. We walked in greeted by a "Please Remove Your Shoes." There wasn't a piece of lint on the rug, not the slightest smear on the studio glass, not a mark on the walls and a "Please do not touch" sign on the perfectly polished black grand piano. How does one play a piano you can't touch? We didn't take note at first, walking in, but during the tuning up I began to look around and felt a little too clean and nervous.

The studio recording process is nerve-wracking no matter how relaxed you are going in. You shake your hands, wag your head to keep loose, tune up and go silent waiting for the sign from the engineer in the booth to give the finger-pointing signal. The tempo is mouth counted silently and the intro to the song you've played a thousand times crashes.

First I blow it. On the next take Burnside blows it. Finally we're off. The third take of the first song is pronounced a take. Eleven more to go in one night. Incredible. It's not done like that anymore. There's something about getting a song down without multi-tracking. "Everybody all together now!" We were stiff, but eager to be ourselves. We tried to joke it off. We cut two more in several takes. We hit a snag. Jack told a new joke I can't repeat and from then on it was all down-hillbilly from there. Belly laughs. The silence between was not freezing us up. We became ourselves. Don wished he had brought a bucket of dirt to set on the rug. Either he wished so or he did, my memorywars fail me.

The freezing-up in the studio is common. Leo Kottke has recorded numerous albums. He played the Big Top many times and at first let us record him live for *Tent Show Radio*. I think the first time he forgot he was being recorded since permission would have been signed off months before. The last time he played when I was working the tent and *Tent Show Radio*, he said no to our recording request. His words–"I can't be myself in a live recorded show. I choke when the red light goes on."

In our session we found our sound and finished the recording. The title of the record is simply *Lost Nation String Band*. The cover is a painting of a Dodo bird, our new Lost Nation logo. It was painted by our friend Ken Frazier. The back cover was a photo of the Lake Superior beach at the Sioux River mouth, taken by Don Albrecht. I still love the record. It was re-released on CD a few years back but is now out of print. I hope we can print it again.

The Famous Bottle of Yugoslavian Plum Brandy

In all my years in Lost Nation, I only knew Burnside to buy one bottle of booze.

It was a purple hazy liquid that was soon matched by the color of the cheeks of anyone who would dare to drink it. Burnside took a sip or two and passed it to Don, Jack and me. We each had a shot and gave up. The bottle bounced and rolled around Stub, our bus, for over a year, maybe two, until one night in Fairmont, Minnesota we were invited for a private very late showing of a movie at the Fairmont Opera House after a club gig at the Redwood Lounge. Wanting a bump of anything available, we remembered the Plum Brandy and fetched it. Much laughter abounded as we passed it slowly around. We felt very Yugoslavian. Don took the final brave gulp, and on the way to our cars we parked the famous bottle in the narrow alleyway between the theatre and a flower shop. Two years later we were booked again at the Opera House and there was much mentioning on the drive down and soon great anticipation of whether or not the famous bottle would yet be standing in the alley. There it was, a lone ranger. It could still be there for all I know. I know it's still in the alley of my memory. It should have been enough to make me stop drinking at the time but I didn't. I recommend Yugoslavian Plum Brandy to any of you with a drinking problem; declare it your only alcohol and you'll never take another drink.

Survivors of the North Woods & The Sport Show Mini Tour

In 1981 Jack Gillespie, a Minneapolis friend of Jack and mine, called Jack to book Lost Nation on a sports show tour with appearances in Duluth, Minnesota, Cedar Rapids, Iowa and Omaha, Nebraska. We had known Gillespie since the 1960s. He was a great trumpet player, frequently playing in big show orchestras in Las Vegas as well as convention and club dates in the Cities. We were good pals with Jack G. We enthusiastically accepted his proposal. The sport shows were good paying gigs and got us back on the road; they ran three days in each city.

Our vehicle then was a used, small, retired Air Force bus we named Stub. It is legendary in Lost Nation history, used for gigs all over northern Wisconsin. It was a twenty-seater with plenty of room to spread out and occasionally invite friends and fans on board. Don was the mechanical keeper of the bus but we all drove it. Don tuned it up for the big tour and we were off.

Gillespie wanted us to have a new PR photo taken for the

tour so he came up and found an old abandoned hay wagon at the edge of the woods out along County C for the photo. The advertising for the entertainment for the sports show featured us as The Lost Nation String Band: Survivors of the North Woods. Wow!

The survivors of the North Woods photo was meant, I guess, to be attractive to the outdoors men and women attending the shows, make us look like we were living in the wild, eating wolves and squirrels, hibernating together all winter in Forest Service caves, coming out for a couple weeks to ravish towns and scare folks. Then we were to play fishing songs on the sports show circuit and return to the woods to root-eating and stabbing things. Don had a beard that looked like it had been glued on his face, Burnside looked like Burnside, Jack was bearded and gruff. I looked like a guy in a wool shirt that just renewed his cable TV but needed a haircut.

We were not the only entertainment. Closing the show every night was Victor The Rasslin' Bear. Victor was an enormous Alaskan brown bear. Sometime before Victor took the stage, a volunteer out of the crowd had been chosen to rassle Victor. Victor's handler led Victor up the steps to the stage; Victor took his seat, and the handler unleashed him. First Victor chugged a Coke out of the bottle holding it with his two paws, his tongue licking it while his handler gestured to the crowd for applause. Then the MC whipped up the crowd with some Star Wars type recorded music introducing Victor and the volunteer rassler with great aplomb. "In this corner, weighing 763 pounds, undefeated champion, Victor The Rasslin' Bear. In this corner, weighing 235 pounds, from Hibbing, Minnesota, Bob 'The Bruiser' Kaworski," or some such name. Victor stood up, his opponent taking a Verne Gagne stance and showing his muscle. Victor stepped towards his man. The man stepped hesitantly towards Victor. The handler acted as referee. Victor put his paws on the man's shoulders and threw him to the floor, the referee slapping the mat and counting to three. Only once, I remember it was in Omaha, did the opponent last more than 30 seconds and that included the old run around the ring trick, showing off. We all gave the loser a great round of applause and the handler led Victor off the stage. "The handler! Man where have I seen him?" Don said to me, "He looks familiar." We could tell he had been a wrestler; he had the moves. He was maybe 60, had lost several teeth, was mostly bald with a stringy ring of long, graying blonde hair, muscular and keeping his weight. "Man, he looks familiar." A light came on in Don. "My God, it's Gorgeous George!" Gorgeous George, the old golden hero of professional wrestling in the 1960s, dreaded adversary of World Champion Verne Gagne, pin up boy for shrieking rasslin'-fan women. We never did let on we knew who he was. He wasn't gorgeous anymore.

Fred Scherer's Lumberjack Show from Hayward appeared every night to complete the big show with a chainsaw contest and tree climbers racing to the top of a tall red pine tree that had been hauled in.

Stub ran great for the tour getting us home safely from the grand two week adventure. As soon as we touched ground in Bayfield County, we ripped off our clothes and went running in all directions into The National Forest, howling, looking for a buck to butt heads with and stabbing things. Lost Nation—Survivors of the North Woods!

The Wagon Train

I loved Wally Gunderson, Jack's dad, whom I met first in

1967 in Minneapolis. Since Jack and I played together off and on for 41 years, I'd see Wally and his wife Jeannie regularly in places we were playing, including of course, Lost Nation gigs. Wally was a working man. He had a cowboy's weathered face from years working construction on the road. He was a crafty left-handed baseball pitcher in his younger days so we were never shy of conversation about baseball, music or anything else. When I heard through Jack that Wally wanted us to play for a wagon train that was traveling fields in northwestern Minnesota, I was ready to saddle up. Wally had a team and wagon in the train and furnished a fold-up camper for bedding down after a night's roundup of songs.

I dragged out my old Justin cowboy boots, found my summer straw, bought a western shirt to cowboy up. The wagon train broke camp a little after dawn and clopped to the next previously determined campsite. We played on a haywagon in the late afternoon as the teams were being unhitched, watered and fed and as the chuck wagon cook was opening the bean cans. I believe Wally was the trail boss. We might have played only one night, I can't remember. It was a riot. We worked hard putting together a medley of Sons Of The Pioneer tunes, each of us choosing a song. Mine was "Ghost Riders In The Sky." Jack put his golden throat to the lead of "Tumblin' Tumbleweeds" while Don and I crooned traditional harmony with plenty of ooohs. Burnside sang "Back In The Saddle Again" and Don took the lead on "Cool Water."

We traveled the next day with the wagon train. Mid-afternoon we noticed the Minnesota sky was darkening in the Southwest. Wally was guessing how long it would be before the front hit us. It looked more ominous by the hour. Wally called for camp, for the wagons to circle and tie up to ride out the storm. It blew in fast with hard rain and high prairie winds. Rating a serious summer storm, I'd give it a rating of 8 1/2 out of ten. The air had the tornado feel. I watched it from the fold out camper set up in the shelter of a grove. Jack rode out the storm for over two hours in the porta-potty. Ride 'em Jack, stay in the saddle. Yippie ki yo ki-a!

Cryin' Ed

Let's face it. Bands booked in a bar are there to play music, attract and keep a crowd, but foremost to sell booze so the bar owner can make a buck as well as pay the band. That's why you don't say, "No thanks" when someone offers to buy you a drink.

"Can I buy you another?" "Of course." Let's face it; that's why bar musicians often end up in trouble with booze. Just ask me. We played a Saturday night in a resort bar somewhere on a lake near Phillips, Wisconsin and the small crowd was a disappointment. We were probably getting three hundred bucks for the gig. The owner/bartender was a wispy fellow, nice enough. I loved the old timey resort with its little half-log cabins, docks and boats for rent. We played well but to very few customers. Came the time when all was packed up to approach the owner for our pay.

Ed stood silently behind the bar as I approached him. It was always my job to grab the money at the end of the night. Don, Burnside and Jack came over as Ed offered us a nightcap. We were staying in the cabins so no sweat on the driving. "You guys are good," said Ed. "Thanks Ed," I said. "Sorry it didn't draw like we hoped." "Yeah, there was a big wedding tonight in town," said Ed. "Oh, that'll affect it," I replied. Ed asked if we wanted another drink. "Yeah, thanks. Could we get paid Ed, Burnside's driving home."

Ed went droopy-legged to the till and came back with a

stack of bills, lots of ones.

"Was that three hundred?" "That's right Ed." "Business has really been down lately." "It'll get better, Ed, when summer is in full gear." Ed began counting, "I barely have enough here I think." Ed's face was sad, I was suddenly sad. Did his wife just leave him?

"What if I gave you two fifty...?" "Sorry Ed." Ed counted out the three bills slowly, his face lowering almost to the bar top. He looked like he was going to cry. I never liked it when the bar didn't make out, but it was our only seventy-five bucks for the week. Ed paid.

I looked back to wave at Ed; he gave me an Emmet Kelley look. I'm a bit sad writing this.

The next morning, Don and I took out a boat with a five horse to troll half the day away. There were a dozen other boats on the lake. From every other boat people were waving excitedly at us. Wow, some really friendly people around here. Wave, wave, more waving. We waved and waved back. When we docked two hours later (no fish), Ed was there. "There is no trolling on this lake," Ed said.

IRS Names

Being paid in cash is the musician's wish. When you're making about $4-5000 dollars a year, I'm afraid to say it, but self-employment income tax tends to skip one's mind. We'd be paid by check half the time. The bar owner would say, "Who do I make the check out to?" "Wayne Nielsen, yeah Wayne Nielsen, that's my name, Nielsen with an e." I'd endorse the check and be handed cash. Thus Lost Nation obtained IRS names. Don Pavel *Dug Shovel*, Bruce Burnside *Bobby Fireside*, Jack Gunderson *Ralph Cumbersome*. FYI those names still hold backstage but not with the IRS.

Moose Jaw Lodge

Moose Jaw Lodge goes to the top of Lost Nation's venues of the past. For two summers (or was it three) we played nearly every Friday and Saturday night in the dining room of the bar/lodge. Located on highway 70 on Round Lake, Moose Jaw (it's still there) is an antique resort, a throwback to earlier Wisconsin rough road days. These older resorts are getting rare. Ken and Sue Head had taken on an incredible project putting the Lodge and cabins back in shipshape. We set up in front of the fireplace, the audience seated at tables with a great view of Round Lake and the huge white pines surrounding it. Ken and Sue had a second floor in the Lodge with rooms that hadn't yet been remodeled. We happily stayed there. We became more of a band at Moose Jaw; having the regular work two nights in a row greases the fingers and loosens the vocal cords. I miss that time. I stopped there three years ago just to know if it was still standing, It's been remodeled a bit but looking good.

Moose Jaw was the place for our famous tabs. We were making fifty bucks a night. Ken let us run a tab for the weekend, dinners (prime rib) and drinks (top shelf). Sunday mornings checking out we'd settle up with Ken. I recall one Sunday: "Ken, thanks again man. What's my tab?" "You owe me six bucks, Warren."

4 B.C. The Beach Club

It was always a fabulous experience to travel over big water and get to perform in a foreign country and so, in the early 1980s, when we found ourselves booked on Madeline Island at the Beach Club, we posed for passports and with great excitement were ferried over. I knew they'd be checking for fruit and other illegal things at the LaPointe dock so I traveled light with just a satchel and my guitar.

My favorite Bayfield-Madeline ferry boat was and always will be the Gar-How. She was a big classy hunk of steel with a classic pilot house over her deck. On subsequent trips, I'd let the Nichevo go and wait for the Gar-How's run. It was an incredible 22 minute voyage. I took lots of pictures and am not afraid to admit that I was a little nervous the first time I landed on foreign soil, wondering how I would be accepted by the people on the Island. I knew the language and that helped immensely. From the very first moment I stepped ashore I could tell the Islanders and we Mainlanders had a lot in common. They were people just like us. Almost.

The Beach Club ran live entertainment on Friday and Saturday nights. They were joyous four-set gigs for us. We were the house band for a couple of summers. Don brought up again his old adage for musicians, "For the best times ever, play where they play." That translates into, "Where the tourists are, happiness abounds; and seek ye gigs where they abound."

Out the window just before closing time we could see the ferry boat leaving for Bayfield for the last trip back. Peppermint Patty let us bunk at her house just up the road whenever we wanted. A few times we slept on the Beach Club's roof. One night Don and I decided to sleep on the Gar-How's second deck. We knew it would be the first boat back over and we needed to return to the mainland early. Footsteps pounding on the deck just after dawn woke us up and we hurried to put our pants on. Don's keys fell out of his pants pocket, clanking on the deck. Someone was climbing the steps. We were found out. It was our friend Sherman, the Captain. "Oh, it's you guys." When Sherman came around to sell tickets he looked at us and said, "If you guys are that hard up, you're riding for free."

The old musician's hunger pains always hit while tearing down. We were left alone in The Beach Club to close up one night. Over my career as bandleader, I always took it upon myself to feed the band after the shows whenever possible. I'm remembering one night in 1971 in Chicago when I courageously entered the main kitchen of the fancy pants downtown million-dollar hotel and fried up some egg sandwiches for my friends in The 10th Story Window. The coolers at the Beach Club were open and showed bread, cheeses, sliced ham, pickles, the works. We ate well after packing up. The next Friday when we were left alone to tear down there were padlocks on the coolers.

In Closing

Tom Mitchell replaced me in 1985, adding percussion and a perfect personality fit. Lost Nation played an annual concert at the Big Top from the beginning year 1986 through 2007, the summer before Don died. They were reunion concerts for Lost Nation's legion of fans who came in from the hinterlands. It was always a great pleasure for me to be invited to join the group again onstage. In one of the years, they decided to mimic a Lost Nation rehearsal which always happens around a table. So, they sat around a table and did the concert. The only difference that I could see was that they actually played some music. The Lost Nation four-hour rehearsals were famous for three and a half hours of talk with a couple tunes thrown in. Don, Jack, Bruce, and Tom recorded two live CDs from the tent.

With the passing of Don, The Lost Nation String Band era seems to be over. I had the greatest times of my life in and out of this outfit of friends. To Don, Cal, Burnside, Jack and Tom– thanks. Thanks again.

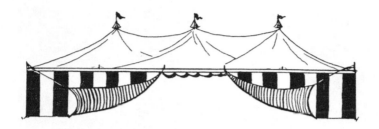

Traditional Chautauquas

People like to congregate on a summer evening. I hope the time may come when public-spirited citizens...may, in the manner of Chautauqua, combine music, the theatre, popular entertainment, with educational, scientific, religious and other forms of discussion into one great program of summer delight. Then the Chautauqua, as we knew it, would live again!

Charles Horner
Co-founder of circuit Chautauqua

EVENING AT CHAUTAUQUA

Long ago before the radio
The automobile was new
There wasn't much to do in this one-horse town I grew up next to
Except work off some shoe leather

Then a little after nineteen five
Those long green summers came alive
For one grand week a year
Chautauqua's big top rose in the air

We got up before the sun and did the chores
Dressed in our Sunday duds and piled in the family Ford
Drove the dusty roads into town
Off to the Chautauqua grounds

We set up our camp for the week
A chance to meet your neighbors and make new friends
Didn't have to say goodbye at the end
Say I'll meet you next year when Chautauqua comes back again

We never seen such drama
We never heard such music played
The singers were all so professional
Shoulda heard those speeches those speakers made

We sat there day and night, night and day
We went every afternoon to every matinee
We sat up straight and paid attention
And fooled around the Chautauqua grounds

Evening at Chautauqua
The old canvas tent show stage
The most American thing in America
Until a new age turned its page
Evening at Chautauqua over the Midwest up and down

Twenty years the big tops travelin'
Twenty years the big tops travelin'
Twenty years the big tops travelin'
To the groves of your hometown
wn

THE WORD CHAUTAUQUA

The most common meaning I have read of the word Chautauqua is "bag tied in the middle with a string." Or consider "two moccasins tied together." Or "jumping fish." It's an Iroquois word of the Senecas who homed on the shores of a lake in what is now Upper New York State. That sheet of water is now Lake Chautauqua. It's a long lake that narrows in the middle, hence the tied bag image. Another translation I've found is "summer tent show nonprofit theatre at Mt. Ashwabay where great shows are presented at 8:15 and where they sell tickets and try to make a profit."

CHAUTAUQUA HISTORIES

The histories of Chautauquas in America are comprised of three separate movements. The first being the Chautauqua Institution, the second being the establishment of regional Chautauquas, the third being the circuit Chautauquas.

In1874 inventor Lewis Miller and Methodist Bishop John Heyl Vincent established a camp for Sunday school teachers on the shores of Lake Chautauqua. Cottages and camp platforms were built along with classroom buildings and a pavilion. The seminars were enhanced with music, plays and forums on the issues of the day. The idea spread quickly throughout the United States. Reading circles were formed in communities, discussion groups similar to the old Lyceums. The Chautauqua Literary and Scientific Circle, the world's oldest book club, was established by Vincent in 1878. From the Chautauqua catalogue, the latest books were mailed out to adults hungry for continued education.

Soon regional Chautauquas were established, permanent sites for the summer programs erected. Many are still standing, two of the most notable being The Lakeside Chautauqua in Ohio and The Boulder Chautauqua in Colorado. Out of the success of these came the circuits.

The circuit Chautauquas in America and Canada, which began in 1905, lasted until the late 1920s. When radio began to come into the living rooms of the masses, making professional entertainment a stay-at-home experience, the Chautauquas began to close shop. Until Edison invented the recording process on cylinders in the late 19th century, all music and performance was live. Would have been a great time to be alive if you were a singer. Everybody had to come to you.

As for the first first in licensed radio broadcasting in the United States, KDKA in Pittsburgh is usually attributed the honor, having gone on the air in 1920. The University of Wisconsin's WHA, however, can legitimately claim to be the nation's oldest continuing broadcasting radio station. On February 17, 1919, station 9XM in Madison amplified the human voice to the public at large for the first time. There was the beginning of Wisconsin Public Radio. Hey, we're not just famous for cheese and for the fact that the cow was invented in Wisconsin in 1848 during the first year of statehood.

Except by train, travel for the common folk was difficult and tedious by horse and buggy. The newfangled automobiles might drive off at an exciting 20 miles per hour, but it would be all over rough roads, some of them barely better than trails. Tent Chautauquas appeared in over 10,000 communities.

Forty-five million Americans experienced the phenomena. The king of the circuit orators was politician William Jennings Bryan known as "The Great Commoner." Bryan was a liberal Democrat who was the enemy of banks, railroad barons and the gold standard. He was the Democrat's candidate for President three times. He believed in popular democracy, was a friend of the farmer and thus the rural crowds loved him. Russell Conwell, a star lecturer alongside Bryan, gave his speech "Acres of Diamonds" over 5,000 times. His theme was "get rich young man, for money is power and power ought to be in the hands of the good people. I say you have no right to be poor." It was a message to all, hope to all, words to the ordinary citizens. Tent Chautauquas were born out of the 19th century disenchantment of wealth being held by the few. Manifestos such as the "Populist Party Platform" championed the plight of the middle class and poor in the greedy face of the rich and powerful. Tent Chautauquas put a light in the eye of all those who attended. Tomorrow could be a better day. Spirits of the hard working were raised.

For years I've thought perhaps we should build a pavilion on Mt. Ashwabay. It wouldn't be a tent but it would still be in the open air and ease the budget of replacing the Big Top every seven years. That's sacrilege for a tent show man but I'm still intrigued.

HOW TO START A CIRCUIT TENT CHAUTAUQUA

Let's say it's 1910, the year Halley's Comet passed through, the year Mark Twain died. You and I are plotting to start a traveling Chautauqua. We'll call it The (your name here) and Nelson Prairie Chautauqua. We've decided to start small, buying six brown canvas tents in the standard Chautauqua size of 125 feet by 175 feet. We will keep to the Midwest, especially Wisconsin, Minnesota and Iowa, the hotbed. We'll follow the proven equation of other Chautauquas, offer a five, seven, or ten-day program, stay to the small towns, carefully routing them to towns reached by the railroad. Our office will be here in (that town's name here), you manning the telephone and accounting while I travel with the tents overseeing operations. I've worked on the Redpath-Horner Chautauqua for three years and so have the inside knowledge of connections for talent and the know how to put up and tear down the tents. I got to know Charles Horner, a founder of the circuit Chautauquas; and he generously shared his experience in the booking and operations. Each tent will have an onsite manager.

Your neighbor, (her name here), is a teacher and you recommend we approach her to ask if she would have interest in working for us as advance girl. She accepts. She will travel to towns we have chosen over the winter, first contacting the president of the local bank to sell him on the glory of bringing to his community a Chautauqua, which for the run they can call their own. He is intrigued and promises to form a committee of local businessmen and others who recognize the value of culture under canvas. (Her name here) returns upon notice of their acceptance of the proposal. (Her name here) shows them the plan to sell advance tickets and thus guarantee its success. (Your name here) and I will handle all publicity.

Our season is booked. Somehow we engaged William Jennings Bryan, the most popular of all orators, for a portion of the summer with his famous lecture "Prince Of Peace." Five of the tents will be up at a time. Upon the closing of a Chautauqua stand, the tent from that show will hopscotch over the other five to the next location. That way five will always be up and the other raised in time for the opening up ahead. The tent raising crew moves with the tents. Local volunteers excitedly join in the tent raising and set up chairs and lights. The railroad connections are good, allowing us to overnight Bryan and other stars from one evening to the next. The other performers will stay in town for the entire run and move to the next tent upon completion of the stay. So we need five complete lineups to perform before each evening ends with the inspiring lecture. We have engaged bell ringers, piano players, Mexican dancers, a women's vocal quartet, a brass ensemble, a theatrical company presenting a Shakespeare play and a variety of other talent. Our crews are hired for the summer, mostly college young people. Volunteers will usher the crowds.

We're hoping, once we sell a community on the Chautauqua idea, each will want to repeat the experience summer after summer. Almost all agree.

The opening day at last comes to (the town's name here). An afternoon parade kicks off the great week. All week there are matinees as well as the evening shows. There is a small children's tent with local teachers and artists taking care of the kids everyday. The children are read to, taught from the latest books, given roles in plays they help create and given time to hold sack races and play games. Everyone is dressed in his/her best no matter what the temperature, women in their white-laced dresses, farmers in the one suit each owns (bought for weddings and funerals); children wear their best school duds. Everybody wears a hat.

Farmers and their families arrive from all over the county by horse and buggy, stabling their teams in the local livery. A few come in automobiles which are examined with great interest by all. Cafes are packed, shops and stores busy as nickels, and hotels are full. Platformed wall tents are erected on the grounds allowing some Chautauqua comers to stay the week. Our site here in (name of town here) is at the edge of town on a grassy field next to (name of grove here). We're praying for good weather. We have a tent in storage in case one should be damaged by wind or hail.

The tent is packed for opening night, the sidewalls are up and folks are standing outside. The elders in the community are given front row seats. There is excitement abounding. For most, this is the first time they have ever seen a professional production of a Shakespeare play. The music is played and sung by polished performers. It's like being in the big city!

As Chautauqua tears down and leaves, onlookers feel a bit sad and start talking about next summer when The (your name here) and Nelson Prairie Chautauqua returns.

I think of the similarities of those old tent Chautauquas and Big Top Chautauqua. We're pitched next to a grove, that grove being miles of National Forest. We need volunteers to sell tickets and usher. We depend on the financial help of local businesses and individuals to exist. We present talent locally that one would have to travel to the big city to see otherwise. Big Top's very existence has proved to be an important part of the Chequamegon Bay economy. Motels and B&Bs are reserved far ahead, restaurants full, gas stations service the out-of-towners. Tourist attractions hereabouts fill the day time for people who have come because of Big Top Chautauqua. A board member of ours once stated lightheartedly, "Without Lake Superior Big Top Chautauqua, Lake Superior would be just another lake!" I have to tell you someone took that quip seriously when I quoted it from the stage and wrote me a scathing letter about our arrogance. Hey lady, lighten up.

The Tent
and
Tent Grounds

Sing...break forth into singing, and cry aloud...Enlarge the limits of your home, spred wide the curtains of your tent. Let out its ropes to the full and drive the pegs home. Then shall your light break forth like the dawn and soon you will grow healthy like a wound newly healed.

from *The Book of Isaiah*

GIVE ME CANVAS OR GIVE ME DEATH

It is said that theatre in its simplest terms is two planks and a
passion. The planks are easy to come by. The passion is rare.
Anon.

I've always depended on miracles. Faith. Higher Power. Fate. What's over the hill.

One summer morning in 1984 on my driving way up 8th Avenue in Washburn, I pulled over at a yard sale sign and after meandering around the tables and finding nothing to add to my rat pack, I began the stroll back to my car. The way out was along the garage and there in the grass lay a single tent pole. It was well worn, ten feet long, six-sided with the spike intact. Where in this world did that come from, from a circus that played and cut town years ago? The sellers had no idea. This was not your camping tent pole. This was a sidewall pole. I picked it up. Laughed. Asked how much. Three bucks. I didn't bicker. I stood there. Took it home. Stood it up. My forgotten years-old dream of someday having a tent show suddenly rose in the air of my heart and yard. This was, as is said of a birth, before Big Top Chautauqua was even a gleam in the eye.

Eighteen months later after a chat with Mary Rice, she invited me to her home to discuss the stupendous idea of building a theatre, to make a home stage for shows like *Riding The Wind*, for musicians like the boys of the Lost Nation String Band– a venue for the Bayfield Peninsula.

I invited Sally Kessler to come along. I respected her knowledge of theatre and thought the idea might come to include all the possibilities of a new stage. I told Betty Ferris a tent show was what I had in mind and carried the word Chautauqua to the meeting. There on the couch I had my say. Though I didn't speak it as such, my ballyhoo was– "Don't build me no stinkin' theatre—buy me a tent!" They did. The MAHADH Foundation. Mary's parents, Bill and Betty Hulings, sweetest of the sweet people and generous with their giving to the arts around St. Paul, were solid behind it. Mary Rice once again was delightfully opening a door. I have always been honored by the trust.

I've been asked many a time, "Did you ever think it would become so big?" My answer—"It started big. It was a big idea with big shows with big casts under a big top." We didn't have time to think. We had to move. The meeting with Mary was in January 1986 and the first show, a performance of *Riding The Wind*, opened July 11 of that year, 8:15 old circus time. More on that later.

A not-for profit organization was in order to accept tax-deductible funding from foundations and other means of support. We were incorporated under the name Big Lake Chautauqua, which I had chosen for the obvious. Couldn't sleep with that. Renamed Lake Superior Big Top Chautauqua with first logo by Don Albrecht.

Tom Johnson, my lawyer, friend and occasional guest MC, once declared from the stage, "I heard they were putting a big tent up on a ski hill and playing historical musicals all summer. Boy, that's gonna work!"

LUST FOR CANVAS

"...it was always there, the thereness of the tent..."
Marian McKennon

There is a great library of books on the subject of Chautauquas and tent shows in America. Recently the word Chautauqua has inspired scholars to publish papers and books on the histories. My favorites are the reminiscences of those who were there, who experienced first hand the long gone years, the troupers, crews and owners.

I don't recall even hearing the word Chautauqua while I was growing up. It wasn't until just before the founding of ours that I learned the stories and became inspired to raise a tent and call it Chautauqua. BTC is an evolution of the idea. It's part Chautauqua and part tent show. In the first years we presented lectures along with our historical shows and concerts. The educational element made us a Chautauqua. Today BTC is more of a tent show. It's become less a Chautauqua and more a concert venue.

Published in 1964, the book *Tent Show*, by Marian McKennon is by far my favorite portrait of the old times. Marian married Joe McKennon and entered the traveling show world in the 1940s. Joe knew the sawdust of the circus, midways, gaming and sideshows along with tent shows. He was a great historian, wanting to keep the era alive.

Marian not only portraits the nuts and bolts of raising a tent and the show but gives the daily struggles and joys of doing so. In her telling, I find I burn with the same passion for canvas that she describes in her man Joe.

A regular opening in the early days of BTC featured Sally Kessler monologuing a passage from Marian's book. She always performed it before I sang "Ballyhoo." A lust for canvas has never been better described than what follows.

From *Tent Show* by Marian McKennon

He can never remember a time he didn't love tents. All his life he has had what I call "canvas obsession." Joe says quietly, "I'm tent simple."

We all know men who are possessed by horses, liquor, women or cards, all the casual, pleasant things a man may become obsessed by. The men who love tents, the lust for canvas, is more rare, but no less violent.

There are hundreds of men to whom the sight of a strange tent is like the sight of a long-sought oasis. A pitiful ragbag of a tent, badly put up, must be investigated. It is a crime against humanity, a sight not to be implored, resented. But a perfectly appointed beauty like our old Tent, the Queen of Tents, or our new Tent, the Little Princess, is an unending joy.

You stroll nonchalantly up to it, controlling your face, surreptitiously thump a rope, though you know already it's just right, not too tight, not too loose. You accidentally feel the canvas as if you were catching a fly, or picking up a stone, casually flip a breeze-tossed scallop of the border straight with a loose line. You saunter around the tent, your hands in your pockets, licking your lips with admiration and envy, talk to the boys, meet the preoccupied canvas boss, and try to find a common ground with him in the long gone shows. You promise to come to a performance, say long-drawn farewells, deliberately turn your back and walk away. Hesitate, turn back as if you just remembered something of importance to tell the crew, and you're lost.

You're there with that tent through the rest of the week, folding, guying. There in the dirty gray dawn, waving forlornly after the last truck leaves you tired and dizzy, to find your way across the trodden ground back to your car. Back to your home, a stupid, uninteresting, solid house. Nothing to slave over, fold, furl, mend, love– just a solid, stupid house. Not canvas!

Every word of our story from now on must be read remembering the thereness of the Tent.

All the time, it is over and around us, a living thing, breathing with every minute whiffle of the air. The ropes creak slightly, the butted canvas edges softly chafe, the bottom edge of the sidewall sweeps back and forth across the grass or sand when there is no wind at all. With every little passing gust, the top billows up between the ropes like a sigh, the sidewall snaps.

A rising wind is ominous: the canvas flutters, drops quiet, flutters again. The canvas buckles, the ropes creak and squeal.

A whiff of rain sounds like fingertips slightly tapping a drum: a heavy rain, like the unending roll of two thousand drumsticks on a thousand drums. Then you begin to watch for water pockets. Anywhere on the top a few drops can collect, then the canvas begins to sag. It can be the size of a baseball, one minute, the size of a grand piano, the next. The moment you see the littlest sag, the side poles below that sag must be "tripped," pulled in, so the water can slide quickly off and away, or you are in for serious trouble.

Always the smell of canvas and rope, crushed grass and weeds. The faint smell of humanity lingers throughout the day, rises to crescendo in the evening, fans back to normal during the night.

Even when you are away from the Tent, it is with you. You are constantly aware, constantly on the watch. You have no peace until you are with it again. If it can be that way to me, who really only met a tent four years ago, think what it means to Joe who has loved and tended tents all his life!

Thank you Marian. You staked heaven to my heart. It's possible I am a reincarnation of Joe.

FIRST AND SECOND TENTS

First Tent

I went to a party, June 1986, at Dave and Jodi Ricard's house in Washburn knowing our tent was on its way from Minneapolis in a sheep trailer delivered by Ken Raspotnik. He said he'd drop it off at Mt. Ashwabay and would be there early evening. About 6:30 I headed to the hill, no one around. Wonder of the world, there lay five big top bags in the grass. Monsters of the Midway, rolled up and wrapped in gray. The big dream was about to unroll. Delight beyond joy. I stepped to the bags and untied one. Felt the canvas duck. It had the sniff of a hundred year old circus. The brittle green rope braids. Blue and gray wide-striped. A big top. So this is how they are packed and hauled. It was a well-used Danville all-canvas square-ender we bought for $3,500 from AARCEE Party Rentals.

Soon to become great friend and fellow roustabout, Paul Buckles, expert tent man with AARCEE, was engaged to come up and oversee the raising and to bring what we needed. Sidewalls were ordered at 10 feet. The normal height for a sidewall is 7 or 8 feet. Remember the old pole I found two years earlier? Raise it. Centerpoles, sidepoles quarterpoles and stakes were ordered through Paul and AARCEE. Brand new sidewalls in royal blue. We were on the wait for the great day.

Somehow I found that God was remodeling a Lutheran church in north Minneapolis and a host of padded church pews, most 24 feet long, were available. I said yes without hesitation. Two semis with flatbeds were loaded with the pews, pumped by my brother and his Twin Cities pals, and the pews headed to their new home. I was pumping gas at Leinos getting ready to drive to Ashwabay when suddenly the blow of diesel was sounding through Washburn. Church pews bound for Big Top Chautauqua, blue covered cushions, meant to be. A gang was organized; we unloaded and covered them in plastic waiting the day. The day came.

Paul was sleeping in his truck when I arrived the morning of the raising. We shook hands and hit it off immediately. I often wondered what he thought of this crazy brave idea of mine. Over time, he told me no one was betting on such a scheme to last long. Jerry Carlson walked up from his house, Carolyn arrived, the roustabouts began to drive in and we were off. I had blown my wild enthusiasm all spring long into the ears of Jonathan Falconer, a sailor who knew the ropes. Paul and Jonathan led the way as they continued to do for the first few years at every tent-raising. They were my canvasmen. In tent lore the canvasman is boss. Jerry Carlson was the third main man, Jerry being a man of many astute mechanical talents. Put the late Noel Meyer on that list. Noel was our lightman and technician from day one. In the early years he made do with what we could afford for lights. He was always, I mean everyday always at the tent, his children in tow.

We pulled out the top, laid the five sections in order, listened as Paul taught us how to lace and lay the poles out. And then the sounds now long forgotten at BTC, the driving of the steel stakes by sledgehammer as it had been done for ages. We got into the three-man rhythm on one stake, three hammers ringing steel, the Anvil Chorus. There was a pure joy in the mystery unveiled, the big hat going up. We learned the clove hitch to tension the ropes from stake to top. As in great circus tradition, I placed a penny under the last centerpole to raise a wish for good fortune, fair weather and straw houses. My goodness, goodness for one and all; I had my tent show. It's time for the song.

Ballyhoo

I can't believe another year's gone around
Is that a big top I see there lyin' on the ground
    ballyhoo ballyhoo
It wasn't but one thin week ago
About 9 a.m. the volunteers began to show
    ballyhoo ballyhoo
Five big top bags rollin' in the sun
What we have here is a half ton of fun
    ballyhoo ballyhoo
Pull it out lace it up step off the stakes
My heart starts to flutter my soul starts to shake
    ballyhoo ballyhoo

To the Chautauqua tent show pack it up let's go
    8:15 old circus time
Never seen such a sight on a sweet summer night
    all canvas music magic delight
It's big it's blue it's Big Top showtime for me and you
    ballyhoo ballyhoo

Up with the side poles don't she look cool
Just like an oversize swimmin' pool
    ballyhoo ballyhoo
Up with the quarter poles see how she bends
Time off for lunch a little chat with your friends
    ballyhoo ballyhoo
Up go the trusses and the centerpoles
It's all uphill it won't be long now
    ballyhoo ballyhoo
Pardon me while I stop and stare
That's the most gorgeous thing I've ever seen in the air
    ballyhoo ballyhoo
wn

The entire first season was adventure. Looking up at the top on the inside one could see constellations of light blinking through. It leaked. It was an old top. We covered many of the pews with plastic every night in anticipation of rain. And it rained. And it rained.

Word began to get around about the hippies on the hill and their crazy goings-on. What's Chautauqua mean? How do you spell it? Chautauqua on Chequamegon Bay? We opened July 11, 1986 with *Riding The Wind*. The band's stage was the ground. The big screen was in place. To adapt the tent for visuals I followed the idea of what was known in the old days as dramatic end tents. A dramatic end tent removes an end centerpole and cables, and ropes the top to hold it up, allowing an unobstructed space for the stage. In our case, we needed to give a clear shot for rear projection. To play it safe for the every worry of insurance, we had a truss engineered by a firm in Ashland. It was an aluminum/steel huge gizmo that was over the requirement for support by at least a million pounds. It lasted I think two years before Jonathan designed a wooden truss which was used for a good many years.

Our friends and relatives took tickets and sold T-shirts. Mom and dad were there. Five bucks a ticket. Good old days. Here's the first year bally–

Premier Season   1986

July came and the Big Top rose,
The old canvas tent-show stage
Came alive on the hill in the Big-Lake air,
The town and the strangers drove up there,
What's all this?—Chautauqua!

It's grass and canvas and 8:15,
It's five bucks a ticket, seven weeks,
About every night, about everything
Of which you can talk, act out or sing,

History in concert on the big screen,
Orchestral, lectural, jazzical, magical,
Comical, festival, reading, revue,
A seat waiting under the Big Top for you!
wn

A defining moment came on a wild, wind-driving raining night when I had booked a one-man show from Minneapolis. It was a dramatic portrait of Edwin Booth, the famous American actor of long ago. Only a few people bought tickets. The actor approached me saying canceling the show would be OK. It was raining in the tent and the poles were shaking like masts. The temperature leaned towards sleet. "No!" I said. "We never cancel. The show must go on."

He set up his throne and Carolyn and I gave notice. Jerry and Carol Carlson came in. Our crew was there. Big Top regular patrons Norman, Judith and Eric Larson were there. We all huddled in the first two rows, all eleven of us, wearing rain gear head to toe and for two hours leaned our ears to the stage. We gave him a shivering, standing ovation and swam home. That night remains at the apex of all my Big Top experiences. You had to be there, but you weren't.

One other grand moment I give you. A very elderly couple came to a show. That night it rained five inches. Rivers and their tributaries rolled through the tent. I had welcomed the couple before the show and noticed the proud way he presented the tent to his wife. He unfolded his arms as if welcoming royalty to the palace. Pointed to the sound system. Pointed up at the top. Gestured to the pews. We called the show early after warning the crowd not to touch the steel centerpoles, lightning was seeking the hill. We pulled cars up to the exit, lights on, to allow customers to see their way out. The tent was now empty. Except. Standing inside the tent was the elderly couple, soaking wet, wild-eyed as I've ever seen humans. I wondered, smiled at them, I was having the time of my life. "What are you doing?" I asked. The gentleman looked at me. "We could die here!" he proclaimed and I sat to my laughing joy. They turned to the night.

5,000 plus people attended during our first season of 40 shows, a small run compared to what would come to be. We ran 7 weeks to August 31. On closing night, the Bayfield Chamber of Commerce awarded us congratulations on this new enterprise that was off its knees and standing up.

Our offices were wherever we found ourselves, mostly in our homes, meetings held at Carolyn Sneed's famous Chautauqua table that surely should be put on the Wisconsin Register of Historic Places. Our business phone was located in my house. For the first many years, calls for information and tickets would come directly to me. I loved it. But of course, as we grew, I found being the receptionist enormously time consuming. Years later I still was receiving calls to 373 5851 from everywhere.

Second Tent 1987

We needed a new tent for season two. Some outfit in Milwaukee, name I can't remember for good reason, took our order for a new canvas top. We were getting nervous come spring when calls weren't coming back and it was obvious they weren't sewing. I called Paul and AARCEE loaned us a tent top for the season. It was a looker and same size but it was a thin, flimsy nylon thing that let in too much light, washing our big screen visuals, especially in June when the sun was still up at showtime. And it pocketed rain. Push-poles were used constantly before, after and during the shows to empty the pools above. Rain is always a hindrance to tent shows, not so much for leaking but for sound. A hard rain during a show makes it difficult to hear, especially during speaking or theatrical plays. The eventual improvement in our sound system cured most of that.

One night emceeing during the show the rain really began to pound. I mean heavy water. I was making jokes but getting a little frustrated. I peered up at the top and yelled STOP! In less than a second it stopped. I mean stopped. Instantly! I kid you not. After the show that night, I went down to Lake Superior and walked on the water, called down the moon, turned the water into wine and fed the gulls loaves and fishes. To guarantee good weather for your next backyard party, maybe you should give me a call.

MADE JUST FOR US

Just in time for the Bill and Betty Show in late May 1988, our first new tent arrived in Bayport, Minnesota and was raised fresh out of the bags on the banks of the St. Croix River. Bill and Betty Hulings, our blessed friends and benefactors, were to be surprised with a 50th wedding anniversary celebration featuring the St. Paul Chamber Orchestra, Philip Brunelle's Plymouth Chorale and Big Top Chautauqua. It was planned by Mary Rice and her family to be the grandest celebration of their life. It was.

Jonathan Falconer, canvasman, and Phil Anich were sent down to raise our new top. It was manufactured by Anchor Industries of Evansville, Indiana, with Paul Buckles as our go-between in the order. Anchor has been in the business as tent maker since the end of the Civil War. The blue and gray striped pattern has a reason. Since they are located along the Mason-Dixon line which separates the northern U.S. states from the southern, the colors blue and gray represent both the Civil War colors of the North and South. Neither could be repulsed. They hadn't sewn a canvas big top in a long while; vinyl was the call with its long life properties. Ugh.

I drove alone to Bayport, all the way down anticipating my first look at the new tent. There it was. I came honking in to the lot. John was walking up the laced seams of the top like a high wire man. Phil and a roustabout crew of volunteers were working on the staging as I strolled in, cigar in mouth. It was a 60 X 120. In less than a minute I said, "Too small." I about faced and drove to the nearest phone and called Paul. "We need another section, Paul. Can we get it in time for tent raising day on Mt. Ashwabay?" He thought so. "I want to hear you say you know so." The call went in to Anchor and it was put on a rush order. It was expressed to our hill a day or so before the Saturday tent up day.

The *Bill And Betty Show* included visuals of the life of Bill and Betty with songs and stories. Some months earlier Betty Ferris and I had spent two days at their home in Bayport under the watch of Mary, copying photos into slides and catching the stories from Mary. Bill and Betty were in Florida. Mary lovingly spoke of her childhood and family life in Bayport along with the Andersen family's long history of summers on Sand Island in the Apostles. My favorite tale was the story of their family running the shore from their place at the old village site of Shaw to the Sand Island Light. They put a new roof on it, thus saving the lighthouse and living quarters from ruin. The National Park Service and all of us owe eternal gratitude for their gift to the future.

We had rehearsed with the St. Paul Chamber Orchestra in St. Paul as we were doing two of my illustrated tunes with them. Quite the experience for all of us, me playing the banjeurine with the orchestra on one of the songs.

Bill and Betty arrived and were speechless as they stepped out of the limo. Bill still had his office in the Andersen Window Corporation headquarters just two blocks away. To prevent him from seeing the setup for the party, his usual road to work was closed with the ruse of a detour no-traffic-allowed under construction sign. Somehow he never knew. The Andersen Window Company is a great story of success dating from the founding in 1903 by Danish immigrant Hans Andersen in Hudson, Wisconsin. Betty Hulings was an Andersen, her grandfather being the founder, and thus so is Mary. Their company's history of profit sharing for employees is generous and rare.

The show was hosted by Philip Brunelle. It was another once-in-a-lifetime experience. Bill and Betty were seated front row in wicker throne chairs, Mary and family alongside. Tears flowed joyously during the two-hour show. The audience had fans in hand as somehow in May the temperature was close to ninety with no wind.

Back to the new tent, our home. I wanted a round end big top and so it was. Since 1988, we have played under four new tents, the fourth being the one standing today. We planned on a top lasting seven years, barring hail or fire. We lengthened and widened it by ten feet for the third tent so making it 70 x 160 feet. I wanted a round marquee entrance added to the second tent as the grand entrance. We added another marquee opposite for the third tent. There was discussion of changing the top to a new longer-lasting fabric but I nixed it loudly. The fabric we use is called Gala Royal. Anchor told us at our last order that there was only one woman left in their employ who knew the ins and outs of sewing a canvas big top. She trained a team of fellow workers to help. We were antique! We were unique! We were peaked in the old ways! In truth, it's cotton ducked but not the old fashioned canvas. New laws prohibit 100% canvas from being used; water and fireproofing are now inherent. Bruce Bowers and his wife, Hope, happened to be in Indiana when our tent was being manufactured. Bruce took stills and a video of the process, our top spread wall to wall in their work room, the seven foot long sewing machine threading the seams. We showed the video on the big screen at Chautauqua during its first summer stand.

The perfect way for me to describe the Big Top is to direct you to see it for yourself if you have never been to Chautauqua. If you have been there, the live picture of it is worth a thousand songs. Get thee to Big Top Chautauqua!

WHAT HATH THE HIPPIES?

What hath the hippies raised on yonder mount
Aside the greenwooded grove?
They tenteth up such music as would sting the night
air.
Harketh their harks!   Thou old dogs barking like
pups for
A ticket sold, howling under a Chautauqua moon at
the padded pews.
Would'st thee and thou wow the patrons of their
purse?
And what return for their arrivals?
Ah! 'Tis a show of live minstrels strumming
Their lutes and tooting their flutes
With all the stage light of heaven
Bloating their struts
As they ride wind and keep light.
Who wouldst have knownst their succeses
Wouldst stay course to
The passing summers.
Forsooth their reveling engages the
Multitudes, each everyman attending
Proclaimath by bespangled applause
The passioned approval.

YOU CAN'T HAVE A TENT SHOW WITHOUT....

Nothing goes better with a tent show than a great cigar. My brand was Canaria D'Oro, a good ol' fat Rothschild Maduro, a dark wrap hand rolled around Dominican Republic tobacco.

Slow burn. Firm. Ouoh. Slow deliberate draw. Box of 50 in two bundles of 25, gold ribbon around. The lovely Dominican woman in her lovely hat at the picturesque shore of a beautiful ship on the inside gorgeous lid of the glorious wooden box. They're extinct now. Not cigars, Canaria D'Oros.

I used to pass them out on tent raising day after the top was stretched, the stakes were driven and the sidewalls were pinned to the Earth. You can have a cigar without a tent show but you cannot have a tent show without a cigar.

It was a P.T. Barnum attitude I lit before most shows in sight of the crowd arriving to the glory of canvas. That music circus feeling. A lot of milling around in anticipation of the big show coming soon to a stage near you. The popcorn popper punching the air, the peals of laughter at some joke you wish you'd been in on, the smoke and scent of grilled burgers.

Kevin Smith is spatuling burgers, the Friday night steam is rising off the waters of boiling fresh whitefish Jerry Carlson is tending. Comes the sight of someone you know, the slip swish of a sidewall Carolyn is lowering on the windward side, the scent of mown grass, the sound of the moon coming through the trees.

And then the clang of the little Great Lakes ship kitchen bell I found in an antique shop announcing ten minutes to showtime.

One must have a cigar in light of all this.

I booked Cubanismo, a 12 piece big band direct from Havana. There were horns, drums of all sizes and sounds, guitars and a string instrument I couldn't name, an old man who was a fabulous lead singer– tango, samba, Latin beat sung in Cuban Spanish, a long time and way from old Spain. Somehow most of the audience stayed seated, though a dozen or so couples headed to the grass to dance. Rare night.

I stood with my cigar, a great cigar, an illegal cigar, just outside the tent.

Rewind. Middle afternoon, I arrived at the tent to find Cubanismo's big bus parked out back, the band sound checking and warming up. I had on my usual Panama straw hat while walking towards the Cubans, smoking my Dominican Republic cigar. One of Cubanismo's crew members walking quickly towards the tent, grinned a greeting at me and said, "Dominican?" I nodded, pulling the cigar out of my mouth and presenting it to the air. We stopped in our passing lanes. He smiled much wider and said, "Cuban?" I squinched looking for his meaning. "Cuban?" I nodded yes at I knew not what.

He motioned in a wave of his hand toward the Spirit Cottage, widened his smile, adding a little wicked curve. "Cuban?" He saw my answering smile and started to walk, me following. We walked through the screened porch and into the meet and greet room. He laid his hand on a satchel, looking about to see if anybody was watching. Cuban embargo and all that. We were alone. He unzipped the satchel and pulled out a cigar box. On the lid was COHIBA 10 Cigars Havana. These were not only Havana cigars they were COHIBAS– King of the roll.

We hadn't yet spoken other than his words "Dominican? Cuban?" Maybe because he didn't speak English and I didn't speak Cuban Spanish. He understood when I asked "How much?" "Hundred Fifty." "Sold!" I quickly answered and indicated I would have to go to the back of the tent to fetch the money. Or did I borrow it? Can't remember. Not important.

I came back with the hundred fifty, we shook hands, I patted him. "Gracias, gracias, gracias."

He headed off to the tent to rejoin the band and I walked slyly like a thief who just got away with the Hope Diamond or a Prince going off alone to think of his coming Kingship.

I nibbled the end off (I never use a cutter) and lit it, hiding the box from passersby. Angels started to flutter their wings, the grass began to sing, the stars came out before dark, and a pillow was laid under my soul.

I rolled it in my fingers and stared at the smoke rising between each puff, kept an eye on the perfect spun gray wasp nest forming at the end ash of the cigar, such a long, long way away. An hour smoke at least, longer if one wishes.

I offered one to a friend whom I shall not name. I told him the story. I offered him a wooden match light. He took his first puff and burned an eye at me. I asked would he like to buy a box. "Hundred fifty" I whispered. "Where?" "Ssshhhh." I told another acquaintance of mine whom I shall not name. "Hundred fifty." "Where?" "SSsshhh."

I sold two boxes that night. It was dark for both of the other exchanges. That wonderful Cuban man had to unlock the cargo area of the bus to fetch them and we walked nonchalantly to the Spirit Cottage. The deals were unsealed.

Those cigars remain dreams away from any other cigar I've ever smoked. Well, maybe except for Canaria D'oro Rothschild Maduros, an extinct breed.

I auctioned off one at the Madeline Island's Fourth of July celebration in LaPointe for a worthy cause. I named the cigar and proclaimed its illegality. It sold for a hundred bucks.

All the summers I dropped the butts of my cigars in rings around the tent or parked them (parking is when you lay down your unfinished cigar to later come back to it). As Bruce Bowers declared once, looking down and pointing– "Tent Show Manager scat."

In my summer neighborhood this afternoon along County C
a summer song was being stacked in bales of hay
green- cut and twined, a stack of hay bricks.
This is the third year now that I have been
surprised by a poem of this field on my way to the tent.

I pull over and gawk, making me late for sound check
but that's what you do for love out hunting song.

Those three young men throw, stack and sweat
this August summer day. I wish I had such good work.

My day in the song mines came not to much.

Down in the song mines down in the song mines
People wonder what it's like chipping away way down there
I write it—it writes me— in come words with a melody
Lord have mercy on us hacks down in the song mines

Nothing much happened all day down there.
If I could have found a main vein
I'd have written a song and put it over my name.
Those three young men throw, stack and sweat.
The song of my day was on that wagon.

Ladies and Gentlemen, the song of the tent tonight
is The Bobs, please welcome them.

THE NEWSPAPER BROCHURE

It proved to be impractical and so it was the perfect publicity piece sending out Chautauqua's schedule to the world. It fit the spirit of the tent, a yearly newspaper, old-fashioned and black and white.

The puzzle of what we started atop Mt. Ashwabay, we needed to clearly publicize, not withstanding that word of mouth has always worked as well or better than anything we could pitch in print or on the air.

Don Albrecht had the idea of the newspaper. He was our first advance man, a circus term meaning the show is coming to town and here's when and where and what time and here's the guy doing the ballyhoo. The brochures were bulky, hard to find counter-space for in retail establishments, and a pile to mail.

The first years our seasons were sparse, we hadn't yet sought sponsors for shows, and so the layout was relatively easy. Don was working at Northland College in the publicity department and knew the processes. Well-known as a topnotch photographer, he understood the eye of designing. He also drew the Big Top's first logo, which to this day I love and still exhibit on a well-faded T-shirt.

Carolyn, Betty and I were overseeing the plan. Money for advertising was thin. Don also designed the bills we postered around town. At that time we were advertising one show at a time and so had to keep up with the up and down billboarding around town. My favorite memory of the first week, indeed the first night, was the small stack of *Riding The Wind* posters, still smelling of fresh ink, piled on a seat backstage. It was an hour before the show and I had thoughts of running downtown Bayfield and putting them up. Either that or putting a road closed detour sign on Highway 13 with an arrow pointing up Ski Hill Road.

The newspaper layout lasted through the 1997 season, always with a picture of the tent on the cover with no commercial advertising inside. There you would see the performers and the description of the shows. That makes twelve seasons we sent them out. When they arrived from the printer we followed our ritual, which once again depended on volunteers and Patsy and Wayne Avery of Patsy's Bar. Sitting at the bar and at the tables, we sat for hours putting address labels on the brochures while being careful not to spill margaritas on them. We kept at it until we were done. Phil Anich, the old postmaster, stacked and stuffed them in bags and hauled them off to be mailed. I think that was the first real feeling of Chautauqua being a community venture, the sense that Big Top Chautauqua belonged to the local people. There was an excitement in the air at Patsy's, a pushing off the dock to the sailing of a new season.

That was not by any means the only major contribution Don Albrecht gave to us. He was also our in-house photographer. His photos have been well used over the years. It was his brilliant idea to photograph patrons arriving before the show, developing the slides on the spot and giving them to Betty to project on the screen during "The Chequamegon Waltz," the end song of *Riding The Wind*. This was first done during the debut performance of *Riding The Wind* in the Bayfield Gym. The tradition continues, only now eased by digital photography and computerized projection. Back in the old days, Don used Polaroid instant slide film and would be seen in the T-Bar shortly after the show started, developing and mounting the black and white slides. It was always a treat for us performers knowing what was up ahead; during the last two choruses the audience would be surprised to see themselves up on the big screen. Ahs, applause, oohs, wows rippled the tent air.

1
Summer fall winter spring
Chautauqua
The five seasons of the year.

2
Steel stake pinned through grass
Clove hitched tent rope
Holding up a summer corner by the Earth.

3
Dressing rooms the mirror of vaudeville
Performers up the steps
Hand on the curtain.

4
Rain on the top
Finger heaven drumming
I don't mind the weather when the wind don't blow

5
Lucky so, lucky me, dreams made clear and alive.
Big Dipper pours night.
Stars come out under and over the tent.

THE NIGHT THE LIGHTS WENT OUT

It was the usual crowd of 700+ for *Riding The Wind* on a beautiful night. The show was going really well, my jokes at intermission were working and the second half was beginning. And then God (or the power company) said. "Let there be no light." The stage went to black, as is common with a light cue, problem was so did the entire tent and grounds.

I was singing the second verse of "Down At The Docks" and just kept singing as we all were assuming a breaker would be thrown and the lights and sound would come back on. They didn't. I kept singing, the band rejoined acoustically. We finished the song as the crowd began murmuring. What to do? "Stay calm." I said. Since no one could see, no one moved or knew what to do. I began to babble and make light (ha ha) of the situation. It wasn't but a minute and our stage manager and crew reached for the flashlights and headed towards the crowd. What to do? Well, we informed the audience that we would be driving cars up to the exits to shine the way out. Someone from the audience yelled "On with the show!" Two people left. The rest of *Riding The Wind* was performed at the edge of the stage, lit by flashlights.

The hour went by with much mirth and merriment, especially from the performers who played loose with the script, standing on chairs and projecting their voices in the old time show business way. The night remains legendary as multitudes of people in the after years claimed they were there that night and will never forget it.

It happened again in a performance of *Take It To The Lake*, but only the tent lost power and the cast stepped to the lighted beer tent and finished the show. Another "favorite" evening, we heard from many in the audience.

Not quite the same but before a Greg Brown concert (tent population over 800) I had to inform the audience the toilets were not functioning, as there was a problem with the water lines. No, we were not going to cancel and lose the gate and show. Once again, only in a tent show. We left rolls of toilet paper up and down the hill against the woods for the women and I told the men, "You know what to do. The world is your urinal."

THE BEER TENT, THE BIG WIND
AND THE INSURANCE MAN

It was the late 80s, the year the big wind blew across Madeline Island clocked at a hundred miles an hour, a fresh water hurricane. For a tent show man, sitting at home listening to weather warnings on the radio at night, is a nightmare. What are you gonna do? Drive up to the tent and pray?

Our first new tent was in its second year. The beer tent was two sections of our first tent, the old warrior that was on its last stand when we bought it. We knew we were due to order new canvas the next year.

The wind brought us damage. It could have been devastating but the big ski hill breaks the wind; we were in the lee of the blow. The big top collapsed at the rear to one side, a quarterpole and sidewall poles were broken, light fixtures at the pole and along the sidewall were disabled. The new canvas had a tear or two, could be mended. We were lucky that was it. A day's work and we were set for showtime. The beer tent was not so lucky.

Carolyn called our insurance agent from Ashland, an assessor was promptly sent over to take a look. Sitting in the beer tent, I saw him with Carolyn and Phil at the back of the tent and let them walk about their business. Above me, in the old hang, was a huge rip, the old top shredded. I'm thinking there won't be much of a claim here; it's not worth much, if anything.

Carolyn and the insurance man with his briefcase approached the picnic table where I sat. We were introduced and he began filling out forms. Right above us was the big hole. I pointed and looked up and said, "This old top is done for but it isn't...." Ouch, Carolyn loaded a sharp kick at my leg under the table and kicked me again. I shut up and let her talk. "This tent is not repairable," she said. He asked while he was shuffling his papers, "What exactly do you do up here?"

I said, "Well, we put on shows, original musicals, concerts, lectures and plays." "Oh," he said, "I've been in a few plays." Carolyn smiled at me with her Cheshire Cat grin. I took the look. "Oh," I said, "so you're an actor." "Yeah, I've done a few plays in college and in Duluth." "Oh, that's interesting, you're a performer." "Yes, but I'm mostly a musician." "Oh, what do you play?" "I play the bagpipes." "The bagpipes!" I quickly retorted, "That's my favorite instrument" (I had just discovered the bagpipes were my favorite instrument). "I love the bagpipes. I bet you're good." "Well, I've been playing quite a long time." His face was now changing from the insurance man look to a Barney Fife aw-shucks look. Carolyn's Cheshire Cat grin widened. "Wow, you play the bagpipes, my favorite instrument. Do you play the uilleann pipes or the type you blow?" "I play the highland pipes." "Well, I'd sure like to hear you sometime, the bagpipes are my favorite instrument." He was asking what this damaged top was worth. "Ten thousand dollars," Carolyn immediately replied. He wrote that down on a new sheet. "Boy, I'd love to hear you play your bagpipes. It's been a long time since I've heard the bagpipes played by somebody who knows what he's doing."

"Well," his face was now shining. He stopped writing. "I just happen to have my bagpipes in the trunk of my car." "You travel with your bagpipes?" "Yes." "Wow! The bagpipes are my favorite instrument. I'd love to hear you play." "Well, OK."

He marched to his car with a Scotch-Irish step. Carolyn, with her Cheshire Cat grin stretched to its limit and her eyes ready to bite down, stood up to follow and I ran to catch up with him. "Wow! The bagpipes, I can't believe it. Did I tell you the bagpipes are my favorite instrument? What songs do you play?" He never heard the question; he was entering a different world.

We stood beside the trunk as he assembled the pipes. I wished he'd put on a parade hat, one of those Scottish high barrels with a plume. I was hoping he was going to put on a skirt, one of them kilts. He began to tune the pipes in those drones that can stop a charging dog. When he finished tuning, he took off, marching to the beat of a Scottish air. Carolyn's Cheshire Cat grin began to eat up her cheeks. I began to nod my head to the beat of the bagpipe. I should tell you now that the bagpipes are my favorite instrument.

He marched along the sidewalls with his full-blown cheeks huffing. His step changed into a more straight-legged Heil Hitler kinda step and suddenly turned about face in a precision parade move while he began the second melody of a medley. I'd say ten minutes he huffed and puffed and blew the song out. We applauded from slightly afar.

The insurance man disassembled his bagpipes, closed the trunk and turned, walking back towards the beer tent. I shook his hand. "Thank you, that was great. That's a first around here." Carolyn said, "That was wonderful, truly." "Well, thanks. I don't get to play them enough these days, too busy."

We sat down at the picnic table. "Tell me again, what is this torn tent worth?" "Ten thousand dollars," Carolyn answered quickly. Her Cheshire Cat grin had disappeared into a business look. We waited for him to speak. It was a while. He was writing to the end of a page and signed his name. "Here Carolyn, would you please sign and date it." Carolyn quickly signed. She kicked me gently under the table. "I think I've got the sum of your claims. We will pay for the wind damage and lighting fixture damage in back of the big tent. And send a check for ten thousand dollars so you can replace your beer tent. I'll have the check mailed over immediately, you can count on that." Carolyn returned to her Cheshire Cat grin, this one a friendly, soft, warm grin that a cat gets after it's just eaten.

We stood up to shake hands and say goodbye and watched him drive away. No words were necessary between us.

The bagpipes are my favorite instrument.

My Big Mouth

Be ye careful what you say from the stage. Show me an audience, my lips flap and slap at any hint– of a joke that comes up the throat.

Some mode of construction was going on at my house and I had a dumpster delivered, my first dumpster, what a thrill. So, of course, I made some mention of it, telling the audience "Hey, anybody got stuff you need dumped, I got a little room in my dumpster, bring it on over." You may or may not know that the charge for a dumpster is determined by the weight of your trash. A couple days later I came home from rehearsal to find someone had indeed taken me up on the offer. There atop the load were tracks from a bulldozer. I mean two steel treaded Caterpillar tracks– hundreds and hundreds of pounds.

Glad to be of service. Somebody somewhere is still laughing. So am I.

DON JONES AND THE SPIRIT COTTAGE

The beautiful cedar cottage on the Chautauqua grounds was a gift from a man named Don Jones. Two years before we met him, he was riding his motorcycle up Highway 13 and saw the sign at the bottom of Ski Hill Road, rode on to Bayfield and discovered Kathy Mattea was playing that night in a tent. Unknown to us, he was impressed and would return.

The two years passed and I was told the man named Don Jones, with a plane-load of friends, would be attending a show and wanted to meet me. As always we were wide-awake to anyone who was well off. We had no ideas of the generosity he would show us. Every not-for-profit arts group wishes what happened to us could happen to them—a benefactor out of the blue. No grant applications, no pitches, no waiting.

He had been flown up to the Ashland airport in his private DC-3. I knew DC-3s as they served the Fairmont, Minnesota airport. The DC-3, first flown in 1935, proved to be one of the great leaps in air travel of that time. It was designed to fly with only one engine, if necessary. It became a major passenger carrier of the 30s and continued to work commercially well into the 1960s and 70s. Still considered the safest plane in the world, it served the Stars and Stripes very well in World War II.

Don and his group arrived and we were there to welcome him in the late afternoon, three hours before showtime; we hit it off immediately. "Show us around." Carolyn and I started backstage and gave him the grande tour. All the time he was asking about the business side of our operation as well as listening to my ballyhoo about what a rare venue an all-canvas tent show was. Carolyn knew every nickel and dime of our struggle and success. And, of course, my flapping lips were famous for selling.

Unknown to me, Don had made his fortune in communications, being on the ground floor nationally with fiber-optics. His home office was in Fond du Lac, Wisconsin where he owned several radio stations. Don said he had heard me many times on *Tent Show Radio* and enjoyed my banter. After a peek at the canvas dressing rooms, the stage, the seating, and the concessions area, he asked about our recording studio for *Tent Show Radio*. I told him the details of getting our show recorded, edited, mixed and distributed.

"Where do you record it?" "In a little trailer; Don, right this way." The small trailer sat up against the woods across from the tent. It was covered with a blue plastic tarp to keep out the rain. It was home to mice, mold and Mark McGinley. Mark was our live recording engineer from day one. Don was impressed with Mark's mixing board and setup. As for the trailer, he smiled, turned his head and said to me "Warren, good things happen to good people, those that deserve it. I need to build you a studio." Whoa! I was speechless for once.

I also informed him we had used the trailer as an emergency dressing room for Judy Collins during her two-show day at the Big Top. It was 95 in the shade that day and we showed her the dressing rooms (canvas curtains creating a space back stage). I think it was Mark that suggested she move into the recording trailer that was air-conditioned. She rested on the couch in good humor. Judy Collin's *Tent Show Radio* hour, by the way, is absolutely one of the best shows we ever produced.

Don was still smiling. We were instant pals beyond the astonishment I was feeling. "So," Don said, "you need a dressing room for these big performers and a kitchen to take care of them."

Don flew off after the show and Carolyn and I informed the Board of this tremendous gift. We immediately thought of Jill Lorenz, a Washburn architect, and began meeting with her, describing the project and asking for an estimated cost.

> *When I talked with Jill to ask for her help in designing this cottage which "might" be built, I explained that we had no guarantee that the finances would surely be provided .. and that only if Mr. Jones agreed to fund the project could it be built; and then she would be paid. Otherwise, we would have no money to pay her, and her time spent on design could not be compensated. Jill graciously and generously agreed that her drawings might have to be a donation. Thank you, Jill!* from Carolyn

She drew up the beautiful building that stands there today. The estimate was $120,000. We wondered whether Don would agree to this. Our people (Carolyn and I) began calling back and forth with his people and after the drawings were completed, I headed off to Fond du Lac to meet with Don.

The offices of his company were alive with energy. It was a delightful and friendly day. I've never felt more comfortable with anyone talking in such figures. The day went on. An assistant of his was assigned to be in charge of the business between their process and Carolyn.

Don suddenly stood up, "Warren, I have another idea. I think you also need a meet and greet room for your sponsors, to give them special treatment for their help. How about we add a good size room? A place where sponsors could meet privately with the stars after the show." "Great idea, Don." I was up to speed on cost by the square foot and we looked for paper to draw up a rough sketch. Yes, we drew it on a scrap of paper. "Let's call it the Spirit Cottage," "Don—perfect, it's the Spirit Cottage." Don agreed to that addition along with funding a septic field that would be needed for the new bathroom building to be constructed by BTC to replace the porta-potties. His gift was at least $150,000.

The rest of the day we talked and talked of many things, getting to know each other. Our celebration at Chautauqua upon completion of the cottage was joyous; dinner, toasts and a show. Don was there, flying up in the DC-3 with friends. It is truly a classy place. Architect Jill must be forever delighted as she sees her design standing in the Chautauqua air. Our guest performers have been duly impressed, made to feel at home before and after the show. The meet and greet room is also a rehearsal space for the Blue Canvas Orchestra and Singers, and for guest artists warming up.

I shall never forget seeing Earl Scruggs and Del McCoury sitting at dinner together in the Spirit Cottage before our *Big Bluegrass Saturday* show. Big Don was a frequent guest of ours over the next few years. He flew Michael Doucet and Beausoleil up when their tour schedule was otherwise impossible.

The absolute unforgettable memory of Don and the DC-3 is the day he picked our band up and flew us to Oshkosh to perform in his hanger. We flew down and back in the same day. I was invited into the cockpit to put my hands on the joystick. Oh sure, I've flown DC-3s in my time. Handling a DC-3 is like wrestling a cow to the ground by the horns. I heard the band was laughably terrified.

After finishing our performance in the hanger, Riders In The Sky closed the show. We were taxiing out the runway. Don had arranged for all his guests to step out of the hanger and wave as we circled after take off. And yes, Don requested they sing "Happy Trails" as we flew north to home, the folks on the ground waving.

One more Don Jones tale. He was active on the Board of the Smithsonian in Washington, D.C. and pals with James Hadley Billington, the Librarian of Congress. Don's idea was that I would put an ensemble together and we would go over to his hidden retreat near Wild Rose and perform a selection of my historically based songs for an audience of four: Don and James Hadley Billington and their wives.

They seated themselves in luxury leather chairs and I introduced Jack and Phil and we began. I could see the dignified quiet look on Billington's face liven up a bit. We finished the first song and began the next. "Hold it!" said the Librarian of Congress of the United States of America; "Let me get my hearing aids." That is still one of the greatest compliments I have ever received.

We've lost track of Don, but he is always on the hill with the Big Top.

Do me a favor. Whenever you see the Spirit Cottage, just say Don Jones. Goodnight Don "DJ/Too Tall" Jones, wherever you are.

THE FIRE

Dateline Friday, June 15, 2000.

On a soggy night we all packed up and left the tent in a hurry after possibly the worst performance of *Riding The Wind* ever. The band and crew to the man and woman were all in ugly moods before, after and during the show. Maybe it was the weather, maybe it was the grind of the schedule, maybe it was all just in the clouds for us that night. I remember plopping myself on the couch at home and falling asleep to TV.

Sometime past 3 in the morning the phone rang. My answering machine took it since I was in the grog and fog. I mean who calls at 3 am unless it's an emergency. It was. It was Carol Carlson's voice over the tape cutting to the quick. She was crying and talking excitedly at the same time, "The tent burned down, the tent burned." Carol later told me she doesn't sleep well and was up when she heard a popping sound. She thought it was a light bulb breaking. Out the window she saw a light and at first thought it was one of the pole lights near the tent. The tent was on fire.

It took me a staring minute or two to process what I just heard. I lay back down not knowing if I was dreaming or? Phone rang again. It was Chris Engfer. Carol had called her thinking she could get the message to me. Chris repeated the message. I hung up the phone, lay back down and went immediately back to sleep. Within minutes, Chris was at my house. She drove me to the hill; we got there just as daylight arrived at the tent. Carolyn was already there as was Betty. Phil Anich arrived, his boat hooked to his truck getting ready to head out for a few days off. Carolyn told him to go on; there was nothing any of us could do now.

I had nothing to say to the ash-charred skeleton and to those who were standing stunned at the sight. The stage end had burned first. I walked through it. My first thought was how do we mount the show scheduled for that night. All else was only stuff, valuable stuff. We lost the complete visuals backing *Riding The Wind*. Bruce Bowers lost his computer box full of programs he used for his violin. The Ojibwa flute that the late Walt Bressette gave me, the flute Mr. Bowers played in *Riding the Wind*, was gone. The beautiful podium, handmade and carved by Matt Scheider burned. All that was left of the piano was the brass sounding board. Most of the pews survived though seriously smoke damaged. The Bayfield Fire Department had put out the blaze not long after it started. We cancelled only one show and the story beginning from there is an astounding, loving, tribute to the tent from the Chequamegon Bay community.

Waiting until the 8:00 a.m. start of the business day, Carolyn called our insurance agent in Ashland, Terry Burns, who assured us our losses would be covered. We then had to wait for the fire marshal's report before beginning the clean up. Meanwhile, we kept tack to the cause of doing the coming shows.

The Bayfield school gym came immediately to mind as temporary home for the shows. Indeed, *Riding The Wind* had first been performed there in 1985 so we knew the space. One show with Cheney and Mills was cancelled: the next night we were back at it and finished the week's run unbelievably believable.

It was discovered that a mouse had chewed a junction box in the piano and an electric spark charged the blaze. The insurance check came quickly; the new old tent went up. It was a white vinyl big top, ugly in comparison, complete with bad sound, but it was ours and we were back at it on the hill a week later.

C &W Trucking, owned by Randy Erickson who was also on the volunteer fire department, donated labor and equipment to scrape the lot; and bulldozers were waiting to begin the instant the fire marshal gave the OK. Ed Erickson, bless his soul, brought his equipment to raise the vinyl top. Once again volunteers by the score from everywhere showed up to raise the tent and do whatever else we needed. People brought in food. Most importantly, people brought in the unquenchable spirit of "nothing can stop us."

It was wonderfully apparent that the community had the heart to say, "This is our Chautauqua and we're not going to lose it." Of all the gifts we had been given over the years, the hard work shown in that hard time was the apex.

"Long Live Chautauqua" had a new bell to ring.

I'd like to add a foot note here of very special thanks to Jim Allen, who was our lightman for the season. Luckily he had come back to us after a few years away in other jobs and luckily he had some knowledge about the most effective ways to document losses for insurance. Jim was the leader in those first days of transition from total loss to getting set up in time to put on a show in the Bayfield Gym in less than 48 hours. He also told me how and what to record as far as related losses and expenses, equipment, loss of income, time spent on transition, etc. When it came time to hand over lists to the insurance company, because of Jim, I was able to pass on information that was all in order and our compensation was quick and complete. Thank you, Jim Allen, -from Carolyn

The Shows

Chautauqua is an institution
where one can be both entertained and educated
and not know the difference.
Mark Twain

LECTURES READINGS MOVIES

Starting from year one we presented Tuesday night lectures and readings in the tradition of the old Chautauquas. We also thought classic movies might draw with our large screen and top notch sound. The lectures and movies were sparsely attended and thus they faded from our programming. Too bad too bad; in 1988 we presented eleven nights of lectures, readings and film.

We set a new record for low attendance on a Sunday night showing of the film *Top Hat*. Susan Soucheray was our lone customer and I think she had a pass since we were borrowing her 16 mm projector. Jerry Carlson closed shop and brought in pop and popcorn for Susan and our crew. Here are some highlights of evenings well given to the summers.

Paul Schurke   Power of the Human Spirit

Paul had just returned from the Steger-Schurke journey to the North Pole, the first ever accomplished unmotorized. The media kept track of it. I gobbled up news of it every day in the paper and on television as did all those worldwide whose direction is north. Paul's face showed the sting of the journey.

He came with Isaac the lead sled dog who was by now famous. Isaac was not your classic Husky sled dog, he was a big black furry lover boy. It was an 8:15 show on a cool June night. Paul arrived at 6:30 and by the time he took the podium the temperature had dropped 30 degrees, we could all see our breaths, something too true perfect about that. They had trained for a year in the Arctic Circle to prepare for the expedition, working the dogs, choosing the teams, getting used to relentless below freezing temperatures in high winds.

His account was spellbinding, as you'd expect, the ultimate armchair adventure for us stove lovers. His book *North To The Pole* is out there if you want to go along. One of the questions to Paul by an audience member was simply "Paul, what was it like? Tell me again." "It was like pushing your pickup out of the ditch fourteen hours a day for twelve weeks."

A sidelight of the story for me involved Patti Steger, Will's wife, who had taken to my "Whale Song." She asked me to record it on a cassette. She carried it to the Arctic Circle, and at the ocean's edge of a glacier lifted it to the waters and played the song for a pod of whales breeching in the Arctic Sea.

Meridel Le Sueur

Meridel came to us at age 87. She was an important voice in the proletarian movement of the 1930s and 40s. Her father founded the Industrial Workers of America; her young life was surrounded by activist friends of the family. She was blacklisted as a Communist during the McCarthy witch hunts, finally being appreciated as a great American voice in the 1970s. Her writings, in the giving hope of human compassion, in the plea and demand for workers' rights, in the light of putting the human soul on the page, in the song of the common man and woman, in the word marching in the telling of American history has earned her the distinction of being one of America's most important 20th century writers. Her voice sang in her readings, her conversation like poems being lifted into the air.

She was never mainstream due to her outspoken unabashed criticism of the darkside of greed and profit of American enterprise. To the "haves" she spoke for the "have nots." We need her today. We have her in her books. We had her at Chautauqua. Sitting on our stage in the yellow lamplight, she bit right into her reading, culling from her poetry and lyrical prose. She spoke as a grandmother of wisdom. I looked around the audience knowing the full range of political persuasions was present. Her message was socialistic, claiming the ownership of the bounty of our country for all. "Let's realize," she quipped, "it's liberty and justice for some." There was, surprisingly, no apparent uneasiness in the audience. In any other circumstance I could imagine anger rising in many in strong disagreement. Were they hearing her? A humored gentleness carried the message. If you've never read Meridel, I highly encourage you to gather her books around your fireside. The book *North Star* is a masterpiece of historical telling put lyrically to the book of America.

Robert Bly

I first met Robert in 1978 at The Conference of the Great Mother and New Father in Minnesota. It was a weeklong soul-enriching, granola-eating gathering of poets, writers, storytellers, musicians, lovely fools of all sorts. We came from the far corners of the country to renew the spirit life, to learn by listening and to practice the great art called life. I had read his poetry covers to covers over the years; he became a teacher of mine thereafter and remains so to this day. In 4 B.C. he gave a reading at Northland College in Ashland; and Betty Ferris and I had the pleasure of his company at our cottage in Bayfield, on Ski Hill Road of all places. In my Chautauqua time, I brought Robert to the tent three times. He gave us a solo reading the first time, a reading with tabla and sitar the second time. His third visit was memorable for our troupe. After we performed a warm-up set, Robert asked members of the Blue Canvas Orchestra to play under some of his poems. It was a geological experience, the country and the world of imagination carved in spoken boulders of truth. To have a worldwide renowned and respected poet in our midst made a treasure of the night. Robert's poems always come to one conclusion– Wake Up!

POEM FOR ROBERT BLY

The wild flame of a true poet
Stepped before us
And with a hand of his voice
Opened a palm of the Midwest
Full of this world.

"Should I read it again?"

Recite to us again a
Hint of what's behind the curtain,
What's over the hill we're climbing,
What's in the jar of the soul.

He is growing during the reading,
At last chewing on the beanstalk
Jack climbed.
He's a cave eating the hill,
A hole in the river
For fish to come walking.
He's asking for music under the poem,
The cello is playing Ed.

He has been my teacher for so long,
He is our prayer flag tonight.
He has made a way within us.
wn

Slide Jam

What a hoot! Simple as this: We invite you to bring to the tent slides of stories of your illustrated life, be they trips to far off lands, photos of the glory of your backyard or secrets you finally want to let out. We will project them on the big screen while you take the stage and we'll ramble on with you. The slide jams were very well attended and pure fun. As neighbors we got to know each other better. What a great idea!

Howard Sivertsen Isle Royale Fisherman

Howard is an extraordinary painter; he puts to canvas the depth of Lake Superior and the color of the people who live along her shores. He grew up in a commercial fishing family on Isle Royale, keeping a fisheye on the old times of life by the lake. This evening was a seagull's view of work and travel on the rolling waters. Howard could go into comedy as a monologist when his paints dry. We used his beautiful paintings of voyageurs to illustrate a voyageur's song in *30th Star*.

Pie and Politics—Tomorrow Tonight

The first annual *Pie And Politics* Chautauqua Community Forum on the Land and Water future of the beautiful Chequamegon Country .. free to all .. was held on June 11, 1997. Bob Hastings, Executive Director of the Door County Chamber of Commerce, who has a clear understanding of the need for thoughtful, well-planned development, was the first speaker. This became an important annual event, a discussion about how to direct and control development in a manner that strives for sensible economic growth while providing for a quality of life similar or better than that which currently exists. The forum in the tent was followed by pie and coffee in the beer tent along with continued discussion. The League of Women Voters of Ashland/Bayfield Counties and Alliance for Sustainability were partners in making this a successful event every year.

RECIPE FOR NEW HISTORY MUSIC SHOW

Set Timer: *to the day and time of show*

Grease: *your mind liberally*

Pick: *stories from, books, newspapers and interviews*

Slice: *into subjects...set aside to let cool*

Sprinkle: *in some quotes from folks you've interviewed*

Gather: *fresh ideas and stir*

Blend: *photographs into storyline*

Peel: *at least a dozen melodies from the guitar and*

Cover: *with words, slice into verses and choruses*

Simmer: *all for six months*

Halve: *the show into two equal parts*

Stew: *on it all*

Saute: *the can of worms you've opened and ignore it*

Boil: *all ingredients until show is finished*

Throw: in *some musicians*

Add: *a quart (oops! quartet) of singers*

Bake: *under stage lights for two hours*

Serves: *1000*

MARTIN COUNTY HORNPIPE 1976 (10 B.C.)

The year was 1976, and I was putting together a show for a celebration of my hometown in Minnesota: *Selections From Lost and Found Fairmont Histories: A Martin County Hornpipe*. Original songs, readings, historical photographs projected on a large screen. Sound familiar?

The *Hornpipe* is really the start of Big Top Chautauqua. Nine years before the tent show rose the equation of our original shows was born. I was running on blind faith writing the songs and script. I had in mind members of my former group, The Tenth Story Window, most of the performers originally from Fairmont.

Betty and I had moved to the mountains for a year along with Don Pavel and my sister whom he had married. We lived two cabins away and thus he was up to the minute on the *Hornpipe's* progress. I was traveling back and forth from the mountains to Fairmont doing research, collecting stories and photographs from the Martin County Historical Society. Betty was in tune with the day-by-day birthing of the project. In the final months she traveled to Minnesota to work with me. John Larsen, an old Fairmont pal, did the photocopying in the old time way, copying photos to slides with close-up lenses that were screwed on and off.

There were many miracles in the coming together of this show. One such miracle happened in Denver. On my way to Minnesota, I stopped at the house of a friend of mine, Michael Stanwood, an autoharp player/singer, who agreed to play the show. I wrote the song "A Home On Lily Creek" for Michael to sing and was taking it to him. Jeff Gilkinson, a cello and harmonica player touring with the Dillards, happened to stop by to visit Michael. He was standing near, smoking his pipe and listening as I sang the song. I looked over while I was singing and Jeff's pipe was steaming like a locomotive in full throttle. I finished the song. "Now, what's this show all about and when is it?" Jeff asked me. I gave him the info. "Minnesota, huh?" "Yeah, Fairmont." "Well it just so happens that I have that week off. I'll be in Minneapolis visiting my mom. Mind if I come down?" "Jeff, I'd love it but I can't guarantee how much you'll make." "Doesn't matter." Jeff came down and played banjo, cello and harmonica in *The Hornpipe*. He was an extraordinary player. I couldn't imagine now that we could have done *The Hornpipe* without him. It was fate I also met Bruce Bowers at that time.

The show was a grand success. The Angels came down that weekend. After the show, we all said our good-byes and went our separate ways.

I can't believe it did not come to me to pursue a career in producing more of these types of shows until seven years later when Ann Christensen and Gary Holman heard the LP of *The Hornpipe* and struck on the idea that Betty and I should produce a show for Washburn's Centennial. We played *The Hornpipe* at BTC in 1995.

SOUVENIR VIEWS 1983 (3 B.C.)

"Just a little town on the big lake,
But it's home sweet home to me."

In December 1982, Ann Christensen and Gary Holman of Washburn were thinking ahead to the Washburn Centennial and somehow had put their ears to the vinyl album of *A Martin County Hornpipe*, the prototype of all the illustrated history music shows to follow. I was invited to a meeting of the Washburn Centennial Committee, chaired by Gary and Carol Anderson, early in 1983. A short time later the project became real for Betty Ferris and me. The first budget request was for $3,500 for our six months of 12-hour-a-day work and that was to include all expenses for the cost of producing the show. One of the committee members asked, "What? Thirty-five hundred dollars for a slide show?" The budget was increased but not much. It was a labor of love for this town we now called home. We began research. My answer to how one begins such a huge endeavor is to say, "We just jump off the end of the dock into the waters of history and begin swimming around, without putting a toe in first to check the temperature. Ideas and spirit float to the top."

Early in our research I discovered Washburn had an opera house soon after the town's founding in 1883. Troupes traveled through by train—minstrel shows, dramas, comic shows and concert companies. There was our name, The Nelson-Ferris Concert Company. We needed a title for the show. I found it in a Washburn antique store, coming across three packets of small colored photos from long ago showing views of cities, towns and natural beauty, *Souvenir Views*.

Of all the elders we have met in our work over the years, there has been no greater pleasure than meeting and getting to know the late Charles "Chick" Sheridan, a life long resident of Washburn. Chick began his career as a journalist in the 1920s, writing and photographing as a correspondent for Milwaukee and various newspapers from his perch in his family home. He was our secret. He had a life's work of typed stories to share and he was a born storyteller, knowing the Chequamegon Bay area better than anyone. We started what we called The Tuesday Night Club. Every week Betty and I sat down with Chick to long nights of brandy and history, inviting friends of Chick's to come over and give us the goods. Patsy's Bar, The C-Side and The Firehouse Tavern were lively "research" centers, the Centennial year being all the talk about town for months before the July celebration. There we met Chin Swanson, Elmer Dagsgaard, and barstools of others who raised glasses in the toast of the Washburn story, blabbing as long as we sat there. I sat there. I want to mention Hugo Ungrodt here, one of Washburn's all-time authentic characters from a family of hardware merchants. His father, Ben Ungrodt was one of Washburn's founders.

I was astounded to find in the Washburn Public Library six bound books of the first newspapers of Washburn dating from 1883. Therein were complete daily portraits of the earliest times. I don't think they'd been opened for years. We were allowed to take them home; and so we sat down every morning to coffee and the daily news of the 1880s. That led to our discovery that the *Washburn Times* office had nearly complete bound issues of all years after. Leslie and Dan Satran, publishers and editors of the weekly, were completely accommodating to us, allowing us full access.

It was a sweat shop project. Our home became the basement of the library, our three year old daughter, Medora, with us for the hours, sleeping on the floor. It was hard on her. And on us. There is a pressure ridge to get over getting a show ready. People of the town were in great wonder of what was going on. "Who are these people putting our big show together?" Once rehearsals started in the gym the question was "What are those hippies doing in the gym?"

We put together a cast of familiars and locals. We located Bruce Bowers after not being in touch with him for seven years. Don, Jack, Bruce Burnside, Lost Nation members, sat at the heart of the show. Sally, Phil, Josh Mark and Jane Thimke from the bakery joined. Great friend and photographer Kelly Randolph partnered with Betty and me in the work on the visuals. Bob Strawn and Craig Kronstadt and a woman named Beth ran lights. Tom Draughon did the sound. We recorded it on tape and released cassettes as soon as possible. Gary Holman led the Washburn City Band. Then I heard of the Sentimentalists. They were a female eight piece barbershop group who were known well in the area. I worked up two songs for them to sing in the show, bringing them to rehearsal. It was there (drumroll, please)! (add a brass trumpet fanfare)! that I met Carolyn Sneed. The rest is not only history, it was destiny.

Washburn has had a homecoming every five years since the 1920s. Former residents from all parts of the country return to rekindle their ties of friendships and family. I can honestly say I have never felt such a fever as the love of Washburnites for this little town. Never.

When we declared the script ready, complete with song lyrics, we found Chick and sat while he read through it. He had no reaction. That hurt. I know he had no idea what it would be like live on stage. We asked him to be a narrator along with Carol Lattimer; and he agreed. Once the lights went down on opening night and the show opened the musical window into Washburn's story, Chick lit up. He later declared it was the best thing he'd ever seen. We used his story of a passenger train arriving in Washburn on a Christmas Eve to intro my song "Where Are All The Railroads." The memory of it still wonderfully haunts me. Miss that man. Betty and I kept up with him through his remaining years, especially me since I knew where Chick could be found every afternoon

We played five shows in the Washburn School Gym. It was 90 degrees outside so you can imagine the sauna of the gym. Didn't matter. It was a smashing success. Saturday afternoon after the last show, I was as ecstatic as I've ever been. We cruised the night with cast and Washburnites, my grin stapled to my cheeks.

Souvenir Views led to *Riding The Wind*. The hippies in the gym done good.

RIDING THE WIND 1985 (1 B.C.)

The success of *Riding The Wind* in 1985 led to the founding of Chautauqua. I've often referred to it as the show that bought the tent. The name Bayfield is romance to all Wisconsin and territories beyond. Picture postcard town. Gateway to the Apostle Islands. Place everybody would like to move to.

The big doings that led to another show for the Nelson-Ferris Concert Company was the All School Jamboree in Bayfield in July '85. Our contract was with the Bayfield Heritage Association and The Apostle Islands Foundation for the Arts for $25,000 which was meant to cover all costs from the beginning of research through the creation and the rehearsals and five-day performances. From beginning to end those line items would include research, writing, film and developing, office expenses, travel and all fees for sound, lights, screen and performers. Bowers flew in again from California.

Upon signing the contract we began reading, knocking on doors of elders, extensively working in the museum of the Heritage Association in the basement of the National Lakeshore headquarters. Kate Lidfors, Park Service Historian, guided us through the files. It was before the digital age so we again shot slide film in the tedious process with close-up lenses. The show was titled from the song I had written a year earlier for *Dance Of The Seasons*. We subtitled it "With Secrets of Red Cliff and Old LaPointe."

The Bayfield Heritage Museum was and is a gold mine. From the earliest settlement, the area history has been carefully written down, kept and organized. We were left alone to sift through original manuscripts, lighthouse journals, photographs, diaries and newspaper clippings. By far the most important discovery was the writing of Eleanor Knight. Eleanor wrote newspaper columns beginning in the early 1950s for the *Bayfield Press*. Her detailed knowledge and lively writing came out of her own experiences growing up in Bayfield and from interviews with homegrown and imported Bayfielders who lived with a boundless love for their picturesque town on the shores of Lake Superior. There wasn't a subject she missed. Thanks to Bob Nelson of Bayfield, Eleanor's columns have been compiled into a wonderful book entitled *Tales Of Bayfield Pioneers*, making them available to all.

I've always been hypnotized by the forgotten language of earlier times– marine and shipping idiom, lighthouse lingo, logging and sawmill talk, daily antique conversation.

Several lines of the song, "Keeper of the Light" were taken word for word out of the *Outer Island Journal* of the 1874 season. I wouldn't call it plagiarizing; I'd call it bringing true voices of the past ashore.

The fabulous Madeline Island Museum was equally important to our work. Therein, on the site of John Jacob Astor's American Fur Company Depot, is a wealth of artifacts, documents, photographs, journals, books and papers. Think on this: before there were missionaries five miles out of Boston, the French had arrived at Madeline Island, built a fort and Jesuit mission. The French were the first contact with the native populations and unlike the following English explorers, melted in to the wilderness life and habits. Jeanne Teisberg, the curator then, was a long time islander, knew her stuff and was delightful. Digging in the backroom I came upon the Madeline Island yell– "Kemo Keimo Dare-O O Mahe Mahi Marumski Poodle won't you knit cap Polly won't you Keimeo." It's the traditional push-off yell to Islanders who are leaving their summer residence behind for their winter homes. I used it in the song "Over To Old LaPointe." I later found the cry in a history of Ohio River 1840s traffic. It's a call across the waters.

Most importantly, Madeline is the spiritual home of the Ojibwa people who migrated here from the East. I've always heard voices on Madeline Island; an ancient air seems to be singing. They are old voices, Native, French, English. They talk to whomever is open and really listening. During a visit to Madeline I caught a melody, carried it home with me and put it to guitar to back up the sequence of Ojibwa photos we collected for the show, for the piece we called "Ojibwa Portrait." The musical key was E. Shortly afterward, the late Walter Bressette, a wise, spiritual voice of his people, called me to say he was stopping by my house. He drew pictographs of the islands with a stick in the sand. He had brought a gift, a loon flute, hand-carved. I played the guitar piece for him. He handed me the flute. It was in the key of E.

Those we have to thank for sharing their Bayfield lives include Ernie and Millie LaPointe, Marjorie Benton, Dawson Hauser, Grace Butler Nourse, Roger O'Malley, Bill Wheeler, Bill and Betty Hulings, Jerry and Mary Phillips, Dick Bodin, Jimmy Erickson, Mary Rice, and many more we met out and about traipsing the Bayfield trail. I regret enormously we didn't sit down with Ed Erickson, Mr. Bayfield. Over the years following I got to know Ed well. Born in Bayfield and raised on the big lake, he had a dry wit in the all-wet working stories of his life on the big lake. His was a lifetime on the water. Up to the end he captained the barge Outer Island, building docks and break walls, hauling whatever whenever wherever it was needed. The Maritime Museum in Bayfield chronicles Ed's life on the lake.

The opening night performance of *Riding The Wind* was all we hoped it would be. The Bayfield Gym, hung with colorful spinnakers for sound and decoration, was packed. It's immensely rewarding to let new songs into the air for the first time when they rise, float and fly and land safely. Most of the audience knew faces and could recognize hundreds of the photos in the show. A gasp, squeal or a giggle broke out often, making the show their own. In the audience were Bill and Betty Hulings who thus first saw what we could do and their love for us began there.

From the start *Riding The Wind* was the centerpole show of Big Top Chautauqua, holding up the tent. Chautauqua debuted on July 11, 1986 with the show. For the first several years it was common to see 700 or more people in the seats no matter if it was Thursday or Saturday. There are dozens of people who have seen *Riding The Wind* dozens of times. Something new is always seen on the screen or heard in the lyrics after repeated attendance. RTW's 100th performance was presented July 1999.

Gerry DePerry, a member of the Red Cliff tribe, strengthened *Riding The Wind* when he came on board. With eagle feather in hand he stepped to the stage to tell of the Anishinabe migration, following their guiding star of the Megis Shell. Gerry often left the trail of his story to ad-lib, mostly at the expense of "old you-know-who." Example– I showed up one night with laryngitis. Sally said from the stage, "Maybe you should say a prayer for Warren to recover his voice." Gerry's snapback, "Let's just enjoy it." In every performance after Gerry left the stage, *Riding The Wind* seemed to be less of a constructed show and more of a circle of storytelling and singing around a fire.

From the end song, "Chequamegon Waltz"

> *LaPointe to Buffalo Bay, by Red Cliff among the Islands*
> *Back to Bayfield on the mainland*
> *I'm upbound drawn to my freshwater home*
> *On the south shore of the Upper Lake*
> *In the Bay they call Chequamegon.*
> wn

Riding The Wind remains our best-known show. Betty Ferris and I had no idea its popularity would last so long. We were simply out to piece together the stories of Bayfield, the Ojibwa and Madeline Island truthfully into one great heart.

The last stop in a new show is the accounting of the final costs. We threw receipts in a cigar box on our way out the door. I have always trusted my intuitions when it comes to budgets for shows. In the final month of push-comes-to-song, anything for the show, no matter what the cost. I thought Betty and I might have to eat the cost above the twenty-five grand budget. A week after the show closed, I met with Sheree Peterson in Bayfield to count out the final costs. The cigar box was dumped on a table and the counting began. The final sum to the penny came to $24,994.00. Gol-darn anyway, we missed by six bucks.

TAKE IT TO THE LAKE 1986

The first original show commissioned by Chautauqua, featuring our band, also included Peaceful Women, a local quartet who appeared often in the Big Top's early years. Tom Mitchell, playing the con man, Dr. Third Eye, is the star of the show. What's up with the good Doctor is penned in my portrait of Tom elsewhere in this book. *Take It to The Lake* is a revue washing poems, songs, and skits ashore. The show is a prayer for caretaking of the Freshwater Sea Superior and Good Mother Earth. A speech by Chief Seattle spoken in 1855 at a ceremony in what is now Washington State gives Governor Stevens instruction on what he and the white man must do. Seattle was signing away his people's homelands.

CHIEF SEATTLE'S SPEECH

Every part of this Earth is sacred.
Every shining pine needle, every sandy shore,
every mist in the dark woods,
every clearing and humming insect is Holy.

This we know: the Earth does not belong to people,
people belong to the Earth.
You must teach your children that the ground beneath their feet
is the ashes of our grandparents.

This shining water that moves in the streams and rivers
is not just water but the blood of our ancestors.
So that they will respect the land,
tell your children that the Earth is rich with the lives of our kin.
Teach your children that the Earth is our mother.

This we know: all things are connected
like the blood which unites one family.
All things are connected.

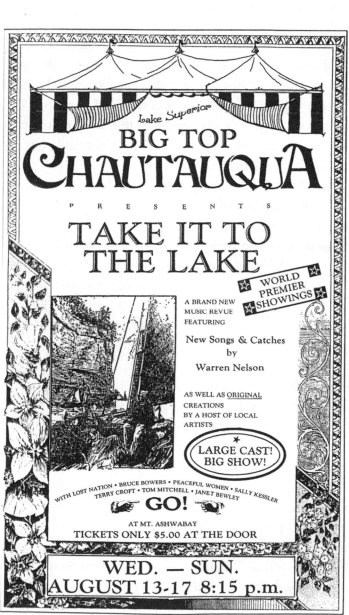

A production of the Sioux River Song Farm

WHISTLE COMIN' IN 1987

Ashland, Wisconsin, I believe, is the only city in the world that celebrates its Centennial every thirty-four years. And so, since the first one paraded the city in 1954, it was time again in 1987 for another Centennial. I liked that. Gave us work and the great chance again to mine the tunnels of history of a Lake Superior port, this one once ruled by big-time shipping and the iron ore trade.

OK, if you're wondering the why and how, here it is. 1855 was the year the first white man row row rowed his boat onto the site and built a shack on the shore of the promise of big things to come. An early speculative boom fizzled in a time of a national financial panic and the town site emptied only to rise again in the 1870s with the discovery of iron ore in the Gogebic Range of Upper Michigan and around Hurley in northeastern Wisconsin. Then began the logging rape of the great white pine forests and the laying of rail from points inland to the lake. So the good people of Ashland centennialed the first landing and now were hundred-yearing the act of the city's incorporation in 1887. Betty and I enthusiastically accepted a proposal to get up another show.

Chautauqua was in its second year and was for the first time partnering with The Nelson-Ferris Concert Company in producing a show. We figured out an equation which earned income for the organization, the accounting for the creation, costuming, props, sets, rehearsals and performances would be handled by BTC as producer and the creation costs raised by Nelson-Ferris. *Whistle Comin' In* was presented by the Ashland Centennial Committee and the City of Ashland.

The process to raise a show was by now very familiar to Betty and me. Once again we were blessed with enthusiastic committee members and residents who were anxious to share personal stories. John Chapple Jr. of the *Ashland Daily Press* was one whose family had been in Ashland from the earliest days; his father founded the *Press* which gave us in print the heart story of the rise of Ashland, The Garland City. Herbert "Chuck" Wilson is worth mentioning here. His inspiration I tell of in the chapter "Song."

We left the tent for a week to play the show five nights in the Ashland Civic Center. It was a task to make the hall into a theatre but turn off the house lights and spotlight the stage and the setting is soon forgotten. The cast was the biggest yet, seven on the bandstand, eight actors, actresses and singers, seven dancers in the Penokee Mountain Cloggers, Ravin' Dave Bloomquist on ragtime piano, Keith and Jackie Dallenbach waltzing during the end song, making 25 in all. Jack Gunderson arranged and directed the vocals. Sally Kessler directed the acting. A huge flat that was painted as a mural depicting Ashland's heritage beautifully back dropped the show. The invocation I wrote for the show was:

> *The door opens, 1854.*
> *Nothing tonight of what went on before*
> *Along thousands of years on this same Bay shore*
> *Tonight we call the moon down that measures*
> *The months that mark the years*
> *We call old Ashland up*
> *We ask shadows to step forward*
> *Silent voices to speak*
> *Frozen moments to move*
> *Ghost ships to sail*
> *Torn-up railroad iron to ring*
> *Now let Ashland, the hundred-year city, sing!*

The door in the mural was gateway to the show. The huge flat was painted by Jan Ramsey. The original painting from which the set was copied is hanging in the Vaughn Library in Ashland behind the checkout counter. Take a look. It's gorgeous. A century of history on one canvas. There was something new in the songs I wrote for *Whistle Comin' In*. It was the first costumed musical. I took more chances with the music. The songs haunt me. This show seems so long gone.

Second Street

First of course with horses it was all red clay
In the new town fever in the slap bang days
Clapboard wooden good an' strong frame buildings
Big bay windows under white false storefronts
Hang out your sign bow tip your hat
Uptown walk around this is where it's at...Second Street

Always been the main drag mercantile sale tag
Hub of the wheeler dealer main street market place
Need a lawyer or your face shaved with a haircut
Step up the boardwalk store hop window shop
Get all spiffed up see and be seen
Pull out the greenbacks find what you need on Second Street

1887 when the streetcars came
First of course with horses with the cars in tow
Nickel fare open air rockin' down the row
Even in the snow clip clop close it up
Then you see electricity came
1893 a new spark on Second Street

Forty more years on the Shanghai rails
Car number 18 ready for you all clean
Lake Park Sunday pack a picnic lunch and go
With your family all the way up Cemetery Road
Old Frank Bartz starts you on your way
1933 last street car up Second Street

Every morning 8:30 at Parson's Store
Fatty rolled Sitting Bull out to stand by the door
It's my understanding then the men rolled in
To sit by the stove and their own bull begin
No femininities no hankies sold
Just fat cigars one day old on Second Street

Holy cow wow how could they tear it down
So grand a stand in the very heart of town
If those brownstones could talk what they could tell
Of the golden days in the Knight Hotel
If only we could once more be
Standing in the lobby just a step off Second Street

Pile in the car let's drive on downtown
Park on Second Street do the walk around
Sure to catch some rumors and the latest news to go
Tell everybody absolutely everything you know
Have you heard what happened yak yak yak yak yak yak yak
How is business buh buh buh buh buh buh buh buh
Yak yak yak yak buh buh buh buh yak yak yak yak buh buh buh
Mosey down the sidewalk tell it all again

Stop right there look up and stare
There's a lot of architecture in the air
Everywhere on Second Street
Hang out your sign bow tip your hat
Uptown walk around this is where it's at...Second Street
wn

WILD RIVER 1988

I took a call in the fall of 1987 from Ms. Jean Daniels of
Wild River State Park on the Minnesota side of the St. Croix
River. Jean thought of me during a meeting of Park personnel
planning for the 20th Anniversary Celebration of the St.
Croix's designation as one of the first six American Wild And
Scenic Rivers. Specifically, a Congressional Act protected the
Upper St. Croix from further development.

"Could you do a show on the river?" Without hesitation I
said yes. The usual research I began immediately. One of
Jean's assistants sent me a bundle of info to get me started. It
was addressed to: "Juan" Nelson, Washburn, WI. Si, senor,

gracias. By spring of '88, I knew I needed to get out of the books and get on the river. The first week of June, I put in a canoe with David Hall at Riverside Landing, packed for a week's float down to Wild River State Park. The privacy created by the lack of other paddlers (we saw two others in one canoe the entire week), the sense of being far away from civilization and yet so close, was shocking, calming, magnificent. Egrets, eagles, hawks, cranes, songbirds, deer at the water's edge, otters chattering on the banks, huge catfish wagging under the canoe, the night sounds of crickets and bullfrogs, how impossibly this wild alley was hidden from towns and the freeway just a few miles off. A few old-fashioned cabins occasionally stood the shore. David could only camp two nights; so Phil Anich met me on the Wisconsin side to complete the paddle with me, five nights to go. The water was low; we did plenty of rock walking, but the weather proved perfect. To spend five full days and nights with someone in a canoe and at a campsite is to get to know your companion very well. After we pulled out to unpack and drive our way home, I had the sudden realization that I would never marry Phil! He did, though, teach me one of life's great lessons—how to put frogs to sleep. Ha! We were a fine team and it remains one of the great weeks of my water life.

As the process of conceptualizing rolled along, dreaming on the show, I came upon the waterfall of an idea. I would write and compose the historic part of the program making one set. For the first half of the show I would have Chautauqua commission several of our artists to create original performance pieces, be they musical or theatrical, based on the tributaries of the St. Croix. The assignments were to choose a tributary, visit it, bring back a jar of water, a gift for the St. Croix bag, and write or compose the segment. I thought the show should flow like the river. So center stage I had a ceremonial jar on a pine stump into which the performers would offer and pour the water from each of their tributaries, all done in the order of the tributaries entering the St. Croix. Their introductions to the audience were very personal as well as informational, leaning to the comedic. The making of the river in the jar was a religious experience. At the end of the show a huge jug of Mississippi River water was carried to the stage. As at the confluence of the St. Croix and the Mississippi at Prescott, I poured the St. Croix into the Mississippi. The cast and audience all stood in closing to sing Pete Seeger's "Of Time And Rivers Flowing," the lyrics he had put to an old German melody. It was a choker, a tear runner, a watery end.

We put up the show two other summers. Moving on with new stuff, we never brought it back. We did bring a few songs from it to the Festival Theatre in St. Croix Falls in spring 2008 on the 40th Anniversary of the Wild River Act. Twenty years had gone by! Twenty Years? Time like a river like a drink of water go down to the sea. I pray *Wild River* plays again, but like others of our big shows it's expensive to rehearse and stage.

I'm looking for a place and a time for this one to return so we can:

All go down to meet the Mississippi
We all go down to meet the Mississippi
We all go down to meet the Mississippi
In the holy rolling waters
Of the singer sweet River St. Croix

KEEPER OF THE LIGHT 1989

For the 200th anniversary of the United State Lighthouse Service, three sites nationally were chosen to host national celebrations: The Point Judith Lighthouse in Narraganset, Rhode Island, a California Pacific coast light (can't remember which) and the Apostle Islands Lights in Lake Superior.

Historian Dave Snyder of the Apostle Islands National Lakeshore was at the tent one evening and approached me about creating a show. The Nelson-Ferris Concert Company was back in business, funding going through Big Top Chautauqua. The collections of The Park Service in Bayfield, The Bayfield Heritage Association and The Madeline Island Historical Museum provided almost everything we needed to research the show. The joy in this one was boating to the Lighthouses of the Apostles, walking through the residents' quarters and climbing the towers.

For the August celebration people arrived in Bayfield from all over the country—lighthouse enthusiasts, lake lovers and kin of keepers who had once tended one or more of the Apostle lights. Excursion trips boated crowds out among the Islands. The trip to Outer Island was spectacular. Children and grandchildren of former Outer Island keepers were among those aboard telling of their young lives at the lights. The boat was abuzz. I met a 19-year-old young man who had come all the way from San Francisco. "Are you a great grandson of a keeper?" I inquired. "No," he responded. "I'm a lighthouse keeper; I was just born a hundred years too late." I used those lines in the script of the show. When we rounded a point and the Outer Island tower came in sight the crowd became hypnotized and still. More than a few eyes misted over.

The images Betty and I collected were fabulous. *Keeper of the Light* was the first show we presented that was a musical theatre piece, all characters were dressed in authentic costumes and speaking lines and songs were memorized. It was the first time I put my hand to writing for theatre. I was pacing backstage when the first laugh flew out of the audience. For the first time in my life I felt like a playwright. Parts of the script came out of the Lightkeepers' journals. The set was ruled by a re-creation of a tower top. Noel Meyer's design for lighting was superb as was the work of stagehands changing sets and running the fog machine. Opening night of the show brought a huge, overflowing, sellout crowd. Standing room was hard to find.

Three years later when we remounted the show, Dennis McCann, travel writer for the Milwaukee Journal, reviewed it. To this day it is the best description I have ever read for one of our shows. Dennis has written several Wisconsin-themed books which I highly recommend. I reprint here Dennis's column from the *Milwaukee Journal*, Sunday, August 2, 1992.

A Beacon Out of History
by Dennis McCann

It is an audacious idea in this age of water slides and mini-golf and a rush to relax. Put up a big striped tent, a huge tent, a Mickey Rooney-style show place, call in your friends, open the flaps and put on a show.

Take people for a few summer hours and not only entertain but tell them something, too. Give them a piece of the past, wrapped in canvas and drenched in song. Give them stories of the small towns that crown the tip of Wisconsin, of the settlers and the sailors, the traders and the lake they plied. Give them a dirt-floored museum of the days when ships sailed stormy seas with only a lonely beacon to guide them through the inky night and treacherous waters.

Audacious, but it worked. I can tell you, readers, I've seen the light. On the night the Lake Superior Big Top Chautauqua told the stories of lighthouse keepers of the big lake, the beacon shone again for all to see.

"There's enough darkness in a man ..

"My God, out here it stands up in your bones,

"And rolls your soul like a stone in the wash ..."

The magic of a tent, co-founder Warren Nelson says, is that you can put everything in and it will fit. For six summers now, the blue and white tent of Lake Superior Big Top Chautauqua has been a lighthouse of its own, shining over the distant border of Wisconsin from a hill called Mount Ashwabay. It is a revival of the famous traveling tent shows of the early 20th Century that carried song, dance, variety, literature and more to townsfolk who otherwise wouldn't find any of that at home.

When you are so far north that Ashland is south, you wouldn't find any of that without Chautauqua. Because of it, you get it all, from concerts to comedy but especially the original, illuminated musical histories of Lake Superior and its shores.

Today lighthouses are for tourists but "Keeper of the Light," a tale of the dark nights and sometimes dark lives of early keepers, recalls a storied period in Great Lakes history. It is not always grim. Old photographs of Apostle Island keepers and their families, backlighted on the big screen, show islands of marigolds and blueberries in summer and of croquet on the lawn.

But the loneliness of those times washes through, in Nelson's songs and in the writings of early journals that provided much of the script, the recollections of men who sold their souls first to a light in the night and only then to the women who followed along.

"Devil's Island?" a keeper's wife demanded.

"It's in the middle of nowhere. Why do you think they call it that?"

A lonely young keeper told a companion going for provisions to bring back a wife for him, as well. "Just ask her one question," he said. "Does she like fish?"

And when a keeper dressed in black stands in the dim light under his tower and demands, "Anybody out there," you wait for an answer, but know there will be none but the rolling of waves and silent darkness, which is not an answer at all.

They are all there, harsh tales of the storm that stole seven sailors' lives the night an ore ship struck a reef in the rain, in a gray-black rain no light could shine through, and of the undeniable advance of knowledge that automated the lights and put men not merely out of work but at the end of an era.

A light is a light, the show suggests, but without light keepers who will plant the marigolds in spring and worry for the sailors at sea? Who will remember the keepers, at least, is answered as eloquently as a Lake Superior sunset.

If you come here and miss Chautauqua, you miss the jewel of the new north, a singing, breathing, laughing, crying tribute to the days when keepers stood watch on lonely islands, accompanied only by duty and the ghosts of keepers past, dancing in the fog of darkness.

EARTH TO WENDELL 1990

Small World was my first working title for this show but as it developed I pasted the title, *Earth to Wendell,* to it. In the storyline Wendell is the Governor of the great State of Confusion and in his ruling he encounters messengers who twist his head to the abuses of human mistreatment of the Earth. David Parmentier aptly played the Governor who was being followed throughout by a Go-Between played by Tom

Gilshannon. Tom was a soft-shoer who danced in the Governor's conscience, dressed in a green coat trimmed with feathers, braids, bones and beads. Poca Adams designed the coat. His birch bark top hat was wonderfully made by Ted Gephart. Masks were created by Hope Atkinson, a master at her craft.

Earth to Wendell was workshopped by the troupe, who contributed to the writing. Members of the Chequamegon Area Choir sang with us. Jan Lee and Ruth MacKenzie were sprites, singing spirits of Mother Earth. On a flight with the Governor, I played Meriwether Lewis dressed in a buffalo coat, gazing out the window at the greatly changed continent Lewis had traveled for two and a half years with the Lewis and Clark Expedition. "Yo Ho Buffalo" was Meriwether's song. The horns from hell played. The endgame of the show sang of the hope that the human population of Earth would come to the sense of taking great care of the planet, our shared home, our only permission to exist.

I have no idea why we didn't play it again. I can't even find the script. I can barely hear the echo of the songs. I remember a chorus:

> *The roar of the rolling ocean*
> *At the shores of the seven seas*
> *The old love moon in motion the tides rising in me*
> *We are all alone as far as we can see*
> *Third from the sun blue eye in the sky one small world*
> wn

ON THE VELVET 1992

In 1991 Buzz and Nancy Neusteter, through the Neusteter Foundation, commissioned the Nelson-Ferris Concert Company, Betty Ferris and me, to research and create a show based on Colorado history. We settled on a railroad show. It was to be added to the main mission of Chautauqua in presenting original historical shows. First called *Baby Road*, it was renamed *On the Velvet*, a railroad term designating luxurious passenger service. I thought the structure of naming the characters Conductor, Engineer, Fireman, Redcoat, etc., the job names of a crew, would give the show a universality within the Colorado story. Researching the show in Denver was a delight, especially meeting and interviewing retired railroad men. Engineer Everett Rohrer was one of the sweetest men I ever met; I used his exact words in the engineer rap scene. It's plum with railroad lingo that's long gone. I also chased down a redcoat, a head cook, and the long-retired Director of the Passenger Service of the California Zephyr.

As usual the writing was not on track until I found a way in. I found it in a model railroad hobby shop in Denver. I bought a used freight car for my antique American Flyer S gauge set. As I was checking out at the counter, I noticed a black briefcase with a complete miniature layout inside. What the? The clerk brought it to the counter. It was a Z gauge set complete with mountains, houses, people, grazing animals, a bridge, a tunnel and a depot. What the? Z gauge is the smallest of gauges. The intricately made locomotive and cars are an inch long, made in Germany by Märklin Trains. What the? $600! I had to have it. My character Traveler was born at that moment. Traveler would be a businessman who carried around his black briefcase, no one knowing that inside was a model train. Opening the briefcase would open his secret life. I had to have it but I waited.

I noticed the American distributor for Märklin was in New Berlin, Wisconsin. I carefully crafted a letter to them telling of the show and how the briefcase set would be the centerpiece and how great the publicity would be for them. Would they consider sending me a briefcase layout gratis? Yes! I wrote back the next year asking them if they could send another set gratis with a winter scene. Yes!

In the show Traveler checks into his hotel room, has a frustrating long distance phone conversation with his secretary, hangs up, orders a shot of single malt scotch from room service and opens the briefcase. The band tickles in some twilight zone music, Traveler puts on his engineer's cap and opens the briefcase, becoming the zany fanatic that most model railroaders are. Traveler sings, as the train set is projected by a camera hanging above the stage:

> *Set these steel wheels on the track*
> *Let this train go round and round and carry me back*
> *To that shining time*
> *Across the nation of imagination to the end of the line*
>
> *Little tiny bridges little tiny tunnels little tiny bushes and trees*
> *Little bitty Z gauge people on the platform look so real*
> *Little tiny Rocky Mountains when you squint look so sublime*
> *Here she comes again around the bend and she's*
> *Right on time!*
> wn

I played Traveler in the debut production. It's not hard to play a role when you're playing yourself. Sue Kuester directed the show. She got it. She nailed it. She spiked it. She creatively engineered a solid production. Thank you Susie! Someday we'll find the ending.

On the Velvet, in my opinion, is a show to grow to go to Broadway. It is my absolute favorite. It's an expensive piece to produce. It'll play again if I have any say-so. Anywhen, anywhere, anytime. All aboard!

30th STAR 1998

Wisconsin knows how to party. Knowing your state turns 150 years old only every 150 years is great reason to; and so in 1998 cheeseheads from the Illinois State Line to Lake Superior, from the St. Croix River to Green Bay cut a rug. Unlike my home state of Minnesota ten years later at their Sesquicentennial, Wisconsin's Legislature recognized the significance and budgeted $6 million dollars to be distributed state wide for the year's revelry. It was helped considerably by Sesquicentennial license plates which proved popular. The state's funds as well as corporate sponsorships supported celebrations involving cities, small towns, symphony orchestras, theatres, artists of all ilk, parades, lectures, discussion groups in the spirit of the old Lyceum, you name it – and a new big show at Big Top Chautauqua.

Tony Judge and I shook hands with the Executive Director of the Sesquicentennial, Dean Amhaus, after a very successful meeting in Madison, knowing $92,000 was in the Chautauqua bank to start the process of putting on a new show. Tony and I had been on the fund raising trail many times together; we had our song and dance down and made a great pair at closing time. I had known Dean from his years as Executive Director of the Wisconsin Arts Board. We always got along well together in the times we'd meet around the state. He was a great choice to hire a staff and lead the Sesquicentennial. Our grant was, I believe, the largest given statewide for a proposal for a project. It was start up money for the show, more would be needed to cover the costs from creation to showtime.

It was another in the line of Nelson-Ferris Concert Company productions in cahoots with the Big Top. Betty and I did what we'd learned to do together, bloodhounding

Wisconsin stories, getting the script, songs and visuals ready for arrangements and rehearsals. We dug extensively into the archives of the Wisconsin Historical Society in Madison for both written and visual materials and also bought and borrowed books.

A show needs a name and I couldn't find it. "Make It Home" was a working title; but it just didn't have the juice. Dean Amhaus was eager to get the story of our project out and called me a couple of times to see how we were getting on and to see if the show had a name yet. It came to me in a flash. Hmmmm...let's see...Wisconsin was made a state in 1848...it was the 30th state to join the Union...there is a star on the U.S flag for every state in the nation...the 30th star is Wisconsin's...*30th Star*!!! I called Dean and told him and he took a deep easy breath and said, "Yeah." I hear there was dancin' in the office at the news.

Although it was another sit down, sing and storytell in front of the photographs show, I wanted to get the performers up and acting throughout. And we needed a hook, a centerpiece, a theme, a signature something. There it was in an antique store in Washburn—an immigrant's trunk. I could see it was old by the hand forged handles, its shape and the ancient brown of the wood inside. The store keep told me it was from the mid 19th century, possibly the 1840s. He found it in Milwaukee. Destiny! The outside was painted puke chartreuse. I thought of refinishing it but I let that go. It cost me $600 but it was worth it because the trunk came with an idea. I would use the trunk as an active symbol of Wisconsin's attic, the place where all the old odds and ends of Wisconsin's history lie covered with dust, ready to be dusted off and handled again and brought into the light. In the show I went to the trunk, opened it, and whatever I pulled out related to the subject of the song to follow. It was one of the best ideas I've ever had, all because I'm an antique lover and saw a trunk in a store. It's another proof that imagination can be found.

In the trunk, during the show, were a railroad spike, a telegraph machine, a book, a sheet of music, an iron ore miner's hard hat, a Ray Nitschke Packers shirt, an empty six pack of Leinies. I can't remember what else besides a very antique Evenrude, ridiculously small, one and a half horse outboard motor. I used the motor in the intro to a segment of inventions from Wisconsin. Ole Evenrude is credited with the invention of the outboard motor though it's a disputed fact. I guess Ole was rowing over one day long ago to bring his girl an ice cream cone and it melted and he thought if only there was a way to propel this boat....aha! (Did you know the typewriter was invented in Wisconsin? And the Republican Party? And the hamburger? [I doubt it.] The cream separator was.)

I think Betty has done her best work in *30th Star*. The visuals are mesmerizing. It's a mind juggling job to find thousands of photos and arrange a thousand or so into the order of a show. It's hard to remember after a show is completed how it all happens. Sometimes a photo gives birth to a song. Sometimes photos need to be found to match the script or a song. It's a creative fire we feed camping on a subject for six months or more.

As in all our shows, we honor the native Americans. What did the native Americans have to celebrate in the Sesquicentennial of Wisconsin's statehood? I think back to a show at the tent when we presented Ojibwa Night. Andy Gokee led a reenactment of the signing of the Treaty of LaPointe in 1854 which settled the Ojibwa onto the Red Cliff and Bad River Reservations. There was a table on stage with the treaty ready to be signed. One of our back stage crew members played the white man handing a pen to the Indian to sign the treaty. Andy signed and said, "Well, there goes the neighborhood!"

The Native segment in *30th Star* was inspired by a line of a hundred year old poem I found in my scattered reading. The poem is by Mrs. L. Sigourney. "Ye say they all have passed away, but their name is on your waters and ye may not wash it out."

I'm still delighted with the songs, especially, "New Barn Floor," the end song, "Down The Home River" and "Walkin' In Milwaukee." "Walkin' In Milwaukee" is based on the 1886 struggle for workers' rights and the eight hour day. It rings truer than true in the year of this writing, 2011, with Governor Walker's attack on unions and collective bargaining. Back in 1886 the Governor of Wisconsin called out the Wisconsin Guard to quell what he called the riots. Two people were shot including a nine year old boy who was on his way to school. So it seems the circle never ends.

WALKIN' IN MILWAUKEE

We were walkin' in Milwaukee walkin' in Milwaukee
Walkin' in Milwaukee for the eight hour day May 1886

In the dark of dawn I'm up and gone
To my job in the grime of the mill
Six days a week 12 hours a day
Sweat like steam to pocket the pay
To pay the way of my family
A family I hardly see
I come home to a lamp in the night
My children they are deep asleep

Got the one day Sunday
But there's not much left of me
It's just not right at the end of the week
Workin' late on Saturday night
I start to heat up like the boiler I throw coal in to feed
I'm the one gonna blow any minute
Twist my fist grind my teeth

And I'm not a man to hurt anyone
But I took to walk with the union
I just joined the day before
I walked out the door of the Rolling Mills
And I never knew the whole story until after
In the Milwaukee Daily Journal I read
They didn't just fire over our heads
Five bleeding in the street lay dead
wn

We debuted the show at Chautauqua in August 1998, playing to sold out crowds for six nights. *30th Star* was the official show of the Wisconsin Sesquicentennial. We embarked on a thirteen city tour in the fall of the Sesquicentennial year; highlights included performances at The Pabst Theatre in Milwaukee and The Oscar Meyer Theatre in Madison. We were the largest selling show at the Oscar Meyer for year 1998, topping 61 other shows including the Russian Ballet. There were over 1200 in the audience, standing room only. I wasn't surprised but I was overwhelmed. It made me think back to a previous performance of ours at the Oscar Meyer in 1992 on a mini tour. I called the Exec after we were booked and explained by telephone who we were and what we did. His reply "What is this? Some kind of Mom and Pop Show?" When I stopped to see him at his office a month later I was wearing a custom made T-shirt that read– THE MOM AND POP SHOW. We got the last laugh and a laugh after the last laugh.

Thanks to a Federal Education Grant acquired for us by Dave Obey, our U.S. Congressional Representative, *30th Star* was filmed at the tent (without audience) for a few days and made into a DVD by Betty Ferris and Bruce Bowers in Mr. Bowers studio. Check it out. They're for sale through Chautauqua.

From the song "30th Star"

This ship of State launched 1848
On the Union flag flying
Count up to where we are
We are sailing altogether on the good ship Wisconsin
Under the 30th Star

OLD MINNESOTA: SONG OF THE NORTH STAR 2004

On the road to old Minnesota,
Up the ways down the days gone by...
Knowin' I be goin' by the old road,
I keep the window open deep in my eye...
                              From the song "Thereaway"

During and after the great success of *30th Star* I began to think about Minnesota's Sesquicentennial a decade away in 2008. I felt the call. I named the show *Old Minnesota*, the deadline was there and so I could feel it—here we go again. After telling Carolyn, I brought it up to the Chautauqua board and they were enthusiastic.

Seed money was received thanks to Ron Lund of Medtronics. Once again, Mary Rice, Minnesota born and bred, supported the project. A light went on. I'd initiate steps to form a new non-profit presenting organization in my hometown of Fairmont, Minnesota. I talked it over with Carolyn and with John Larsen, an old hometown pal of mine. We traveled to Fairmont for a meeting and the process was begun. We named it Minnesota Shows, Inc. of Fairmont. Board members were found, the application for the Corporation sent in and approved. Bob Wallace, head of the Fairmont Chamber of Commerce, was (and is) Treasurer of the Minnesota Board. We needed his immaculate bookkeeping and straightforward let's-do-it-right manner. State representative Bob Gunther secured funding from the legislature at a time we desperately needed it to kick it off and carry it on.

It was a Minnesota show that needed Minnesota money. If and when someone would agree to support the show, what would I say when they asked "Where do we send the check"? "Oh, the check, send it to Wisconsin."

It seems everyone involved with BTC but Carolyn and I were confused by the new approach. That kept up all during the *Old Minnesota* show's history. It was clear to me– Minnesota Shows would handle the accounting and initial fundraising for the creation. BTC would handle the presenting and touring, and pay the performers. Any crossovers or confusion would be discussed and clarified by contracts. It became a partnership from the beginning to the end.

I had been wondering for a couple years how I could lighten the load of my Chautauqua wagon. The answer came in conversations with Terry Meyer. At the time Terry was Executive Director of the Door Community Auditorium in

Fish Creek. She had been there for several years and annually booked us for performances. She expressed a desire to leave her position and would there be a job at BTC? Terry's hometown is Fairmont, Minnesota, (same as mine...is there something in the water)? Around 1990, while she was an intern at Ravinia in Illinois, she wrote a letter to me introducing herself and wondering if she could intern with us. It impressed me that she was charting a professional career in show business. So, in my usual manner, I did not reply immediately. That's because I lost her letter. I had used it as a bookmark and stashed the book back on a shelf. (It wasn't until 20 years later when I found the letter. By then, of course, she had been with us for several years.)

I mentioned Terry's interest to Carolyn who knew I needed to lighten my load. Writing shows, booking, making *Tent Show Radio*, fundraising, performing and/or emceeing every night at the tent and keeping track of everything was simply too much for a guy passing fifty going a hundred miles an hour. The issue was again money. Chautauqua, as always, was running on fumes in the off-season but still going strong. We couldn't afford to create another full-time position and hire Terry. Another light went on. How about Minnesota Shows hiring Terry to work on *Old Minnesota* half time and BTC hiring her for the other 20 hours a week? It was agreed it would be a two-year contract, the salary to run through the Big Top's accounting. Scott Unke, a board member of Minnesota Shows, had facilitated a $50,000 sponsorship from the Agstar Corporation of Mankato, so moneys were in the bank. It was incredible to me and highly appreciated that Agstar agreed to support our proposal before the show was written. BTC has Minnesota Shows to thank for bringing Terry over here. We fundraised together and she booked the touring. Terry had joined the circus!

Another major sponsor was needed to help. I called American Family Insurance Company, headquartered in Madison, with a proposal. They had given $30,000 to get *30th Star* on the Wisconsin road in 1998. I called from my driveway and asked for $75,000 that would include credits for both the show's touring and a DVD to be filmed later. I had never thought of a film until that moment. American Family's previous experience with us was nothing but the best for both of us. Judy Lowell, their Foundation and Grants person, said yes. I thanked her, said so long and danced with myself.

Fundraising is the job no one wants. Asking for money for major support for a project that has yet to be finished seems rather impossible. I'm good at it. Bold. Fearless. Smooth. My tongue can tap dance with the best of them. It's a performance, showtime at the table. What can they do but say no? It's always been easy for me because I have something to sell, shows I believe in that are earmarked for celebration of the spirit of places, histories, stories of who we were and where and who we are. I'd usually start with a snap of my folding silk top hat. "Ladies and gentlemen, it's showtime! And you're going to help pay for it."

To approach the chairman of the joint appropriation committee of the Minnesota legislature, I bought me a tailored brand new Men's Warehouse fundraising sport coat for four hundred dollars complete with two eighty-dollar pairs of pants, two seventy dollar shirts and a sixty dollar belt to match my hundred dollar shoes. At the appointed hour I showed up for the meeting in his elegant office. He was wearing jeans and a sweatshirt with his feet up on his desk.

It was two years of researching and gathering images. Medora Nelson-Ferris, my daughter, was my main sidekick, photocopying and filling note cards. Chris Engfer worked extensively along with us. We centered our research at the great Minnesota Historical Society in St. Paul. What a well-kept wealth. We worked in Duluth and at the maritime history room of UW-Superior. It was totally enjoyable, but then every major project is in the beginning. The problem is doing something with it afterward; take the overload of info and press all into a two-hour show.

Every project has come with gifts. Two examples: In the first, I was working in St. Paul on the native American story of Minnesota when I saw in the morning paper that the Dakota people from up the Minnesota River were re-creating the tragic walk of elders and children who were forced to follow the Minnesota River to a concentration camp at Fort Snelling following the Sioux Conflict of 1862. The men who were accused of murder were jailed in Mankato. President Lincoln pardoned most, but 38 were hung, the largest mass hanging in the history of the United States. That morning I drove to the bottomlands below Fort Snelling to the gathering at the museum of their people. The Dakota believe the center of their world is at the confluence of the Minnesota and Mississippi Rivers. Holy Ground. I arrived at the hour they were walking the bridge with the Eagle staff to the site. There was a ceremony. It surrounded a medicine wheel that had been laid in rock on the grounds where the people were forced to pitch their tipis in December 1862. In the sting of winter, many of them froze to death. As the ceremony concluded, part in the Dakota tongue and part in English, three women in back of me began to quietly weep. I stepped aside. They were grandmother, daughter and child. All of us were invited to approach and circle the wheel. There was a feast afterward but I didn't stay. Some horse of me gently rode away into a silent field. All the freeway back to my hotel I kept thinking of all this ground under in its fenceless days and what a gift the Earth was and is, even paved and cluttered as it is now.

Another powerful day was spent in the Brown County Historical Museum in New Ulm. On the top floor, with arrowheads and other artifacts of the local Dakota, is a settler's wagon with bullet holes in it. Two settlers fleeing the Dakota were killed in the wagon. They were fleeing the farmstead they had built on ground that had been treatied from the Dakota. Previously, the U.S. government had promised the Dakota the land would be theirs "as long as the rivers flow and the grass shall grow." More like "You can live there until we tell you to go."

In a glass case next to the wagon were pieces of ancient Dakota jewelry and artifacts. And there, next to a pipestone peace pipe, was Little Crow's Flute. It was beaded beautifully. Little Crow gave it to a New Ulm dentist on the Sunday morning before the conflict of 1862 began. The Dakota had had enough of broken treaties and the white man's promises.

> Little Crow, Thayota Duta, was a chief of the Mdewakanton Dakota, a principal in the 1851 treaties of Traverse de Sioux and Mendota. Little Crow never wanted war but was forced to lead the Dakota, recognizing that the rapid destruction of their ancient way of life would leave them starving. The attack on settlers was their desperate last gasp at holding onto their homeland. I heard that flute in the museum air that day in New Ulm and the song flew in.

The logo for *Old Minnesota* is the state seal which shows the North Star, the Falls of St, Anthony, a native riding towards the setting sun, a farmer with hand on the plough. My song, "Little Crow's Flute," was born out of the images.

LITTLE CROW'S FLUTE

Oh say can you see by the leaving evening light
How so proud the Indian rides into his coming night
And the ploughman looking back his gun against the tree
Oh say can you see how a nation lost its country

Beside their home river at the ancient crossing place
The Dakota put quill to the treaty
Statehood will soon seal their fate
And beside the home river at Mankato they hung thirty eight
Oh say can you see how a nation lost it's country
wn

Old Minnesota debuted at the Fairmont Opera House on May 7, 2004. Unheard of, me having a show ready four years early. It was a five-night run, new born, clumsy and needing work. Half into the first performance I was thinking of changes and rewrites. But it worked.

We began touring *Old Minnesota,* doing school shows in the day and concerts at night– Worthington, Grand Rapids, St. Cloud, Mankato, Duluth, Austin, Glenwood, Sauk Centre, St. Paul at the Historical Center, and Minneapolis in the beautiful antique Pantages Theatre and further out, up and around. The show never drew much under the Big Top. I guess badgers and gophers don't get along.

I loved the show if I do sing so myself. The vocal, instrumental and string arrangements by Ed Willett and Severin Behnen were done in their usual brilliance. Our bandleader, Don Pavel, led the rehearsals, conducted the shows and also composed a piece of music for the show, his instrumental inspired by St. Paul, his hometown. Ed, as always, directed our vocal rehearsals. Betty Ferris helped gather and once again expertly arranged the complicated visuals, mixing film and stills to the script and music.

I hope it plays again. All these historical shows may have been created for specific celebrations but they tell stories that need to be carried on.

STATE FAIR CHAUTAUQUA

Minnesota State Fair August 21 – September 1, 2008

> *Papa says so Mama says let's go*
> *Everybody's gonna be there*
> *For the see it all stroll and the Grandstand Show*
> *At the Great Minnesota State Fair*
> *Leave the tractor and the baler in the hayfield*
> *Work today don't you dare*
> *Shine the midway lights on me tonight*
> *At the Great Minnesota State Fair*
> wn

Oh the Midway! And the tattooed carny barkers! The exhibits of horse-grooming 4H'ers and businesses in their booths. The screaming rides! The backlot trailers! The Grandstand Shows of thrillcades and races! And famous singers! Here comes Ricky Nelson (1957 I was there). The painted banners of the side shows—live on the inside! A barker ballying a sideshow cage of Giant Man-eating Communist Rats! (they are muskrats in a box of barbecue rib bones). The strong man and sword-swallowing fire-eating tattooed men. The girlie shows with a peephole in the canvas! (Oh what I learned there.) The step-right up and win a Teddy Bear. The diggers and balloon stands. Ring the bell big boy and win your girl a prize! All the bustle, sounds and the long day and night din dizzied me. Firecrackers were going off in this young boy's soul all the livelong runs. No one ever attends a fair with a frown. I never wanted the midway to load and leave and the food booths to close their wooden awnings.

My fair career began when I was around age 8 or 9. I organized neighborhood carnivals/fairs for several years of my boyhood, complete with games of chance with prizes, rides and a spook house. No surprise then that a dream arose for me to have Big Top Chautauqua play the Minnesota State Fair.

My boyhood pal, Dave Mortensen, was my main partner in the neighborhood carnival/fair. The money we made we gave to a Fairmont charity, sometimes raising over twenty dollars. The spook house was in my basement, dark, with bowls of candy corn as teeth of a dead man, a bowl of chicken livers were hearts of witches who had been boiled alive, bones from a human skeleton (from Mom's roast beef of course), shooter marbles offered as eyeballs. Always someone was hidden (usually me) behind a blanket to jump out shrieking in the face of some 4-year old, scaring the weasels out of him or her. I used the old trick of cutting out a hole in the bottom of a small cotton-lined jewelry box, my thumb sticking out from under it covered with ketchup. "Look—here's a bloody thumb I found this morning out along the railroad tracks." The carny games of chance I copied from those I had seen played at the Martin County Free Gate Fair— softballs tossed into bushel baskets, darts at balloons, marbles under walnut shells. I liked the sound of pennies and nickels jingling in my pockets.

What a long road it was to get *Old Minnesota* to play the Fair. Minnesota Shows Inc. of Fairmont was at the top of the list with BTC in making the whole *Old Minnesota* show/State Fair Chautauqua happen. Terry Meyer was made consultant for their Board. We traveled extensively to Fairmont to meet with them. For a couple years Terry answered her phone with

"Terry Meyer, Big Top Chautauqua and Minnesota Shows."
The Minnesota Shows board never hesitated in backing the
Fair run. Hats off especially to John Larsen, Bob Wallace,
Scott Unke and Marnie Brodt.

I had taken the idea to the State Fair office two years
before. I met with Renee Pearson in St. Paul and she
immediately showed interest. One thing I knew for sure was
that it would be in a tent, not our tent since it would be up on
Mt. Ashwabay for our season running concurrently with the
State Fair setup. The Fair staff came to Duluth to see the show
playing at the DECC theatre in 1997. After the show we met
during tear-down and their enthusiasm only increased. I
knew that night it was going to happen.

The scope of the project was enormous. We had a year
and a half to get the tent, sound, lights, a big screen and
projection equipment. Yes, we could play the twelve days but
we had to raise the money. The State Fair would help
publicize the show and give us the lot free.

So I traveled frequently to the Twin Cities to make
connections and chase funding. The first important meeting
was with Kay Hellervick who had just been appointed
Chairperson of the Minnesota Sesquicentennial Committee.
Kevin Kasper, a friend of mine since Junior High, had joined
our campaign as co-presenter/seller of the idea to
corporations and the Committee. As soon as it was a reality,
Terry and I began the campaign. Carolyn Sneed, as
indispensable coordinator for the creation of *Old Minnesota*,
carried on as my ear and organizer for travel and meetings.

The Agstar Corporation, who had first given funding to
the creation of the show, loved the idea of its place at the Fair
and once again was lead support, pledging $75,000. Terry
and I met with 3M. They were in. We were on our way!

By far the greatest Minnesota partner we had was a woman I loved and respected immediately, Jane Leonard. The Minnesota Legislature waited until the 11th hour to give funding to hire a staff to organize the Sesquicentennial. Jane was made Executive Director. As I remember, they designated a paltry $100,000 for Jane to pay herself and put a staff together. "We know you'll find the money to keep you and your staff going." The legislature was saying, "It'll be easy, don't bother us, here's ten bucks, throw a great party for 2,266,214 Minnesotans." So for Jane, like us, it was go go go for the money. Jane worked unbelievably long and hard to bring it all home in the end.

But we weren't there yet. Jane carried the spirit of our show along on all steps of her crusade. We were written into the overall budget which included sponsorship of such diverse companies as Travelers Insurance, The Miller Brewing Company, The Minnesota Vikings, among a dozen or more other major sponsors.

With the guarantee it would happen our Big Top staff, Terry, Carolyn, Phil, Therene, Jamey, and I kicked it in gear, all while keeping up with our summer schedule on Mt. Ashwabay.

Terry, Phil, Therene and I met with the grounds chief on the fair grounds the fall of 2007 A site was chosen near the Grandstand where an old horse barn that forever had stabled race and show horses for the track had recently been damaged beyond repair in a windstorm. The lot needed leveling with a small slope for drainage. It was our lot.

Terry found a tent to rent in Florida, a two color, vinyl, circus round with seating for 700+. Chairs would be set up front and center with bleachers three sides of the main floor. The tent rental for the run was $45,000. Add to that the sound, lights, projection equipment and I would guess it was

80 grand plus for the 10 days. I loved it at first sight. Terry had noticed in a picture of the tent that they had circled it with translucent panels tied to the side ropes. When backlit the panels showed historical photos. We selected images from *Old Minnesota* and copied the idea. It was an astounding sight, especially at night. Keep that idea.

I met Phil at the fairgrounds just before the setup. A semi loaded with the tent, poles, sidewalls and stakes was parked near our lot. I couldn't believe it. I couldn't believe it was happening. I lit a fifteen-dollar cigar and paraded around the truck like P.T. Barnum. So my State Fair dream wasn't all smoke rings after all.

The owner of the tent had driven it up from Florida with his wife and child, setting up a small travel trailer in the backlot where they lived the two weeks, from setup through teardown. We had a true carny backlot. A covered fence surrounded the backlot to hide the trailers and generators. There was a trailer for volunteers who worked ushering and staffing a Sesquicentennial booth in the tent that gatewayed ours. There was a trailer that was all ours, complete with pop, bottled water, beer, snacks, chairs, two dressing rooms. It was a tent show green room.

The cast and crew arrived the night before opening day to sound check and play a special performance for sponsors and fair personnel. I felt at home. Home for our cast and crew was the Radisson Hotel on the University of Minnesota campus.

It was a great moment on Thursday, August 21, to stand opening day on the State Fair Chautauqua tent show stage. A bus was leased to transport us back and forth everyday. The schedule was told to all. I chose to drive each day to get there early, leave late and squeeze in every minute of the experience.

When I arrived early on opening day, Betty was there at the projector playing films scheduled by Minnesota Public Television.

Thursday is the traditional opening for the fair and I was ready. OK, where's the band? Noon came and no bus, no band. I was furious. Our grand opening, the tent was mostly full, the stage was empty. I stepped to the stage and did what I do—ad lib. I told a few Minnesota jokes and then had Betty play the DVD of our Minnesota Public Television film of the show until the cast arrived.

We played a vaudeville schedule, four shows a day—noon, two, four and six. I cut down the two-and-a-half-hour concert show to one hour. Hour on, hour off. That left an hour between sets to wander the Midway. There was some wondering in the band if the schedule was too much for our voices. I did get laryngitis on the first Monday but missed only one show. The great energy of the crowds kept us up. The twelve days went by too fast for me. I could have played there the rest of my stage days.

The show was free to all fair goers. Perfect. It had been decided that air conditioning was needed, this being August in the Minnesota summer. What we hadn't planned on was the noise of the air conditioners. It sounded a lot like a 747 taking off. The show goes on.

Word began to spread around the fair that the show was something special to see and hear. Almost all our performances were played to a full tent. The run that seemed to be so long skipped by in a whiz. It was as much fun as I've ever had and it was rewarding to be singing and telling the story of Minnesota in the bulls-eye of the state's 150th birthday. I began to get thoughts of doing State Fair Chautauqua every year. Alas, it wasn't to be, but like my years at the Big Top I can say, "Been there, done that."

The State Fair run was not only great exposure for Big Top Chautauqua, it was major income for both the organization and the performers.

It was a tragedy Don Pavel didn't live to play the fair. He and I were the only two in our troupe who had been Minnesota State Fair junkies all our lives. We knew all the spots from Machinery Hill to the Arcade to the Tunnel of Love to the Midway to the Grandstand. We were Pronto Pup mustard-licking veterans.

Now that I've had my spell, one of my last big dreams in the life I have left is to travel with a midway carny. I'm betting on it. I'll need a tattoo. Step right up.

CENTENNIAL GREEN 2005

The Over and Understory of The U.S. Forest Service

SONG IN THE PEOPLE'S KEY

Oh say can you sing with me, a song in the people's key
From the Eastern Region sea of leaves,
Over all to the western sea
Oh say can you see the National Forests
For more than the trees
For the greatest good for the woods, wildlife and waters

Whose woods these are and grasslands I know I know
The U.S. is us all of us each and every one by one
By hands on the public lands the planted promise grows
For the greatest good
For the greatest number for the longest run

We who hold and have here now this time on our hands
Green and wide tall or small leaning toward the light
Caring for the land and serving people
For the greatest good
For the greatest number for the longest time

We must like a river deliver tomorrow today
Keep a tower-watch and lookout
For a future stand we will not see
Conservation a rhyme with nation to leave a legacy
For the children of the children who follow
wn

Centennial Green came about from a phone call from Susan Nelson, Steve Hoecker and Steve Schlobohm of the Chequamegon-Nicolet National Forest. Carolyn and I met with them at the Northern Great Lakes Visitor's Center and the idea was rolled out. OK, in six months it's the Centennial year of The U.S. Forest Service and the subject is fabulous, how 'bout a show? I'm signed up to complete a *Tent Show Radio* season, perform at the tent and on tour and catch managing duties. The timeline is impossible. Perfect. "Sure, I can do that" I said in my cavalier voice, not being able to imagine I could turn it down.

I'm always a bit afraid of looking Carolyn Sneed in the eye at times like this. She knows me too well. There is more than a good amount of suffering, anxiety, fear and desperation giving birth to a new show. I've always been one to say, "No problem, I've got six months, how 'bout a beer?" "Tell you what, it's coming slow but tomorrow I'm going to write all day and night. How 'bout a beer?" We couldn't talk ourselves out of it. Oh, it seems so easy when it's a finished script with a dozen new songs. I want you to know again how much I owe Carolyn for her unblind faith.

The highlight of the making of this show for me was a 3,200 mile trip my daughter Medora, my son Rowan and I took in the spring of 2005 driving a trail through most of the National Forests of the U.S. Eastern region. We left Washburn on a muddy gray day and motored south through Wisconsin to Prairie du Chien and on along the Mississippi towards the springing green.

Our first destination was the Mark Twain National Forest in southern Missouri. The route took us through Hannibal, home of Sam Clemens, Mark Twain, hero to every writer. The river blood of the Mississippi silents me as deep as Lake Superior; I love to be put in my place. Everyone has to visit Twain's boyhood home and the whitewashed Becky Thatcher-Tom Sawyer picket fence. I thought of the young Mark Twain saying, "It's time to strike out for the territories." That's what I was doing, striking out for the territories, for country I had never seen. If there is a better feeling than being out on the loose at the beginning of a trip, I don't know what it would be. The idea and start of a new show is always free and easy for the first while and then at night, lying in bed, the deadline suddenly begins to loom. You wonder how you ever signed up for such an impossible project. Mission: put the history of the Eastern Region of the U.S. Forest Service into a 90-minute show.

We cut southwest of St. Louis, the Missouri air a delicatessen of the scent of spring. The roads curved through the Missouri hills as we approached Rolla, the headquarters of the Mark Twain.

Missouri showed trees and ditch flowers we didn't know on the soft rounded hills. "Beware of Bull" read the sign up ahead. The field was surrounded by electric fence. "Where is he? Holy...!!! .It's Ferdinand." The largest black bull I had ever seen was lying in deep shade. We stopped to stare. He gave us the slow eye so we walked closer. He began to focus. His tail began to sweep dust. I wondered just what he would do if I took him a bouquet of flowers. There were a dozen other Ferdinands in the next 50 miles, all the size of hippos, all lying down resting up to mate with the herd I suppose.

We had moteled it up to arriving at the Mark Twain but now it was time to pitch the tent. Our first camp was at the edge of a sharp cut river ravine. Our team took to our jobs, Medora photographing, Rowan unloading the tent and packs (he earned his nickname "Mule" on this trip), me scratching notes and listening for new winds of songs blowing in. The night came in cool and we fell asleep to the sounds of Missouri.

I lost my wallet in Maggie Valley, North Carolina with all credit cards, cash, ID. The next day Rowan lost his wallet. Medora's debit card was found to be expired. Here we were in North Carolina looking under the car seat for loose change. We found about a dollar and a half. Fear not, the great

Carolyn Sneed Western Unioned the money to keep going and go we did on our blazing journey.

Too bad we had to move so quickly to cover the ground of our trip. It would have been a pleasure to stay a week in each of the National Forests. We stayed the longest in the Blue Ridge Mountains of North Carolina. Here is the "cradle" of the National Forests, The Pisgah, where a young man named Gifford Pinchot was hired to manage the great expanse of land owned by Cornelius Vanderbilt. Gifford Pinchot and Theodore Roosevelt are the two most important names in the story of the National Forests. They were the founders in 1905, Pinchot becoming the first Chief. (I played Teddy Roosevelt in *Centennial Green*, I look like him, giving a bully bully speech. It wasn't the first time. In 1967 while playing the Gold Seal Amphitheatre in Medora, North Dakota with my folk group, I stood as Teddy for 70 nights in the show.)

I had met most of the Superintendents of the forests of the Eastern Region previously, first in Milwaukee at their annual conference. Upon arrival at the headquarters of the National Forests we visited, I would sit with the Superintendent, tape recording and taking notes. He/She would introduce me to staff members, specialists in forestry, water quality, wildlife, geology, fire fighting, recreation. All of those I met had undeniable passion for their jobs, for what they were doing. Several were kind enough to take the day and drive us about. In Ohio, Superintendent Mary Reddan, gave us a day and half of her time and knowledge.

The debut of *Centennial Green*, with hundreds of Forest Service people at the tent, was a complete success. Opening night of a new original show that has never seen the stage is a private, exhilarating joy for the creator. I'd find myself before the first performance wondering if the jokes would work, the drama would dramatize and the songs ring true. This one was especially so since the audience knew their story and wished it done right. "OK, Warren, this is our big year, our big story, it better be good!"

In December of 2005, our troupe took the show to the Jefferson Auditorium in Washington D.C. to cap the Forest Service's great centennial year. The Chief introduced us. The honor was all ours.

Discussion began with our closest Forest Service friends to make a film of it. Susan Nelson, Anne Archie, Becky Dinsmore, Sandi Forney, Cathy Fox, Steve Hoecker, Teri Pues, Steve Schlobohm and Pam Wiese led the way to finding the money. Steve Dunsky and Dave Steinke, filmmakers for the Forest Service, were put on it along with Milwaukee Public Television. MPT's Raul Galvan would direct the cameras. Dan Braovac was our liaison with the station. The Pabst Theatre in Milwaukee was reserved and we kicked back into rehearsals.

Add this to my huge experience pile. The big TV network truck was gurgling outside the stage door; it was big time big time. I was as nervous as I've ever been. I had more than butterflies, I had pigeons flapping. This was a one shot movie with no retakes. We sat for makeup, we circled as we always do before a show, and we took the stage and nailed it.

The DVD *Centennial Green* is one I'm very proud of. It really shows off the beautiful opera house theatre and the band and singers. It is tough to see Don Pavel in the movie alive and picking.

Later performances did not draw well at BTC, but most of the mattering to me was in the enthusiasm I had for singing and telling of the incredible history. The National Forests today are places for all to recreate in and soak in a spiritual sense of first Earth. They are open to all, from motor sporters to the silent visitors. They belong to all of us and hopefully, to our children's children and their children too.

Will this show ever play again? I don't know. I will say, it's my pet and perhaps the most meaningful, gratifying experience I've had in putting an important American story to song.

THE YO HO BUFFALO HOUR 2007

Terry Meyer called me with an idea for a one-hour show that would gather all the songs I had written about Native Americans and circle the music around my song.

Yo Ho Buffalo. "It's already done," Terry said. So I thought so. "Yeah, I'll just make up a show order and read a little on the history of the American bison to throw in some stories between songs."

I must tell you the buffalo has become my helping spirit. It's a symbol of the untamed West. The bison were the lifeblood of all Native peoples in the buffalos' wandering range, providing food, tools, robes for clothing, and hides for tipis. I sat down to think on the show and suddenly a big herd of ideas approached and began chewing on me. I saddled up for the long ride into the buffalo hour.

I consider the hour to be the 10,000 years of this wild, free-ranging continent.

The decimation of the great herds of American bison is an unparalleled tragedy in the history of the world. Indeed, in all our planet's history, there has never been one species covering such a vast land in such great numbers. From an estimated sixty million running free at the turn of the nineteenth century, there were less than five hundred at the turn of the twentieth. Read the last sentence again. It was a sentence of death to the old free ways of the Natives of North America.

The common phrase in the U.S genocide of native peoples in the middle to late 1800s was "Kill the buffalo, Kill the Indians." Or as the Army's General Sherman said, "The only good Indian is a dead Indian." In all our abhorrence to crimes committed towards innocent people, like 9-11, we should remember the U.S. government's treatment of natives, supported widely by the white populace. Our history is discolored with great injustices as well as filled with great accomplishments. There is an abundance of truthful books on the American West. The courage to write the truth is honorable.

I got the call. I worked the show. I wanted to relate through song and story the centuries' old life of the great herds and the humans that followed them. The energy of the show was not meant to wallow in bitterness. I wanted it to educate and celebrate, somehow, the great free running life of the long time. It was sung to be a hymn to Mother Earth.

The Yo Ho Buffalo Hour included a beautiful beautiful chorale arrangement by Severin Behnen of the old song "Oh, Shenandoah." When I read of the dwindling numbers of Western Meadowlarks, the bird with the call of open prairie, I passed on a recording of their song and Severin and Don Pavel composed a piece based on the bird's melody. Tom Mitchell monologued the history of the horse. Scott Kuester spoke as Buffalo Bill. Jack Gunderson in his buffalo robe coat told of the present day threats to the last wild pureblood herd of buffalo that roams Yellowstone National Park. (Go to www.buffalocampaign.org to read of it.)

The Yo Ho Buffalo Hour thus became a full show. I look back and see the show yet grazing in my memory. Ideas of how to round it up and run it again are still chewing on me. I was graciously sent a full bull hide by a woman from North Dakota who heard of the show. On winter nights it covers my bed and my dreams.

And I think on a story a pioneer told of watching a great herd crossing the Platte River in Nebraska. It took five days for the herd to cross. For miles and miles, they drank the river dry.

DRANK THE RIVER DRY

It was hot and dry noonday July
When the big herd come to the stream
They bowed to the water and they drank the river dry

10 20 50 thousand side by side
Wide as you can fit in a swipe of your eye
They bowed to the water and they drank the river dry

In the summer the herds come together
In the running season rut
They bowed to the water and they drank the river dry

Time beats slow when all you own is you
Stand chew eat and drink is all you gotta do
They bowed to the water and they drank the river dry

Who gets there first gets to slurp their thirst
Upstream on the downstream end
They bow to the river and all there is to drink is mud
wn

NEW FIRST NIGHT / OLD LAST NIGHT

"Gonna be dead for millions, billions and zillions of years
why not stay up late tonight?" wn

Every first Tuesday in August the Chautauqua Institution in New York celebrates its founding. They call it *Old First Night*. It's been a tradition for decades.

Every opening of Big Top Chautauqua is called *New First Night*. Every closing show is called *Old Last Night*. I guess you can see how I named them.

New First Night always features the Blue Canvas Orchestra and Singers and presents a guest or two to kick off the season. The song "Ballyhoo" always starts it backed by pictures of the tent going up. There is an air of excitement; another season up ahead that seems so long, that goes so quickly. We've had The Washburn City Band, a bagpiper, a juggler and other assorted novelty acts performing outside the tent before the show. In the old traveling tent chautauqua days there was always a parade on opening day to stir up interest in the weeklong program up ahead. I always thought we should have one but it never happened.

After nine months of no shows, stepping to the stage to welcome a new season always gave me the sensation that no time had passed. "Wasn't I just here?", I'd think, pinching my self. The roll began down the hill of the summer. It seemed to me the joy ahead would never tire; but by season's end we were always ready to roll up the top and tuck it all away in the storage shed.

Old Last Night, that's another story. A long story.

For years it was a total benefit night for the Big Top as we faced an off season with no income from ticket sales or concessions. The resident performers and crew generously donated their talents to the night. It wasn't long until it became a tradition that many of our guest performers expressed desires to come back up and join in. Finally, we had a parade of our own. It's all different now; outside acts are booked in at their regular fees.

I would sit down with Carolyn and we'd whip up a show list of five full sets. We always wrote down how many minutes each performer would play, add up the sets to go an hour each. We'd plan on four breaks during which Jerry and Carol had different food specialties to offer at the food stand. There were always the drawings from raffle tickets sold throughout the summer featuring prizes donated by local businesses, the grand prize being a season pass to the Big Top. You needn't be present to win. I loved it when the season pass was won by somebody from California. No lie though, one of the passes was won by our own Jack Gunderson.

The audiences learned to bring blankets for the long night up ahead. The northern nights near Labor Day cool down when the sun sinks, a full tent keeps bodies warm with the sidewalls closed. A little nip now and then has been known to help.

The audiences at the beginning of the night went bonzo. The early performers received resounding applause and always looked at me for an encore. It took me a few years to learn to say no. An extra ten minutes here, ten minutes there, ten minutes everywhere elongated our master plan. The result was that the performers scheduled for the late sets would still be pacing backstage well past 2 a.m. waiting to go on. The audience dwindled set by set and began to run out of gas. Oops, it's way past 3 and the show is not over. Finally, it's time for the jam session for the performers who are still around and can still stand up. I often sat. Wonder why?

At the start of the last set, Jerry Carlson would light the bonfire he had set up in tipi form in the parking lot. A keg of beer was tapped, the bar stayed open late and songs were raised at the fire. The light of dawn wasn't far away and those of us who knew we would see the new day rise actually appreciated the late late shows. It made it easier to stay up all night.

In the last decade or so, *Old Last Night* began to change. The show was shorter, the dawn further away for us diehards. In fact, compared to the early years, *Old Last Night* had become a rather sparse ring of fire keepers; hordes of wimps had gone home. The "Survivors" as we called those who stood all hours of the night and early morn were fewer, mostly the same faces of those who kept the tradition.

The Survivors. Ah, back in the good old nights. The ultimate reward for those who stayed up all night was to be included in the Survivors' photograph taken every dawn by Don Albrecht to be printed in the following year's brochure. There were sometimes 60 people or more there for the photograph, beaming at the camera. There, it was proven for all time that YOU WERE THERE!

I'd say for ten years or so the energy was strong. Half in or half out of the bag, the Survivors' laughter rang the hill. It was like being pinned by a fraternity or sorority. It was a select few that proudly served. Then, gradually, the cheating began. I used to count those who stood late at the fire and those who sat in the pews while the late late music was being played. People walked back and forth from the tent to the fire and sometimes climbed Mt. Ashwabay to view the sprinkling lights of Madeline Island. The crowd seemed to dwindle all of a sudden. Then at dawn at the cry of "Survivors! Survivors!" a surprising number of people showed up at the flatbed trailer for the photograph. Aha! Cheaters! Pitching a tent in the dark and sleeping until photo time. I even heard of people going home and driving back just to be in the photograph. Shame! Shame! Wimps!

I miss *Old Last Night*. The REAL *Old Last Nights*. Rain or shine, another era come and gone.

TENT SHOW RADIO
UNDER CANVAS OVER THE AIR

I am the eldest son of Radio Al and so listening to the radio was an everyday part of my growing up. Our house was full of radios—transistors, table radios, kitchen radios, a Philco floor model, and of course the great pull of the car radio. They were tuned in morning, noon and night. My father slept with his bedside radio on all night. I do the same to this day, or should I say to this night, all night.

The old wooden one on my bed table included short wave. Lying in the dark by radio light, listening to Japanese, French, Spanish voices traveled me to sleep nightly. There is nothing better in this world than a baseball game on the radio. My fanatic love of sports, especially baseball, I can joyfully blame on my dad. The clearest reception for a major league team in the fifties was from St. Louis and so I grew up a Cardinal fan until Minnesota became home to the Twins in 1961.

My solid memories of boyhood include lying in bed with my Dad on Saturday nights listening to Dick Enroth broadcasting Minnesota Gopher basketball games. We'd lie back with a bowl of popcorn, my dad reacting to the action with a nervousness and small noises. Saturday afternoons in the fall we listened to Ray Christiansen play-by-play Gopher football games while we walked the cornfields pheasant hunting. Sitting with Dad in the old '50 Mercury in the driveway after coming home from church Sunday nights, listening to Amos and Andy, was the cat's pajamas, the cricket-chirping southern Minnesota summer starlit night out the open window. In the dark car, I'd stare at the lights of the dial, and the voices and laughter coming from within. What a miracle to be everywhere, from anywhere it came over the air to play to me alone.

That's the secret of good radio, to have the voice(s) inside talking or singing only to you. The same secret holds for live performance where every audience member feels like the show is meant only for him or her. I grew up on AM radio, ads and static and all. I declared a Radio/Television major at the University of Minnesota. I became an FM man with *Tent Show Radio*.

By the early 1990s, our Chautauqua resume was spreading statewide. *Tent Show Radio* came to be out of an idea first proposed by Washburnite Dale Baggerly to the rest of the Wisconsin Public Radio board, and then endorsed by Director Jack Mitchell.

The fact we were singing and telling Wisconsin stories was a foremost reason for the show to be a weekly part of the network schedule. We recognized we could only present the original musicals once with limited repeats, adding touring performers and the Blue Canvas Orchestra Shows to the programming. As for the cost of producing a radio show, we already had the studio (the tent), a crowd, the talent, and a post-production resource for editing and mastering in Bruce Bower's recording studio. We were off.

I was always happy with the name I gave it, *Tent Show Radio*, but perhaps the word Big Top Chautauqua should have been more up front. In the first few years we were on both the Classical and The Ideas WPR networks, following Keillor on Saturday nights. Our times changed over the years.

Our budget the first year was $130,000 for expenses. Well documented by Carolyn, they came in at $116,720.

The process was (and is) an interesting one. Because we weren't "live" over the air, it did open up an approach that allowed for post-recording creativity, allowing us to edit for the show. I would have loved to have done the weekly broadcasts truly live but we didn't have a satellite on the grounds to send it. We did send one out live on a Saturday evening after Michael Feldman's *Whad'Ya Know?* show broadcast from the tent that morning. It was a thrill. Even though we recorded live, to me there was always something missing. Screw-ups could be fixed. What fun is that?

First things first: we immediately bought a recording board, snakes and mics for Mark McGinley, our recording engineer. I had known Mark for years. He had been a sound man for local groups and had built a recording studio in the basement of the Music Center in Ashland. In the Chautauqua years previous to *Tent Show Radio*, he was house sound man with Andy Noyes, and then moved to the studio (first a little trailer) when the radio show began.

Mark's task was a difficult one, mixing live sound onto two-track tape, DAT (Digital Audio Tape) was used. He would come in early to the soundchecks of the guest artists as well as for our shows but he was mostly riding the sound balance and the passing of solos, vocal and instrumental, on the fly. His performance was truly amazing considering he did not know the groups' arrangements.

The great advantage was that we recorded the performances from beginning to end. I often think of the extensive catalogue of music we have in the vault of contemporary artists that played the tent. They should be sent to the Smithsonian. They are a backyard portrait of music of our time. Almost all gave us permission to tape in the early years, some with a clause that allowed them to take a tape with them to approve broadcast. Emmy Lou Harris and John Prine were the two main performers who wouldn't allow us to broadcast.

Here's the story from tapes to broadcast. We have the tape of the full show in hand. As producer and host, I led the choices of who and what and when. We have 55 minutes to fill. The tapes were catalogued and selections arranged by my editors, the maps given to Bruce Bowers who put them into 55 minutes to the second. I did the voice overs, Phil Anich sent them out to the stations who played us. We made many friends over the airways. My signature was, "If you would like a tape of this show, you shoulda pushed record an hour ago!"

FROM TENT SHOW RADIO
"Under canvas and over the air"

Every year in the week of St. Patrick's Day we broadcast a Celtic music hour. We regularly presented Celtic performers at the tent including The Drums Of Ireland, Natalie MacMaster, Piper's Crow With Bruce Bowers, The Barra MacNeils, Willowgreen and Carmel Quinn.

Writing a voice over for one of the shows, I hit on a poem that has remained one of my bulls-eye quickest shots. I wrote it but an hour before I headed to the studio. I've been meaning to put a melody under it– someday soon as soon, as I learn to play the fiddle and jig at the same time. This one boils my Scotch-Irish blood.

GREEN STEP

The only thing I wonder is with all of us doin' so right
The only thing I wonder is will I ever get home tonight?
For tonight the fiddler's on the bow
And the pipe and the whistle are rollin'
And the floor is swept up clean for the dance
And if I see her I'll ask my chance
And if I see you I'll dump my pockets and buy you one
Ale dark as the night is out or a double-shot or a pint of stout
I'll pour it and toast the glass of your eye that shines that certain way
Especially when you're all in green
On old St. Patrick's Day
For all some those of us here
This is the night we roll up the year
Give a step and a hand to the band
Sing to the moon and the wild land
And I wonder, and I wonder, when shall we meet again?
For a true love and a great friend
The only two that never end
And I wonder, and I wonder, with all of us doin' so right
I wonder and I wonder where are you tonight?
wn

Where Else But In A Tent Show

In 1989 Sally Kessler picked out a wonderful one-woman play, *Planting in The Dust,* to present. The scene was a farm kitchen. While she performed her kitchen duties, she was telling of the life of a woman much alone on the farm. The monologue referred to her husband on his tractor out in the field plowing back and forth in the rows all the while.

During an afternoon rehearsal, Jerry Carlson was mowing the hill grass up and around the tent, the sound of his tractor ever present. Voila! Jerry and the tractor were added to the play.

While Sally delivered her lines in the performance, Jerry drove the hour back and forth, up and down the hill, unseen. The sound faded as if at the end of the field and rose in volume as Jerry turned around outside the backwall of the canvas.

Lake Superior

BIG TOP

CHAUTAUQUA

All About Us

8:15 old circus time–
Center ring I give good evening,
pass the wand to
Don Pavel who counts a one a two,
The Blue Canvas Orchestra
grabs the trapeze of the evening,
their fingers flying through the air
with the greatest of ease.

wn

A DAY IN THE LIFE OF...

Today will be a long one. We're doing two morning shows for elementary school groups that are being bussed up from Washburn, Ashland, Red Cliff, Solon Springs, Superior and Hurley. Call is 8:30 a.m. for the band. For musicians an early call is dreaded, but it rarely bothers me. I'm a morning man. Half the band though has the drip-cheek zombie look when they step into the back of the tent; laughter slowly begins to bubble out as they head to the caffeine. We are playing a cutting of *30th Star* for the school shows and the full show tonight. Makes for a good paying day for the performers in this first week of September, the last week of the Chautauqua season.

The air has the crisp cool scent of the coming fall, red tipping the maple leaves, yellow popping out in the popples. The pond, better known as Lake Superior, shows a different hue of blue come fall. This morning it's a flat sheet of water perhaps resting up for November. I'm knowing a week from today I'll be lolling at Northland Lodge on Lost Land Lake with nothing to do but fish, read, fish, read, fish, fish. The end of every summer's run on the hill is always bittersweet. I gaze at the Big Top with the two masks of drama, one has the wide smile, one the turned down frown. The wide smile wins. Unclip the ropes, ease down the poles, drop the top, it's time. The saving grace is knowing, God willing, that in a blink another summer will rise.

The busses are arriving, fourth graders jumping out, teachers herding them towards the tent. Andy Noyes once described their landing as flocks of birds migrating in. The theatre becomes an aviary. Andy was always in the audience running house sound, in the middle of it, hearing and seeing all. On the *30th Star* tour in Green Bay's Weidner Center, 900 fourth graders were squirming and chirping in their seats before the 9.a.m. show. We walked out to high-pitched screams that never let up. Teachers were standing and giving the kids the ssshhh sign but to no avail. I waved with one hand, they waved back, I waved with the other hand, they waved back, I patted my stomach, they patted their stomachs, I patted my stomach and rubbed my head, they........all was suddenly quiet. I use that trick to this day.

The students this morning are wriggling with joy, the teachers are even happier not having to settle the herds down inside a schoolroom on a beautiful September morning. The sidewalls are up, the show is on. The first thing I do is tell them, after I count to three, I want them to shout out their names. Now we're all introduced. Never talk or sing down to youngins. Give them what you'd give an adult audience. DO NOT encourage clapping along on the first song. If you're playing Beethoven's Fifth, they'll clap along. Give them soon a song to sing along with. They're yours.

The kids notice two large video cameras being carried around the tent, aiming frequently in their direction. "You're on TV!" They all stand and wave and shriek. I let it go a bit and settle them down. They suddenly sit up a little straighter as the show begins. About a half hour into it a boy in the front row yells out, "It's my birthday!" "My birthday's next week!" "My birthday is in December!" "My mom's birthday was yesterday." Carry on. After the show I invite the kids to walk up the stairs and across the stage. "Take a bow." I parade them through the curtain to backstage and out the stage door. Betty waves from the projection stand. Some of the musicians are waiting outside, soon surrounded by the wired-up students. "Hope you liked the show." "I go deer hunting with my dad." "Will you sign my shirt?" "Grandma's coming tomorrow." "Wanna see my tooth?" "I just got these shoes." "My mom knows you guys."

What's better than this? The busses pull out, the band right behind. Carolyn and I talk in the sweet sunlight about the show order for Old Last Night. The tent is empty. It's like a balloon just popped. There's another show at one. In the hour school show I try to look at every young face from the stage as I sing the *30th Star* end song

> *What shall we leave our children to live on?*
> *What shall we leave our children to dream by?*
> *Leave a deep garden with clear waters blue*
> *To their children's children and their children too*

I wonder what they shall live on as they grow into the modern world. I think of how lucky I've been to be born in a less crowded time. I swear it was simpler, an easier age to make a living way back in the fifties, sixties and seventies. The country was not as paved physically and spiritually. Singing for attention to the health of the planet is at the top of the reason I sing. Maybe I ought to stop singing of anything else. We need Homeland Security for the Earth for the future of these kids, from our generation's terrorism on our natural resources.

Ed tells the singers he would like them in the Spirit Cottage at 5 (be ready for downbeat at 5, don't come straggling in five minutes later) to run through vocals again before the evening sound check at 6. The original shows are spread out for one-night plays throughout the summer and thus it's impossible to have the songs and scripts memorized for each show. We need the brush-up.

I stop at the coal dock in Washburn on my way home to see if the browns are in yet, the usual gang of old geezers are car fishing, three lines each, in the pole holders. So and so caught a 26 inch brown this morning there on the corner. It's always astounding to sit and gaze at Chequamegon Bay on a summer afternoon, a few sailboats up towards Bayfield in full flight. In this busy freeway world it is continually amazing to see the Bay almost empty of boats. Lucky me to call here home.

It's 26 minutes from my house to the tent. I was cutting it to the minute one afternoon heading up for rehearsal, head down charging out the door, when I looked up and saw a big black bear sitting against the hood of my car with a plastic garbage bag in his mouth, He looked like an old man, his arms on his knees, eyes not as surprised as mine. I froze, stepped back, having a small heart attack. He didn't run, didn't move a muscle, and was standing his ground. I stepped back in the house slamming the door hoping he'd leave.

He didn't. I walked back on the deck. "Look, I'm gonna be late for rehearsal. Get! You hear me." I pointed to my watch. "I need to go." He didn't move. "Mukwah! Mukwah! Get!" I stamped my foot hard. He didn't move. I stepped nervously towards him talking all the while. He didn't move. I pleaded some more. He didn't budge. I remembered my son had a bag of firecrackers in his room and fetched a pack of Black Cats, lit the fuse and tossed them at the bear. He ran. I was late for rehearsal with an excuse. "Yeah, sure." I had a mess of garbage to clean up next morning.

Carolyn and I continue our Old Last Night planning on the phone. Afterward, I open the laptop and see if the blank page will spit up some new jokes. Whoa! It's 4 o'clock, time to shower and head back to the hill.

Time left the vocal rehearsal with some untouched arrangements. Time to cross the grass to the stage and soundcheck. There are fourteen in the onstage cast of *30th Star* with Betty at the visuals, Andy and Andy on sound, Lisa stage managing, Chris Berge crewing and Phillip "Cruise" Warren on lights.

The soundcheck begins with the cordless head mics Andy Noyes adjusts for house sound. What a great name for a soundman—Noyes. Then the band runs the song "*30th Star*" once through and we begin the search for instrumental balance for each individual performer. We're using earbuds as monitors. I use only one in order to keep one ear to the audience alive. I turn the volume up max and add to my increasing deafness. I need presence! One by one we tell Andy Okey on the monitor board what we need more or less of. Less fiddle. More mandolin. Less of Jack. More of me. Me me me. We sing the chorus of the end song to hone in vocals. Lisa yells "five minutes" from side stage, meaning the house is opening and we need to vacate.

I'm checking the concessions special for supper. It's a Swiss cheese California burger with chips. Put it on my tab. The crowd is arriving and I meet and greet showgoers. I recognize many who come to the tent at least once a year. Ten minutes before the show, the cast and crew circle outside the tent. It's our ritual. Last minute reminders come up of mistakes made in rehearsal. Clipboard Carolyn speaks out the schedule for the next couple days. We end with the word for the night. "Severin, what's the word?" "Do what you do." I count to three and we all blurt out "Do what you do." It's showtime.

The show goes well. If we don't get it right tonight after being close together for three months, it's time to get a day job. I, of course, stay to all hours in the T-Bar and then move it to the picnic tables with those who have come from near and far to Chautauqua. The moon is silvering the lake on my drive home. Tomorrow is another show.

THE BLUE CANVAS ORCHESTRA AND TROUPE

How did Chautauqua's troupe come to be? How did the members make their way to the Big Top? I give you here stories in the order of how and when I first met each of them on their sidewinding trails to the tent. As I always said from the stage, (while on my knees), I am the luckiest man alive to have this band playing my songs and playing Chautauqua.

Jack Gunderson
The Golden Throat of Hoffman, Minnesota

March 1967

I'm to meet a guy named Jack Gunderson at McDonald's in Dinkytown, University of Minnesota campus. I remember hamburgers were nine cents. We were to ride together to rehearsal of the Edgewater Eight, in which group he had been a regular performer for a good while and I was joining up for only one show. Little did we know.

Agent Fred Smith, while I auditioned for the Edgewater Eight, asked if I had a tenor banjo. I said, "No." He said, "Here. This one belonged to an old vaudevillian we booked for many years. $300." "Sold." It was a 1920s B & D Silverbell with a knee mute. I sold it later when I was hurting for money to buy a new guitar. There's another one of the great mistakes of my life. A lost love. All I have is a publicity picture of me, hands on the Silverbell. I'd die for that banjar now. Gary Schafer, director of the Edgewater Eight, assumed I played tenor banjo. I didn't tell him I had never had one in my hands before, or for that matter ever seen one.

The Edgewater Inn in north Minneapolis was a classy old-fashioned show club. It was an elegant example of all the show clubs that were so prevalent in the sixties. That was an era I'm sorry to see gone; there was work for show groups six nights a week then all over the United States. Jack was the voice of the Edgewater show.

Frankie Oliveri was the band leader. At the first rehearsal, Jack joined the vocalists while I opened the banjo case. I had just bought a method book a couple days before, learned to tune it but that was about it. I had two weeks to the opening of the show to learn how to play tenor banjo. Frankie, at the piano, set the chord charts out and I froze. I made some comments like "I've been having trouble with the tuning pegs." "These strings are old, maybe I'll just listen first." What a bunch of bullshit. Frankie could see through me but unbelievably enough, kept it to himself. I told him I would take home the music to my solo, "Whispering", and woodshed it. Well, I did, staying up all night for three days despite my college classes. Years later, when I saw Frankie multiple times at the Big Top during reunion shows of the Edgewater Eight, we'd laugh about it. I'm as fond of Frankie as anyone I've ever met.

Somehow I pulled it off, made it a comedy piece where I first started to play, hit a wrong note, squinched then kicked off the solo with Frankie carrying the rhythm. I still can play about half of that melody 45 years later. I was a rookie in the Edgewater revue of a Broadway type show. Along with Jack, the cast was patient with me. I learned a new stance of showmanship from the group. Oh no...they dance and I'm in on one. Jackie and Bob Hansen were the lead dancers. (Wow, they settled years later in Bayfield buying the Winfield Inn and were the chief movers and shakers to put together the wonderful Edgewater Eight Reunions at Chautauqua).

Back to Jack. What an incredible voice. I've always been amazed at Jack's talent and stage presence. Still am. Smooth. Classy.

We became great friends during the Edgewater time. From there we've worked decades together, celebrating our 30th anniversary of performing together with a party at Patsy's Bar in 1997. Adding the years to 2008 makes 41 years off and on we stood stages together. Jack was lead singer and bass player in The Tenth Story Window, touring the entire country for two and a half years, and in The Lost Nation String Band. From day one, of course, Jack has been a principal singer and actor at the Big Top and remains so to this day. He was the BCO's bass player until 2005.

Down the years, he has done numerous Big Top concerts with Jimmy Martin and several others with his family singers. It's amazing such vocal talent is found in one family. Their concerts attracted a dedicated audience. I loved the gospel songs they brought to the tent, the church pews and canvas being a perfect setting for an old-time gospel hour. We should have passed the basket. Jack auditioned and cashed in on a dream when he sang in several operas with the Minnesota Opera Company. It was *Othello* I joyously saw in St. Paul. The plot circled around the trouble caused by a handkerchief. I renamed it *Damn Hankies*. It was damn good.

Jack's acting talents equal his vocal prowess. Put a hat on Jack and he disappears into the character. Two of the leading roles Jack played were the chief lighthouse keeper of the Outer Island Light in *Keeper Of The Light* and the Conductor in *On The Velvet*. Jack Norwegianed up and portrayed the one and only Ole in *Riverpants* . Jack has known Ole and his jokes for many years as they were both born and raised next door to each other in Hoffman, Minnesota. I think they're related on his mother's father's side by a second cousin through a marriage that didn't last. Ole died but Jack keeps his stories alive. Yeah then! He is resident joke teller in the Big Top troupe. Here's to Jack with high regards:

JACK

The golden throat of Hoffman
sings in silver,
the setting the stage.
Pure gold, pure silver.
Belltone.

In the left hand the microphone cord,
the right hand gestures,
waving smoke of the song
as a priest wands wet cedar
over the congregation,
as a native American elder
wafts the smoldering sage
beginning the ceremony,
as a fog clears in the throat of the night.
wn

Do wah this guy can sing! A voice like his is a gift of the Bird God. It's showtime. As Jack says, "Time to fool 'em again."

Don Pavel

Don Pavel died suddenly on January 30, 2008. It was a shock to all of us. He was the bandleader of the Blue Canvas Orchestra, a Chautauqua trooper from opening night. He was a thoroughbred guitar player; he could swing from bluegrass to jazz and cover all styles in between. His playing was instantly recognizable, much like you can tell it's Frank Sinatra from the first note on the radio.

Don and I were the founding members of the Lost Nation String Band and so he was on the permanent move with Jack Gunderson and me to the Chequamegon country in 1980. We were partners, off and on, for 38 years, unheard of in the music business. He always declared we were the most unlikely duo to succeed. While we were scrapping for a living around Madison, he had an offer to join another band, popular in Madison, but chose to stay with me. I certainly chose to stay with him. We always said we could change pouches anytime, the pouches holding money and trust.

Here we go on the adventures of Don Pavel and Warren Nelson.

1970. My show group The Tenth Story Window (nine members) was back in The Twin Cites, our home base, and we needed to replace our guitar player. I can't remember exactly (more memorywars) how I came to hear of Don Pavel. I think our drummer knew him. But I remember the day well when he came to the London Productions, Minneapolis office of our manager, where I had my own office for tomfoolery. I had my customary derby hat on and as Don would later remember, was constantly twirling a pencil.

At the time, Don was gigging in a rock band and working regularly; I could tell immediately he was in the music business for life. His guitar came out of the case and he began playing. I was astounded and confused. Would this style fit our group? I had never heard the guitar played quite like this before. I was like a frozen dog tilting his head at a sound that was curiouser and curiouser. We talked music, me a folkie and he a rocker. Don said from the beginning, "They're all the same notes."

I didn't make an offer; he wasn't sure he wanted to land and travel with us. We agreed to meet again the following week. He played again but didn't have to. The game was on.

And so we traveled the U.S. together for a year and a half playing show lounges and concerts with The Tenth Story Window, covering the hits of the day as well as a few original songs of mine. What a time it was. Gas was eleven cents a gallon; we were always provided with lodging; life was music and driving and staying in a city for a week or two or three— Chicago, Cleveland, Denver, Montreal, Cape Cod, Louisville, Des Moines, Minneapolis, etc. It was a great life being a visiting resident for two or three weeks, getting to know the locale and the locals. Montreal was my favorite.

He drove a used Cadillac, a beautiful boat that fit his style. I say again, what a time. There is nothing like it anymore. Work was easy to find for talented groups, six nights a week, four shows a night, pack up Saturday after the show in Cleveland and open in Allentown, Pennsylvania come Monday. Another six or twelve nights and leave for the next lounge.

For all those years, I always stood next to Don on stage. I spent half the show time watching his fingers dance. There was no hesitation between his mind, soul and fingers. The music moved through his arms at the speed of light, never playing a solo the same. Seemed like he never knew where he was going on the solo road until he arrived. Every transition from solo to accompaniment was given with rhythm, taste, rarely missing a note. Don's ear swallowed sound. We both came to have hearing loss over the years, a sure sign along with calluses that you're a musician. When someone tells you he or she is a guitar player, ask to see the fingertips of their fingering hand. Look for calluses. You'll know.

After The Tenth Story Window broke up, Don joined other traveling lounge groups until he moved to Denver in 1974 with John Pinckaers, an incredibly talented and wonderfully eccentric piano man who was also in the Window. They came to a gig Michael Kotik and I were playing, Michael being another true musical partner I met in Colorado. After two years, our duo broke up and Don, Pink and I formed a trio, Nelson, Pinckaers and Pavel, playing ski resorts, especially Vail and joints around Denver.

We were playing the Holiday Inn in Dillon and on the schedule letter board it stated– "Playing nightly from 9 to 1 in the lounge, Nelson, Pinckaers and Pavel." Somebody overnight took a look at our name and switched the letters around. "Playing nightly—Pelvis, Pancreas and Navel."

We changed our name to Goat Marbles. My sister Sharla and I shared a house in Arvada, a suburb of Denver. It had a funky field of a backyard and she bought a goat she named Josephine. Hence Goat Marbles became our name and the goat was included in the publicity picture.

One of the supper clubs we played was the Hungry Farmer in Boulder. Yes, the bright light marquee advertised, "The Hungry Farmer Proudly Presents Goat Marbles."

During this time, Betty Ferris and I were living together; she quit her good job in Denver and we moved up into the wilderness of the Gore Range outside of Silverthorne along with Don and Sharla and the big Pink. Pink married a woman named Evelyn who had been traveling with a musician. She was delivered to Dillon by her previous boyfriend and out of his Jeep came 17 or so suitcases. Like clowns out of a tiny clown-car, they kept popping out the doors.

The trio broke up but we remained friends. We always said we never really broke up; we were just taking a break.

John and Evelyn moved back to Denver to an apartment. When he joined an ensemble in Alaska, they kept their apartment. We hadn't heard from him in six months when I got a call. "Hey, would you please go check our apartment. Evelyn thinks she left a casserole in the oven." Wow! I went to their apartment and there was the casserole. At least she had turned off the oven.

Don and I became a duo in a very spontaneous way. He was working on crew at the A-Basin ski area and I was writing and not gigging. He came to our cabin one afternoon after work and said, "Hey, you wanna play a gig?" "When?", "Tonight." "OK." We had never performed as a duo before. "How much?" "Fifteen dollars a piece and all the booze we can drink." "Great." I packed up my sound system and we left for the Snake River Saloon.

On the way down the mountain, I suggested we needed a show order or at least a list of songs. We got quiet for a minute. I started writing a list. We looked at each other, laughed and threw the list out the window. We tuned up to start without a clue of what we were going to play. Punch line, we were the first live entertainment they had ever had and we were a hit, packed the joint Friday and Saturday nights. I would call out the titles and we'd travel with the songs. It wasn't at all curious to me that Don knew hardly any of my lyrics. Songs that we'd played hundreds of times, he carried on the wings of his strings not knowing the storyline. Our common love was sound, live sound. The sound of words to me, the sound of the music to him, put the glove on the hand.

It was there I tried my first attempts at playing lead. I had always been a rhythm player. Don suddenly yelled out "Take it." "Yeah, right, Don." I waited for him to play another solo but he just kept playing backup until I began to plunk plunk.

I'm still plunk plunking, though noticeably better I hope, at least more courageously.

Don and I never forgot the Peppermint Schnapps night. Shots were a quarter. It was a sticky situation. I mean everyone and everything there, including the barstools, were glued together by Schnapps by the end of the night. The dancing was a sight to see. Every lift of a boot or shoe had that little zipping sound. And tapping my foot, as I always do while playing, caused erratic tempos I'm sure. My God, did we laugh often and brightly in those days. I guess you had to be there. I'm glad I was.

Don and Sharla had found a little cabin on the Snake River on Highway Nine. It was 18 miles home from the gigs. I was driving my 1954 Plymouth station wagon that got 40 miles to a quart of oil. After every Snake River Saloon gig, I would chug the 18 miles, park at the highway, strap on my cross country skis and make-way for Betty and our cabin two miles up the unplowed road. I hated the first quarter mile with all my boozed up heart, but by the time I hit the first flat span, I began to wake up. Those mountain nights were incredible, nine thousand feet closer to the stars and the Milky Way, Keller Mountain's peak looming over the valley. Often, ahead in the darkness, I would hear a herd of elk crossing the road.

The story of Don and me founding Lost Nation is another chapter in this book. All along the way Don helped to mold my new songs. He played and sang in every new big show. He was a great singer, his voice glove on hand with his playing. Many of you also know what an excellent composer he was. His CD *Glade* features his compositions.

I don't remember us ever getting into an argument during the Tenth Story Window years or after including all our years at Chautauqua. He was always a close-the-bar pal of mine.

Every day now when I practice and play my guitar, I start out with a scale exercise that Don designed and warmed-up with, a very melodic travel up and down the strings and neck. Everyday I think of Don Pavel. I miss, miss that man. And I will to the end of my time on this globe.

Betty Ferris

In spring 1971 while playing the Continental Plaza Hotel in Chicago with my showband, The Tenth Story Window, I took a stroll up Michigan Avenue and entered a bookstore that was stacked with poetry books. I pulled a paperback off the shelf. It was the *Collected Poems of Dylan Thomas*. I opened it to whatever page and began to read. I was stunned. The force of the first poem I read let loose some power within me that was opening a morning curtain on I knew not yet what. Dylan's lyrical lines were a map of the same country of the empty page that I had been wandering in since I first took pen in hand in teenhood. It was like I found the King of my country.

Unbelievably, at age 24 I had never heard of Dylan Thomas. Outside of the classic poetry I was assigned to read in high school (and enjoyed) I had found poetry in the song lyrics of folk singing groups I listened to. I say now that's as good a writer's upbringing as there is but there in my hand in Dylan's poems was a thunder of sound that made me want to take cover, go in a cave and wait until I was good and ready to come out with the courage to take a new trail to the high country of poetry and follow rivers into the valleys of song.

I suddenly felt an orchestra in me tuning up, waiting for something to play in words.

When I met Betty Ferris I met a soulmate who knew well the country of poetry.

It would be three years before I encountered her. I broke up the Window in September of '71 having come to the realization that I needed out of the lounge circuit. Looking back though, I have great regrets of not keeping our show group together, traveling in the worlds of fun we had on the road. Jack and Don were in the Window with me and the rest of the group were also great friends of mine. The trail out of the cave took me to Colorado.

I moved out with Rex Loker, a former group member who had just been discharged from the Army, and Jenny Fetzer of Denver. We shared a trailer in Avon, Colorado a mile from Vail. Jenny worked and supported us while I scouted those rivers of song. I began cleaning condos which produced a meagre income, but the benefits of taking home the leftovers in refrigerators full of food the high-rolling tourists left behind kept us in steaks and expensive wines. Jenny and I stayed together for a year, moving to Denver, eventually breaking up.

My first Colorado gig was solo in a little club/bar called the Robin's Nest. My memorywars fail me here recalling how I met Otto Hallgren but he was there that night, being a new fan of my songs. I soon met Otto's wife, Betty Hallgren, maiden name Ferris. No hanky-panky here. It would be two years later after Betty and Otto were separated that we began our beguine. I worked for Otto and his partner Brian Elgart remodeling a funky apartment building. All the while I was thinking music.

My sister Sharla had moved out and we were sharing a house in Arvada. She was waitressing at a club called the Port of Entry where I met Michael Kotik, an extraordinary guitar picker and songwriter. Michael and I zapped on each other within 30 seconds of meeting. I was playing on his off night when he showed up. The pay was $10 for the gig. Michael and I became a duo and played together for nearly two years, mostly in ski resorts. Michael and I were true partners and are back in touch. He played the tent with the band and me in 2006.

As for Betty Ferris and Warren Nelson, hang on, we're getting there.

Don Pavel moved to Colorado with John Pinckaers, former members of Tenth Story Window. We became a trio (see the chapter on Don). Don married my sister Sharla.

Betty and I saw each other eye to deep eye for the first time one evening at a club called the Carriage House in Denver where Nelson, Pinckaers and Pavel were playing. There began a personal relationship that lasted 17 years, our professional relationship going through 2008.

She offered me one of the greatest gifts I've ever had, the gift of time to sit and write and dream. She offered to support us. It was a turning point in my life. For the first time I sat in a year's chair, reading, reading, reading and writing poetry and songs. She was Executive Director of the Denver Association of Retarded Citizens. Her dedication to the rights of handicapped people in the community was a devoted trait which rose again in our later work together in creating shows that celebrate community. I think above all other people I have ever met, she understands the living meaning of the word community.

It was during the year 1976, the U.S. Bicentennial year, when a recognition rose in me that I wanted to do something in the spirit of the great living room of our nation. Sitting in her grandfather's rocking chair one morning I struck an idea. I wrote in my journal:

> *"A THING: Combine your interests in history, old photographs, songwriting, storytelling, comedy and putting on big shows into a concert program to celebrate the story of Fairmont. Put together a large ensemble of musicians, singers and actors."*

There on one page was the causeway of my future career. Writing songs into a show with readings telling history illustrated by historical photographs. The Big Top Chautauqua family tree was planted on that fateful day in the year 10 B.C. Time went by and we decided to move into the mountains. We found a one room cabin in a mountain resort under the shadow of Mount Keller in the Gore Range. Sharla and Don moved up with us, living two cabins away. I began work on *The Martin County Hornpipe*, the story of which is told in this book. We stayed a year in the mountains, moving from one cabin to another, into the next valley. Rent was free. For the whole year we figured our expenses for light, heat and water were between seven dollars and seven dollars and fifty cents. For the year! Kerosene lamp light, gas for the chain saw, water from the mountain creek. Don and I began to gig in the mountains. Betty and I were looking to the future as we left the mountains when Betty became Executive Director of the Wisconsin Coalition of Advocacy in Madison. Soon after the Lost Nation String Band was founded by Don and me; time went by and we all moved to northern Wisconsin.

The Nelson-Ferris Concert Company was founded in Washburn in 1983 with *Souvenir Views*. For understanding "The process," as we called it, in creating shows, see the poem "Recipe" in the chapter "Shows."

The combination of original songs with projected photographs defined the heart of Big Top Chautauqua. Betty is "Queen of the Screen." Our work together, pounding out scripts into a show, has indeed defined Wisconsin. The greatest recognition for our work with Chautauqua was receiving the first ever Wisconsin History Award presented on stage at the tent by Bill Cronon and Jerry Phillips representing the Wisconsin Historical Society. Betty continues to this writing as Chautauqua's Visuals Director. She was the first president of the Board of Directors of the Big Top.

By far the greatest joys Betty and I hold in our lives are our children, Medora Napea Nelson-Ferris and Rowan Newport Nelson-Ferris.

This verse from my song, "Once You've Lived in Colorado," is for Betty in the kerosene light of our mountain time together.

> *Once you've broken trail to heaven*
> *There is no goin' down*
> *Snowshoe away from the trouble*
> *You dropped off back in town*
>
> *Woodsmoke curls from the chimney*
> *Light flares from the kerosene lamps*
> *Up and down around the cabin walls*
> *The shadows flicker and dance*
> wn

Bruce Bowers

Mr. Bowers' path to Big Top Chautauqua was a long and winding road. The year was 1976, the beginning of our partnership was the show, *Selections From Lost and Found Fairmont Histories: A Martin County Hornpipe*. The show called for a fiddler and I knew not who that might be. I didn't know any fiddlers. One night Don Pavel, who was working at the A-Basin ski area in Colorado, stopped at a bar where a group called Succotash was playing. Don introduced himself and somehow got on the subject of the show. Bruce told him that the group was breaking up and he was curious and available. There it all began.

The last gig of Succotash was in Jackson Hole, Wyoming. I called the bar they were playing in and asked for Bruce Bowers. What faith. He agreed to come do the show, money unknown, and mentioned his partner Joe Weed. Joe played fiddle, guitar and mandolin. They borrowed a car and headed to Fairmont, arriving on the Tuesday before the Friday opening. I'll never forget the first time we shook hands in my folks' dining room. Ten minutes later Bruce and Joe were in the basement digging into the songs. The other performers began arriving. Thank God for Bruce and Joe. They wrote out string arrangements. The first time I heard Bruce play I was speechless. I stretched my face into the widest grin of my life. I not only hadn't known a fiddler but the sound system I had would have been totally incapable of sounding the show. Bruce had a huge sound system! Roll on *Hornpipe*!

In 1983, once again we needed a fiddler for the Washburn Centennial show, *Souvenir Views*, and this time we knew one. But where was he? I can't remember how we found Mr. Bowers again. Seven years had gone by. It was likely Michael Stanwood, a singer/songwriter/autoharpist knew where he was. I called. He said yes. He caught a flight from San Jose, California; I picked him up in Duluth.

He was wearing red pants and a headful of long hair. (We later gave him the stage name of Leon Redpants.) We drove to Washburn catching up on seven years of news. *Souvenir*

Views was another great success. Bruce flew back to California.

Two years later in 1985 here comes *Riding The Wind*. Here comes Mr. Bowers back to the Bayfield Peninsula. Another success. Bruce flew back to California.

1986. Here comes Lake Superior Big Top Chautauqua. Bruce flew out from California and the rest is this history. For the first few years Mr. Bowers would play the Chautauqua season and fly back to California, a rather long commute.

Bruce Bowers is woven into the entire fabric of the Big Top's success. How lucky we are to have his incredible talent, musicianship and recording prowess hereabouts. His talents as a composer can be found throughout our shows.

One of my favorite Bruce Bowers moments occurred during one of his annual concerts. He had designed and built what I always called "The Gizmo." It was a box of mystery that could make his fiddle sound a thousand ways. The humid heat of summer can cause havoc with instruments and amps in the tent. The Gizmo froze up in the heat. He pulled out a portable hair dryer and we waited while it did its do on the Gizmo and the show went on,

Bruce and I partnered up in the production of *Tent Show Radio* from its beginning. He was the digital editor, pasting the mapped shows together out of the master Dat tapes with timed spaces for voice overs. I came to trust Mr. Bowers as a director reminding me we were taking a live taped show and making it seem to be live on the air. I'd come in with fully written voice overs or, more often than not, just a few notes allowing me to improvise. That was my jazz. Over the years we worked to define a Tent Show Radio style. To the second…55 minutes…5 4 3 2 1 flap the lips and tie it up.

Thank you Mr. Bowers for the great years I stood the stage and studio with you. Fiddle on.

Cal Aultman

Cal and I have a renewed friendship, first meeting each other in Madison in 1979 when he joined Don Pavel and me, forming the Lost Nation String Band. We circled Madison like we were going to take it but we never quite did. That makes him a founding member of LNSB. We gigged together in joints around Madtown until he left to join Gold Rush, a country-flavored band fronted by Danny Parks, a whiz kid fiddler.

Don and Cal had connected in northern Minnesota in summer 1978 when they both answered a newspaper ad for professional musicians to form a group. That lasted six months, both giving their notice to quit on the same night. Cal gives Don, as we all do, huge gratitude for enriching his understanding of music via the guitar. "It was Don who first made me want to broaden my very limited musical vocabulary and for the short time that we made music together in those days, he was the source of most of what I now know about music."

Jack Gunderson moved to the Madison area and became Lost Nation's bass player, replacing Cal. Cal booked a few gigs for Lost Nation around his hometown Grand Rapids, Minnesota, when he moved back. He sat in with us, as he says, "for punishment." During a job in Grand Rapids, Cal's dad threw out a line to me after hearing me play guitar during our first set. "Hey, why don't you go stand over there by the door and I'll help you out."

The circle goes around. In the winter of 2002-2003, Cal auditioned for Don to be bass player in *30th Star* which we were playing at the tent and touring during the off season. He's brought a solid bottom to the Blue Canvas Orchestra players while they wander around the fingerboards. He sings my song "Hotel Hustle" like nobody I know. I get the good feeling Cal and I will be friends until the final checkout. That's my pleasure.

Professor Bruce B. Burnside

Bruce Burnside opened the window for Betty Ferris, Don Pavel, Jack Gunderson and me to the strong sights and delights of Lake Superior's south shore and Bayfield County.

I met Mr. Burnside in Sauk City, Wisconsin in 1978. I was living close by in Mazomanie. Don and I were gigging Wednesday nights at Potts Inn in Cross Plains. I needed some work done on my guitar and was told of a local luthier by the name of John Reintz. I took my guitar to John and we talked music, me mentioning that besides folk and bluegrass I had a passion for the antique music of classical banjo. "There's a guy living in Sauk City who plays classical banjo. His name is Bruce Burnside, here's his number." I had never heard of anyone else with any knowledge or interest in this nineteenth century era of nylon-stringed banjos. I called him. I knocked on his door one Tuesday morning. As Mr. Burnside commented a time or two after, "one Tuesday morning..."

We hit it off. He had an upstairs room full of instruments including banjos, guitars and mandolins. He played them all. The talk went immediately to classical banjo music and the improbability of the two of us living so close to each other with a knowledge and passion for the long lost time of banjo orchestras. I had bought over a hundred pieces of sheet music in Denver back in the early 70's and started diddling with it off and on. The music was curious to me. It took me awhile to recognize it was five-string music, the notation written a step and a half lower. I was learning to play it on my steel string

OME, never having seen a five string strung in nylon until meeting Burnside. He was soon off somewhere to work and I told him of Don and me playing at Potts, inviting him to stop by and sit in.

He showed up with his mandolin and raised our ears with his incredible playing. Another old dog (not so old then) still barking, making music. It's an immediate brotherhood meeting someone else whose life is making music. He joined our Wednesday nights, getting on the weekly payroll. Thirty dollars each we made for the gigs. We sat in chairs when we played. One night we stood up and Potts told us if we'd keep standing, he'd add five bucks. A guy named Bugsy showed up to play bass when he wasn't gigging elsewhere. A young Madison fiddler, Danny Parks, jumped in off and on. Danny was a whiz on fiddle, banjo and guitar. He left for Nashville and we lost track of him until he showed up in summer 1984 playing in Mel Tillis's band at a mini festival at, of all places, Mt. Ashwabay, soon to be the home of BTC.

Cal Aultman joined up and we became a group, a band without a name. Someone had stolen the town sign of Lost Nation, Iowa and it was nailed to a wall at Potts' place. As we pondered trying to find a name, Potts looked up at the sign one night and declared, "You're the Lost Nation String Band," and so we were.

Mr. Burnside had a friend working at Northland College in Ashland and knew this up north neighborhood. He booked a gig for Lost Nation at Archie's Supper Club in Washburn on a Wednesday night. By then Jack Gunderson had become our bass player. Up highway 13 we drove to where we'd never been before. Coming into Washburn I noticed a bar named Patsy's. It was painted orange, advertising burgers and Walter's Beer. Had to stop there before the gig. Had to stop there for the next 30 years.

The Archie's gig was packed with locals. It was the start of Lost Nation's long run of gigs hereabouts and around the North. We returned north a few more times and it started feeling like this might be home. I remember standing with Betty Ferris at the mouth of the Raspberry River in Herbster and right then and there deciding to move up. The whole band moved up. The history of Lost Nation from there deserves an entire book.

Lost Nation, as I've said, was the musical foundation for the Big Top. Burnside and Don, an odd couple, got to know each other extraordinarily well on stage, passing solos back and forth. The years flying by found both of them at the top of their games.

Mr. Burnside, (I never do call him Bruce), besides playing his fingers off on the mandolin, began composing and writing with a fervor. He put together a Civil War show entitled *Unsung Stories of the Civil War*, a show *Town Hall Tonight* and most recently *Lincoln's Legacy*, a multimedia original song and story history show. He has also been traveling throughout the years to schools all across Wisconsin working with students, teaching and doing workshops.

Bruce Burnside has his own wonderful legacy growing as a leading picker/performer in the Blue Canvas Orchestra, being there, of course, from show one. He's been in all the shows I've led and I've always made note to him how much I enjoyed listening to him fly those fingers over the mandolin neck. The days, months and years whiz by and one comes to take for granted the amazing talent of a fellow member of the band. It's mostly unspoken, the respect one solid musician has for another.

Let me speak it, this being one Tuesday morning in April 2011. You've spiced my life, Mr. Burnside, and for that I am ever grateful and tipping a top hat full of the melody of memory to you.

Sally Kessler

You can tell while playing catch if a person is a real ballplayer or not in the first throw back to you. That notice goes for any gamer, crafter, worker or artist. Shortly after moving to this area I saw Sally Kessler in a play. I saw in her entrance even before she spoke a line that here was an accomplished, experienced actress. Stage people somehow find each other. Before Chautauqua was ever thought of, Sally and I talked of having a place to put on plays and shows.

Souvenir Views was our first chance to perform together, her dramatic reading skills needed in the show. The following year, 2 B.C., we joined up with an idea that Diana Randolph, a Washburn artist, proposed. It was a show titled *Dance Of The Seasons*, a multimedia celebration of the four seasons. Sally, Diana and I put it together featuring original songs, paintings and dance. Diana had applied for an Arts Board grant and we were awarded the funds to get to it. Sally directed the staging along with performing. *Dance Of The Seasons* was the spark for *Take It To The Lake* that debuted in Chautauqua's first season.

When Mary Rice first spoke to me about establishing a theatre, I knew Sally was the one I would invite to come along. My knowledge of staging plays was nil. Sally was there on the couch when I dropped the lovely bomb that I wanted a tent show. I was counting on her to choose and lead any plays we would be presenting. In the first year we were co-artistic directors. She choose *Jacques Brel Is Alive And Living In Paris*, as the first, a revue. In the next years we mounted a few plays and musicals. Acoustically, the tent required extreme enunciation and projection. Rain can drown out dialogue and turn a show into a silent movie. Eventually we bought area mics and finally individual clip mics. At the beginning they were thousands of dollars and a few years away.

All through the early times when we regularly presented plays, Sally was front and center, being Theatrical Director. She attended several of the first official at-the-table planning sessions at the Sioux River Song Farm or at Carolyn's house as we charted the course of Chautauqua's future. I miss, in the lights-down minute before a show, taking her arm, waiting for the violin cue, and walking to centerstage to launch *Riding The Wind*:

> *Old winds are about tonight old steps up the street*
> *It's not long a human lives but the place underneath*
> *Stays through all those changes made.*
> *Now you drive on roads they paved, over tote roads they laid*
> *Over moccasin trails of the first ones.*
>
> *What's new? They loved each other and some didn't get along.*
> *But they kept some different wisdom.*
> *When you see a gander, and he chewing his cud,*
> *Look for a Nor'easter tomorrow or the next day, or the day after,*
> *Or at some future time.*
> *Whenever dogs are seen traveling around with nothing to do*
> *And hop vines won't climb and old maids refuse their tea,*
> *Then expect a light crop of blueberries*
> *And apples won't pay for the picking...and the fishing...*
> *Well, stay on the dock.*
>
> *Old winds are about tonight. For the shores of the past we sail*
> *Our hailing port Bayfield*
> *We could begin under the glacier with the birth of this Great Lake*
> *But let's skip those ten thousand years and start*
> *One singing spring day,the ninth of June, 1856*

Phil Anich

The guy is a Phil of all trades. I first met Phil at the Washburn Post Office; he was Postmaster in 1982 when Washburn became my address. The topic of music must have come up early at some time in my frequent stops. His musical partner at the time was Washburn Police Officer Tim Cheney with whom I had a nice talk late one night through the car window after speeding through town. Tim and Phil were familiar with Lost Nation. In fact, I remember one spring Saturday night, when we were playing at The Voyageur, Tim grabbed me after the gig and informed me of the initiation necessary for any new Bayfield County immigrant to begin the process of being called a local. He pulled a smelt out of his pocket and said, "Bite the head off it." I thought about it. It was the first smelt I ever laid eyes on. "Come on, bite the head off." I put it in the pick compartment of my guitar case. I didn't see it again until a week later when I opened my guitar case. It smelt bad. I'm a local.

Phil informed me he and Tim were singing at the Bayfield Library. He knew of *Souvenir Views*. I was looking for locals to include in the cast. From the first note I heard him sing, I knew his song in the show would be "All For A. A. Bigelow," a bully of a logging song I had just finished. I told him I wanted him to sing one song in the show. I guess I thought the cast was set, but Phil's bass voice was needed throughout.

For the original shows, it was always a delight for me to write songs with specific singers in mind. Here I had found the song and then the singer. It was the start of the great years of sharing the stage with Phil, the next show being *Riding The Wind*. Shortly after, Phil took a job as a detective of some sort with the Postal Service, traveling full time. In the first two years of Chautauqua, he traveled back to do *Riding The Wind* and *Souvenir Views*. We kept in touch by telephone. One night in 1989 I got a call from him saying he wanted off the road and out of the job. He was stressed. I could tell he had the passion of "I have one life to live and I'm going to sing!" It was good news to me. I guess he saw the light of what was to come. It's a once in a lifetime find to come upon a band like we had in place. It's another thing to realize your singing talent is as strong as the musicianship of the band.

I told him we needed help with PR. Don Albrecht and I pushed out the news the first year. Todd Kessler of Cornucopia worked 1987 and 1988. Phil accepted the position and made his way back home, being Ashland born and raised. We were all working out of our home offices. Phil's PR office was wherever he parked his car; his file cabinet was the trunk until we found an office.

Handyman Phil kicked in with tent raising. He's become BTC's canvasman along with Jerry Carlson. We all learned the ropes from Paul Buckles, as I've told elsewhere, with the sailor Jonathan Falconer leading the raising for the first years.

Whistle Comin' In, The Ashland musical, was next in line for the Nelson-Ferris Concert Company Shows in 1987. As for Ashland history, the ore trade ruled. Iron ore had been found in the Gogebic Range of Upper Michigan and the border Wisconsin country before the Mesabi opened in Minnesota. Four ore docks once stood Ashland's shore. Reading of the boom, I came upon the memoirs of a miner named William Williams. "My name is William Williams, I been a miner since I was eight. I worked Hell's Gate in New York harbor, before coming to the Norrie Mine." There it was, the vein was struck for the song "Ore Dock Pockets." I heard Phil's voice immediately in the lyric. A strange dark wind of inspiration came in like a fistful of rock.

The guitar is my shovel when it comes to digging up new melodies. I wander around the neck aimlessly, playing chords I can't name, listening for voice. So goes the weaving of melody and word. Poets and novelists often talk of believing a piece of work is never truly finished, years after a revelation shows a need to revise. Not so with a song for me. I need to know it travels and comes home to stay. Phil also sang my iron ore song, "Mesabi," in the show *Old Minnesota* and carried it like a Great Lakes freighter.

Phil, Jack and I became BTC's ambassadors in the early 90s. We played tourism conferences, banquets, anywhere the call came from anyone who wanted a taste of the Big Top. After playing a gig at Lakewoods in Cable, a woman asked what the name of our trio was. Jack, without hesitation, answered, "We're Los Hobos." "Oh, I've heard of you."

Barb Linton, Wisconsin State Representative from our district, often brought us to Madison to make the rounds in the capital city. We were Barbie's band. She arranged for us to sing in the House chamber at the Capitol at the swearing in of new representatives. I wrote a poem and a song for the occasion. These appearances around the state brought us into a friendship with Tommy Thompson, who was then Governor. We had some hilarious times with Tommy, eventually getting a private invitation to join him at the Governor's mansion. He laid out a cookout and afterward we gave him a private concert.

Phil is also blessed with the natural presence of an actor, dramatic to comedic. He'll become whoever the part calls for, the son of Wisconsin immigrants, a coal shover in a steam locomotive, a forest ranger, or a sailor drowning on the shoals off Sand Island. Phil is also Chautauqua's plumber, electrician, carpenter, pew stacker, gofer, computer-consultant, co-designer of the tent's truss system and all-around fixer. On the staff, he's listed as Operations Manager. I always noted he's the guy with the tent stake punched in his forehead. And if you ever need a hootenanny singer who knows a thousand songs to extend your party into the wee hours, he's your man. He was my right and left hand man.

Tom Mitchell

Can't remember the first day I met Tom but I was at a gathering or two with him sometime in the early 80's when the hippies hereabouts were still trimming their long hair, free waying days and settling down, or at least pretending to.

I first saw and heard him perform as a solo outside the Bayfield Inn on a fine summer night. I immediately took to his wonderfully askewed manner. I mean by that he had the hat of his presentation tilted perfectly. He was telling and singing the truth. He was playing guitar and singing song after song that I knew or wanted to know. His songlist was right up the alley of my ear. I stayed to the end of his gig and remember walking over to him wanting to say without words that he had it.

A year or so later, immediately after the last *Souvenir Views* show in the ninety-five degree heat in the Washburn gym, Tom walked up to me with a soft eye and shook my hand and he said what he wanted to without a word. It was the kind of applause I most appreciate for my work– I could see the show hit the heart.

We first joined up on stage in *Riding The Wind* in 1985. It was there I first saw his talent as an actor, performer and percussionist. When the winds of fortune blew our way with the start of Chautauqua, he was frontline from the start.

My admiration of his quiet, strong manner only grew over the years. Besides, he always gave me a cymbal crash when one of my jokes worked, or didn't.

I wanted a new original show to debut with BTC's first season and *Take It To The Lake* was it! I created a character called Dr. Third Eye and wrote a monologue for the principal carrier of the show. I had meant it for myself to act out my carny barking fantasies but I never got to play it. Unknown to me, it was written for Tom Mitchell. He kept to the script at the beginning but soon added his mind-juggling improvisations and the audiences loved him. They still do. The words I wrote for it are still the essence of the Doctor...Professor...quack...snake oil salesmen. But I've become grandfather to the bit.

The oil the good Doctor Third Eye sells is Lake Superior Wizard Water, fresh-dipped at 12 fathoms. We indeed used 12 fathom (that's 72 feet down) water but soon it came to be water dipped at shore and then it came to look suspiciously like water out of the faucet from the back of the tent. Only Dr. Third Eye knows; his knowledge is beyond us.

Bob Sneed and I first dipped the 12-fathom water from his boat in the middle of Chequamegon Bay. Bob knew the lake. He motored us out to the deep. We had a long rope that was marked at 72 feet and we lowered a pail with a rock in it and yanked up a couple buckets full. Leo LaFernier, an Ojibwa elder from Red Cliff, caught me one night after the show and declared, "Only the white man would sell Lake Superior water!"

In the first couple years Dr. Third Eye had a young assistant, Ethan Cole, who was seven or eight years old at the time. The wonders of the Wizard Water were made instantly known in the young lad. Just a drop in the middle of his

LAKE SUPERIOR

BIGTOP

CHAUTAUQUA

2003 Program Guide

"Old Last Night", 1987.

L-R: Canvasmen Paul Buckles, Jonathon Falconer and two roustabouts.

Early Board, seated L-R: Libby Telford and Eric Kramer; standing L-R: Warren Nelson, Tom Lindsey, Carolyn Sneed and Betty Ferris.

First tent Ballyhoo coat.

Evening at Chautauqua.

Carolyn and Warren.

The Blue Canvas Orchestra and Singers; front, kneeling L-R: Phil Anich, Rowan Nelson-Ferris; middle, seated L-R: Cheryl Leah, Warren Nelson, Ed Willett; back, standing L-R: Betty Ferris, Sally Kessler, Severin Behnen, Andy Dee, Tom Mitchell, Jack Gunderson, Cal Aultman, Bruce Bowers and Bruce Burnside.

State Fair Chautauqua.

"Centennial Green", 2005.

"Keeper Of The Light".

Lightkeepers and family, standing L-R: Tom Mitchell, Jack Gunderson and Michael Stanwood; seated L-R: Lisa McGinley and Medora Nelson-Ferris.

Publicity photo for "On The Velvet".

Cast and crew of "On The Velvet".

June 16, 2000, morning after the fire; inset: found in the fire.

My side of the tent.

Gerry DePerry, circa 1883?

Jerry Carlson at the fish boil.

Anglin' Wayne's Fishtar.

Doctor Third Eye (Tom Mitchell)
with Sally Kessler.

Ritual cast circle before the show.

The Lost Nation String Band, L-R: Jack Gunderson, Warren Nelson, Bruce Burnside and Don Pavel.

The Nelson-Ferris Concert Company under the oredock, 1987.

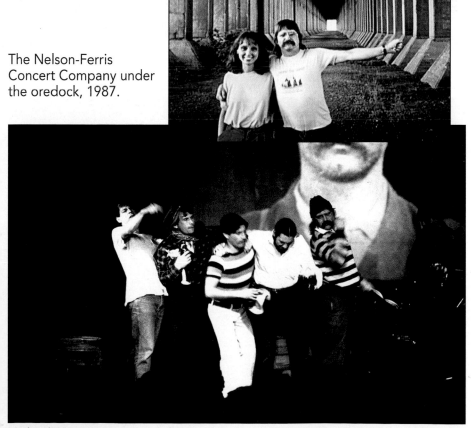

"Whistle Comin' In" Sailor Bums, L-R: Tom Mitchell, Randy Borich, Phil Anich, Bob Donahue and Warren Nelson.

Warren Nelson with poet Robert Bly.

Carolyn and Doc Watson in dressing room.

Warren Nelson and Mason Williams.

With Tom and Dick Smothers.

Father of Bluegrass Bill Monroe amazes us all.

Don Pavel.

Carlene Carter, June Carter Cash, Johnny Cash at the Big Top.

Two great banjo players no longer with us – John Hartford and Mark "Pete" Nelson

Nick Reynolds of the Kingston Trio, Patsy Avery and Star-struck Guy.

"Centennial Green" School Show.

Warren Nelson, Betty Ferris, Bill and Betty Hulings riding the wind.

Big Top being sewn by Anchor Industries.

The sweet smell of brand new canvas fresh from the bag.

forehead, over the Third Eye, and the boy performed mighty miracles and feats right before our very eyes.

I think Tom's monologue on fly fishing with his dad, that he first wrote for *Wild River* in 1988, and later performed nightly in *Riverpants*, is as fine a piece as we ever presented on the Chautauqua stage. It is human, humorous, serious and original. That's Tom Mitchell.

He remains one of the finest actors I have ever had the pleasure of working with. He is also a playwright and prolific journal keeper. When do we get to read those thoughts of yours, Tom?

As for Mr. Mitchell and his legacy in Chautauqua's story, the rest is history as they say, and it continues. Lucky for the Big Top.

Scott Kuester

I would occasionally get the thought of how it would be to have a repertory company in a theatre that stood the four seasons in a city with a population to support long runs of our big shows. What a dream to provide deserving talent with year long contracts, health insurance, retirement program, masseuses, company cars, etc. Sure thing.

Scott Kuester would be a first hire of mine as a musical theatre actor. He had the voice, the presence, and the serious and comedic versatility. It felt secure to know Scotty was in the show.

He joined us in *Whistle Comin' In* in 1987, and following, performed in *Keeper of the Light, On the Velvet, 30th Star, Old Minnesota, Showpants, Centennial Green,* and in our *Best of the Big Top* revues, touring with us throughout the region.

Severin Behnen - The Jazz Problem

Shortly after the first tent season, Susan Dexter called me from Madeline Island wanting to introduce me to a piano player named Severin Behnen. Thanks Susan.

How a Minnesota farm boy got to the piano bench is a mystery. I think he was just too lazy to do chores. Maybe cows had something to do with it. I don't know who first taught him and got him started but they done good.

Florence Skovald, a vaudeville piano player from Bayfield who also became a Hollywood star in B movies, once told me she could play by reading sheet music but she couldn't travel. That's the best term I've ever heard for a musician who can improvise. Severin, or Sven, as we call him, can travel. Far and wide. Sven and his "tinkling ten."

I came across *Etude*, a music magazine issue dated in the twenties that featured a cover page and a long article inside about the "jazz problem" in America. I also read of a woman music professor who years later wrote an essay stating that jazz should be outlawed for its effect on young people, leading them to dance suggestively and act wild. If it had become law, Severin would be serving a long prison sentence. Severin has always been our jazz problem and we love it.

He has no fear and is patient with those of us who can't make our way easily through music that's a little, shall I say, thick. He has been a lead arranger for us for several of our original musicals, including the instrumentals and vocals. He keeps rehearsals on track. He is also one of the finest human beings I've ever met, sense of humor, ready for anything, tireless worker, deadline maker.

We also share a common Big Top history. We both backed our cars over our instruments. I, sad sad sadly to say, backed over my long-owned Guild classical guitar, stone sober. It was with my big 1990 Buick LeSabre. I was in a hurry, leaned it against the trunk, spaced out, and put it in reverse. The sound of the crunch I will never forget. I wrote many songs on that guitar. I think I would have rather run over some of my songs than that beautiful seasoned instrument. Even then Severin beat me. He ran over his portable electric keyboard TWICE!

Instruments are easy to come by. Musicians with competence, experience and ego-lacking sensitivity are not. There's a reason why professional singers warm-up singing ME ME ME. The performer's world is bloated with egomaniacs. Severin is not one. If I could play like he does, I'd bark more.

We have written a couple tunes together, the favorite being our hit—"Can't Wait To Get To Heaven, Won't Have To Go To Church No More." We seem to be up comedy lane as we also penned "The Beer Belly Polka." He's taken to the accordion which is a great instrument in the right hands and easier to play in the boat than a grand piano. If we ever could spend more time together, I would love to be the lyricist for whatever melodies he'd pass along.

I designed the 1988 *Wild River* show celebrating the waters of the St. Croix River, so that the first half would feature compositions from each of our ensemble composers and writers. Severin chose the Snake River. Over a bed of his signature atonal music, we were instructed at one point in the chart to do whatever we wanted. The idea was to bring up long past and present spirits of the river as it eternally rolls along. Kind of a ghostlike float in the fog of time. I'm still haunted by that piece, half in wonder and half in nightmare. It scratched the audience's head. It was certainly like no other piece in the show.

I was always sad near the end of the season when Severin left for his studies in master composition and for his teaching duties. Lucky is the student that has Sven for his or her mentor. He lived in Minneapolis for years but now he calls LA home. The distance also prevented him from joining us for most of our off-season touring.

There is no distance in our friendship and that means the world to me, musically and otherwise.

Randy Sabien

Sabien is the man, and he is his instrument. He deserves all the accolades he's received over his career as a violinist, guitar player, mandolin player, piano player, teacher. He founded the jazz violin department of the prestigious Berklee School of Music (I think he was only 4 years old.) As for multi-instrumentalists, I've never met anyone like him.

Randy has been on the Big Top stage since his first appearance in 1988, most often bringing his Fiddlehead Blues Band, featuring Clyde Stubblefield who was James Brown's drummer. Randy recorded a live CD at the tent– *Paintin' The Canvas* August 24, 1994.

Further traits: generous and tasty as a sideman...easy to go along with....jokester extraordinaire...readily available fishing partner. Chautauqua house show credits include *Show For A Slow Night, Wild River, Riverpants, Centennial Green*.

Despite being an alien, he is one of my favorite human beings. I think he still holds the record for items in the rider we had to promise to before he would sign a Chautauqua contract. We pinned a star on his dressing room flap. All in great fun but humor is just what we needed in the push and hurry of the hectic summer. I mean John Hiatt asked for two clean pairs of sweat sox but check out Mr. Sabien's rider.

Here's one of a three page, long-winded,
highly demanding, don't-you-know-who-I-am document.

D.) Required Liquids - available at all times

   1.) 1 case of Leinenkugels beer
   2.) 1 case of Point beer
   3.) 1 case of assorted Hibernia beers, (Eau Claire All malt, Dunkel Weitzn, Winterbr.
   4.) 1 case of Don Perignon champagne - chilled
   5.) Liquor - 1 bottle each Bacardi Rum, Tanqueray Gin, old Bushmills, Gordon Vodka
   6.) Assorted fruit juices and mixers
   7.) Lots of ice
   8.) Assorted wines, chablis, beaujolais, rhine, California '86 OK, nothing too sweet

E.) Security:
   1.) One guard by dressing room door at all times. No enters without the secret password and handshake (unless it's a stunningly beautiful woman.)
   2.) 5 guards in front of stage during performance. Prefer to use the G. Gordon Liddy Guard service if available.

F.) Stage requirements - in addition to contract
   1.) Lights - computerized laser light show with hologram capability
   2.) 2 smoke machines
   3.) revolving drum cage
   4.) trap door

H.) Purchaser agrees to anything written or unwritten.
I.) Provider reserves the right not to show up at the last minute if he decides to do something else.
J.) Provider will not perform if the ice cubes melt before all required liquids are consumed.

_____   _____
Purchaser   Provider
"I agree to everything"   March 20, 1989

Felix Knox

The main character in the musical *On the Velvet* is the porter. The porter of a train, it was always known, was the unspoken boss of a train's journey. This, of course, was during the time America still kept African Americans from any important positions. Daddy Joe is the name given to all porters, a prototype as Paul Bunyan is to loggers.

The porter, of course, needed to be a black man. Who?

An Ohio traveling theatre company was putting on a play at Northland College, the story of a slave being pursued. In the play, he is hiding in an attic. I went to the play and found Daddy Joe.

Felix Knox was his name. He was enormously talented with an astounding stage presence. After the show, I introduced myself and congratulated him on his performance. I explained our show. Could and would he consider it?

"Yes," he answered with a headlight shine in his eye. "Funny," he said, "My partner and I are leaving in two days for a two week trip on Amtrak." Another miracle was given to the Big Top Stage.

Felix arrived from Atlanta for rehearsals and immediately became a true member of our company. Throughout the play, Daddy Joe and the Conductor (played by Jack Gunderson) interact with a train fanatic, Traveler, a foamer. Foamer is the name given to anyone whose passion for all things railroading is beyond fanaticism. In the first years, I played the part of Traveler.

Felix's solo number was a song I wrote called "Set Of Keys," a set of keys being the old term jingling for those lucky enough to get the job of a porter. The story was intertwined with the operations of Pullman Company sleeper cars. "Set of

Keys" is at the top of anything I have ever written. It is an up-tempo boogie-woogie, 12-bar roisterous singing of the porter working on a train.

To save voice during long rehearsals, most singers cut back. Felix never could. The band kicked in and Felix lost himself. He was singing to the high heaven of an audience that wasn't there. Our director, Sue Kuester, would beg him to save it. He never did.

Felix Knox was as fine an actor/singer/performer as I have ever had the chance to stomp the boards with. The first performance was a staged reading. The following summer we went into full production. It was obvious Felix's health had deteriorated. He even cut back in rehearsals a bit. Just a bit. Those of you who saw the show back in 1992, I'm sure you remember Felix as Daddy Joe. I long to see him and hear him again.

Felix Knox died a young man. His being is often a far away steam whistle I hear somewhere in the night country of the beyond. My God, I miss him.

Ed Willett and Cheryl Leah

It was two for one in my meeting Ed and Cheryl in the early 1990s

I took a call from Milwaukee from someone named Ed who informed me he and his partner Cheryl were playing a gig on Madeline Island the coming weekend at the LaPointe school library and would I be able to make it. He told me their duo was cello and vocals. I had never heard of that combo before.

He told me they were thinking of moving up north, having left LA, and knew all about Chautauqua from an uncle of theirs who had been to the tent. I went to their gig on the island, crossing the ice road on a chilly chilly night, the milk of the Milky Way shining in the snow on the way over. It was January and the reputation of the North being deepfreezed was on. It's an adventure to take the ice road. I always stop midway and get out of the car. It seems the distance to the stars must be about the same distance as it is from the ice cap to the bottom of Lake Superior. Just an eternal thought that joyfully belittles me.

When I walked in Ed was tuning in the corner and Cheryl was singing to herself. It was a small perfect audience at the end of the day's world in this secret place. They took the stage of the floor and introduced themselves. Then I really woke up. Ed started sawing on the cello and Cheryl kicked in. Not only were they musicians from the high sky but they were singing original songs. OK, you're hired.

Chance was the name (and still is) of their duo. Once again, chance had given us miracle musical partners. We've had some times over the years, especially on the road. They are road warriors. In conversation, Cheryl and I found we had been in the business for the same number of years, had played in the same long-unforgotten places and never-ending were the stories backstage.

Ed would job in symphony orchestras in our off-season. He is like Don Pavel in the way he can travel on his instrument, playing all styles of music with ease and an understanding of the feel behind the notes. It's rare for a classically trained player to be able to dip and whittle and fiddle away. He added a whole string section to our ensemble. Not to mention the man can sing, compose and arrange.

For *Riverpants*, I asked him to compose a "Minnowette." As he says, "It's just another cello solo for a fishing show." It's hilarious, accompanied by minnow tank talk. I'd love to see a symphony orchestra perform it.

Ed is presently the bandleader for The Blue Canvas Orchestra. He has a very especial talent for arranging vocal parts and running rehearsals unlike we ever had before. The new songs I put up over the years for the big shows always seemed like dress rehearsals on opening night. Up in the lights by the skin of our strings! Ed erased that habit when he became our director.

We have been great partners (my honor and pleasure indeed) and still are. Ed, along with Andy Dee, produced my CD *Song In Your Hat*. Though I can read music, I've never been one to write the notes down. Jimmy Martin once told me "There are people you can hire to do that."

Cheryl brought us a voice we were missing. She can wail. Her stage presence is her own, quirky and real. Her rendition of my song "Decoration Day" lays me out.

We did a trio mini tour together that we advertised as being "performed without a net!" More of that for me please.

They've settled here, Chautauqua being the open door. They live on Poor Farm Road. What an appropriate address for working musicians nowadays. It was exciting to first introduce them to the old farts in the band. No hesitation in getting right to work.

They have a string of recordings that are a must for you Chautauqua and music lovers. What next? I'm in line.

Liz Woodworth

If I'm needing a comedic, musical or dramatic actress, no auditions are necessary—I'm calling Liz Woodworth. Of the house shows, Lizzie has played in *Whistle Comin' In, On The*

Velvet, Riverpants and Showpants as well as directing *30th Star* during one of its runs. She has also performed in several of the plays Chautauqua has presented. Not sure exactly when I met Liz but it was early in the Big Top's childhood.

During the rehearsals for new shows Liz was never shy in throwing in ideas for rewrites and staging. Much appreciated and used. She was frontline in the productions of *Riverpants* and *Showpants*. Playing the famous Lena alongside Jack as Ole in *Riverpants*, they take the cake, cut it up and paste it in your face all in fun. She is one who I, while creating away, could hear before a line was written.

Outside of Chautauqua, Liz has been successfully extending herself into playwriting, songwriting and recording, with frequent appearances at Stage North.

And oh yeah, I've yet to hear a better vocal reincarnation of Ethel Merman.

Andy Dee

Andy is a late comer to the Blue Canvas Orchestra, joining in 2008 following the tragic death of guitarist, bandleader Don Pavel. Andy took to the road with us to the Calumet Theatre in Calumet, Michigan in February, two weeks after Don died. His name was the first spoken among us to be offered Don's lead guitar chair. Mr. Dee wasn't a stranger to the Big Top stage as he played for years with Corey Carlson and Randy Sabien in their concerts. I first knew of Andy through Molly And The Heymakers, a Hayward based group who made the national rounds out of Nashville. I never had the chance to play with him until he accepted our invitation. Lucky me.

Give Andy a guitar, acoustic or electric, a steel or dobro, a ukelele, anything with strings and he knows his way. He's become an A#1 pal o' mine. He co-produced, mixed and played on my latest CD, "Song In Your Hat." We've just started playing and traveling together with my new band, The Nelson Outfit. Our history together is in its first chapter and I'm looking forward, God willing, to finishing the book of our story together. Check out his CD, *Sweet Soul Sewage*, a tilted, witty, original, enjoyable satchel of songs. Always great to know another dedicated, professional, damn fool musician hooked for life in the net of playing music.

Madeline Hart

Madeline was an original with *Riding The Wind* carrying the soprano parts, soloing beautifully on "These Islands," the small choruses that were the haunting airs of the show's beginning. Her voice gave a distance to the lyrics and the waters. When people left the tent, it was her voice they remembered with the chant of "These Islands." She sang with Peaceful Women in *Take It To The Lake*.

Mary Bondeson

Mary replaced Madeline in *Riding The Wind*, singing and playing on a fiddle tune in the show from 1994 to 2008. Her Chautauqua credits also include singing and playing violin in *Souvenir Views* and performing with Peaceful Women in *Take It To The Lake*. It's hard for me to imagine ever playing in *Riding The Wind* again without Mary. I won't tell you of the night Mary forgot there was a RTW performance scheduled and didn't show up. We created a new phrase for a show business no-show. We called it "pulling a Bondeson."

Lisa McGinley

Lisa, with Mary and Sally Kessler, was a mainstay in RTW, through 2008, singing in the chorus and adding pennywhistle to "Whiskey Before Breakfast." She took the role of the volunteer Lighthouse Keeper in the Ghost Scene during two productions of *Keeper Of The Light* beginning in 1989. Chautauqua has been fortunate that talent abounds in the Chequamegon Bay area and Lisa is top shelf.

Jan Lee

Jan is an astounding talent musically and theatrically. She performed and wrote a comedy piece for *Wild River*, directed and starred in *Keeper Of The Light*, directed and sang in *Earth To Wendell* and sang in *Take it To The Lake*. She is the signature singer for two of my songs—"Two In A Canoe" from *Wild River* and "We Were There" in Keeper. Both Showstoppers. She is founder of Stage North in Washburn.

Marcie Gephart

Marcie joined up with us as a member of Peaceful Women singing in *Take It To the Lake*. She carried my favorite verse in the end song "...you can't drink oil and you can't swallow silver, will gold hold water for the good of this Earth..." She played Miriam *In the Keeper of the Light* and played a hobo sister in *On The Velvet*.

Gwen Baxter

Gwen was a soulful voice as an original cast member of *Riding The Wind*, performed in concert with Peaceful Women and as a soloist in *Take It To The Lake*.

Janet Bewley

Janet performed in original chorus of *Riding The Wind*, sang and acted in *Take It To The Lake* and played a starring role as the upstart Kate in early productions of *Keeper Of The Light*.

Corey Carlson

Corey, grew up with the tent; and to watch him become a premier singer/songwriter/performer has been a joy for me. As his honorary "Uncle Wayne," I'm proud of "The Hippie." He's got it. Corey and his band have become one of the big Chautauqua draws of the summer. The dude is a prolific writer. Seems like every time I see him he tells me he wrote a new song yesterday, which leaves me with the feeling I oughta get home and get to work. He knows he's been lucky, as we all have been, for the exposure to the traveling talent that plays the Big Top.

Gerry De Perry

Ojibwa stories are traditionally told only in the winter. When Gerry stepped to the summer light in *Riding The Wind* to tell of his ancestors, he told us all that he had offered tobacco to "any spirits that may be with us tonight." Good spirit is what Gerry brought to the night air when he arrived at the tent along with a friendship I honor. Megwitch.

ADDITIONAL PERFORMERS IN "HOUSE" SHOWS

Don Albrecht
Monica Anderson
Nathan Bitzer
Ravin' Dave Bloomquist
Rosemary Bodin
Randy Borich
Weymuth Bowen
Annie Bowers
Jasmine Bowers
Bill Bussey
Timothy Burnside
Chequamegon Area Choir
Marc Christianson
Terry Croft
Keith & Jacque Dallenbach
Bob Donahue
David Drake
Jeff Eckles
Steve Eckles
Geoff Ehrendreich
Jonathan & Cookie Falconer
Scott Fuller
Ali Gephart
Gena Gephart
Mark Gonzales
Phillip Hamilton
Gary Holman
Deb Joanis
Glenn Walker Johnson
Addie Kessler
Jeff Kriner
Sue Kuester
Kenn Macur
Sue Masterson

Cassie McCorrison
Llake McCorrison
Wendy McCorrison
Hope McLeod
Vernelle Mercer
Elsa Mitchell
John Munson
Reno Paulson
Kirsten Pedersen
Penokee Mountain Cloggers
Jerry Phillips
Gary Raynor
Micah Ricard
Monica Rice
Rittenhouse Singers
Pat Robertson
Loren Savitsky
Frank Nebenburgh
Jane Nelson
Mark "Pete" Nelson
Medora Nelson-Ferris
Rowan Nelson-Ferris
LaRae Niehaus
Elizabeth Olm
Ann Olsen
David Parmentier
David Siegler
Carolyn Sneed
Michael Stanwood
Jane Thimke
Joni Vaughan
Kitty Wahlberg
Mary Lou Williams
Washburn City Band
Luie Young

WARREN INTERVIEWS CAROLYN

1. You were with BTC from minute one. How did that happen?

It happened because I loved the concept when I first heard you talk about your grand idea of an entertainment venue outdoors under canvas, in these northwoods near my home. I wanted to be part of that dream; I wanted to hear more music by you and the Lost Nation String Band; and felt I could contribute.

2. Pop up memories of season number one.

- The first tent raising: Paul Buckles teaching us how to put up a tent. Warren getting advice from an engineer about how to be sure the truss supporting the top was effective and safe. Most of our house performers and some enthusiastic community supporters helping with the process, sawing on the truss, pounding stakes, lacing the top pieces, hooking up the side walls.
- The first show night: I realized the audience was beginning to arrive, and no one could find the opening to the tent, so I opened the flap and began to welcome the happy customers.
- The first shows: The performers' kids taking over the front row (some of the parents on stage directed courteous behavior of their offspring); the best behaved kids were Noel Meyer's. He supervised as they sat or slept in back rows near the light stand.
- Papers covering my dining room table, my office for nearly a year. Months of dealing with details of acquiring tax exempt status. I hand wrote every check and recorded every transaction of income and expense in 16 column

ruled pads. (I was determined, and proud that my bank statements balanced to the penny every month.)

- Because the MAHADH Foundation was giving us start up money before we had our tax exempt status, from May to October I had to send them a copy of every check I wrote. Since we had no office equipment, this meant going to various businesses (mainly rotating among Tom Lindsey's law office, Bremer Bank, and Bayfield Chamber of Commerce) and asking if they would please make copies for us. All were happy about our new business adventure and were very supportive.

- When it was extremely windy and stormy, the side walls (which at first were not attached to the ground) would flap noisily, so many times I stood with one foot holding down the side wall to subdue the noise. Phil Anich eventually took care of this problem with bungee cord attachments.

3. Planning Process for BTC first years...who and how?

Betty Ferris was the expert leader of our planning process and meetings. Warren, Betty and I usually met around my kitchen table in the fall, to talk about what we had done, what we should change, what we should do. Betty would put up big papers on the windows and walls and then she led and recorded the discussion which determined what categories we needed to establish in order to have an orderly plan that encompassed everything needed to put on the shows. Mary Rice, as our Founding Angel and successful local business guru, joined us in our planning sessions the first few years.

4. Details, minute and otherwise of your handling of the business/ticket end in first years before, during and after shows and during the off-season. What were your jobs not related to the financial concerns? Describe a working day for you during season house shows? Guest artists?

I started out as the Secretary-Treasurer of the original three-member Board of Directors. For the first eight years, as board secretary, I wrote and distributed the minutes of all Board meetings, arranged and attended the meetings. As Treasurer I was also the only bookkeeper, wrote all the checks, designed and distributed regular financial reports, and took the lead in formulating the Annual Budget. I made sure there was always an Annual Report which summarized all the details of each year. I also took the lead in procuring and maintaining our tax exempt status, and finding insurance coverage for our unusual business. I carried out the business of the operation (writing contracts, paying bills, etc.) through my role as board treasurer. I made an appointment with the highly regarded accountant, John Maitland, to get advice on bookkeeping, record-keeping, payroll, etc.; and arranged for John and his office to oversee all our finances and monthly and annual reports. (This affiliation still continues.)

In addition to performing, introducing every show, writing shows and songs, fundraising, and general oversight / leadership of all operations, Warren booked all the shows for the first fifteen years. For the first few years, we hired necessary summer tech staff together. I took care of all the contracts and job descriptions and eventually did the hiring and job evaluations by myself.

In 1990 we added our first new board members: Libby Telford and Eric Kramer. I wanted another person to look over all the monetary transactions I was handling, and to have that individual regularly examine all the books and reports; it was a great relief to have Eric in that role. I continued with my duties as secretary until 1994 when John Fiorio came on board and took over the role; and I resigned from the board.

I fulfilled the duties of House Manager at the tent the first nine years, a good experience because I attended every show and learned what was needed in front of and behind the stage. Geoff Ehrendreich took over that role in 1995, so I had a little extra time for dinner before going to the tent; but my daily summer routine started about 7:00 a.m., and ended, usually well after midnight. I began each show day by checking to see that whatever I needed for that evening's show was in my car: my clipboard! with "to-do" memos, checks, copy of the contract if the show scheduled a guest artist. An array of sweaters and jackets stayed on the back seat all summer. I then made a trip to the office to check on everything, and to the bank to get the correct denominations of change for the ticket seller and the merchandise sales people at our Big Top Shop. After all was in order for that evening's show, I reviewed plans for the upcoming shows and meetings the next night, week, and month, and met with office staff and with Warren to coordinate all the parts.

I would head up to the hill at least an hour before show time, take care of any details there, greet guest artists back stage and individuals in the audience, watch the show, communicate with and pay guest artist managers and merchandise handlers. It was not unusual to still be there at 11:00 or 12:00. Then, at home, I would count the ticket stubs and record exactly how many people had attended the show, and count the money and prepare change for the next day. (One year for a special price we sold a 10-show pass, to be punched each time a show was attended. As I counted the "dots" from the punches, I decided we would not do that again.) Some very special memories are of Jimmy Martin, my house guest with Carmel Quinn, helping me to count ticket stubs and money in the wee hours.

I had a regular hair appointment with Therene Gazdik, and soon learned that she was very interested in the Big Top, particularly the original historical shows about the region, performed by our excellent local musicians. I realized that we would need to use the many volunteers that offered their services to sell tickets, usher, stuff envelopes, and help in many ways, and that they would need leadership and organization. Therene agreed at once when I asked if she would take on the role of Volunteer Coordinator. Our weekly appointment became the time to work out details of this very essential component of our organization.

Therene was perfect for the job because she truly cared about all of it, she was well organized, could see the big picture as well as the small details, and was relentless about letting volunteers know how much they were needed and appreciated.

Tickets at the tent the first year were $5 for adults; $3 for children 12 & under. At first there were no reserved seats. When we saw that patrons were lining up, sometimes for over an hour, to get into the tent and secure a good seat, and then sometimes finding all the front rows covered with blankets brought in hours earlier by local people, we knew we had to begin reserving seats. It was several more years before we would have computers so I drew out the seating chart, and for every show wrote in the names of people who bought reserved seats ahead of time—very time consuming! One year Gloria Maitland volunteered to help me with that job.

In the first five years we did not have an office, so we operated out of our homes until we had temporary office space from 1991-1997. In 1998, after complicated negotiations, and with the wonderful help of Attorney Matt Anich who donated his service, we purchased a building on Washburn's main street just across from the bank. I would go in to the office every morning to check the mail and take care of any messages, talk with other staff, check the books with our indispensable bookkeeper, Bill "Woody" Woodward.

5. *Your part in the launching of new original shows from conception to performance and touring.*

This was one of my favorite roles. I truly enjoyed typing the new scripts; through this exercise I was able to deeply appreciate Warren's remarkable talents as a writer, and it was a delight to copy how he put words and ideas together.

There is a three part outline for development and production of a new show: 1) research, conceptualizing, writing, composing and arranging, 2) visuals, stage and light design; rehearsals, 3) performance. My job was to coordinate all parts, while Warren or Warren and Betty were responsible for getting the script written, music and visuals ready by the first rehearsal.

It was satisfying to prepare the scripts for the performers and techs and help with the rehearsals, and exciting to be involved as the new show came to life. I usually attended the rehearsals for new shows to be available to help with anything needed: script changes, copies of songs, prompter, etc.

6. *Memories of Tent Show Radio in the beginning and first years.*

At the suggestion of Dale Baggerly, the Wisconsin Public Radio Board came to a show at the tent in the summer of 1992. They subsequently passed a resolution urging WPR management to pursue a collaboration with BTC. In September, Warren and I met with Jack Mitchell while he was vacationing at the Rittenhouse Inn in Bayfield. Jack was the Director of WPR, and agreed that WPR would air a weekly radio show to be produced by BTC. In December, we had a letter from Jack Mitchell, confirming our conversations: Tent Show Radio would be a one hour weekly radio program to be produced for WPR to begin airing January 8, 1994; the letter pointed out that BTC would have to raise its own production costs, and that our proposed budget draft of $180,000 seemed "tight but reasonable."

Then, in our effort to raise the money and get things started, Warren and I met to work out details with other WPR people (Jill Schorr, John Munson) in Iron River and Superior, and in Madison with Barbara Linton, our representative in the WI State Assembly, and with aides of Governor Tommy Thompson. It was agreed that WI Public Broadcasting would give us a one time payment of $30,000. The legislators had agreed to add an additional $100,000 from the state budget for this project which they felt would be good PR for the state. The Educational Communications Board forwarded two checks for $50,000 each which would have been reimbursed by the state if the ECB representative had requested it; for some reason the request was never made; and for years we heard rumors that we were accused of stealing the money from WPR.

Warren and I went to the Governor's Conference in 1994 and met Winfield MacDonald, who worked for the WI Department of Tourism. Winfield helped greatly by opening the door of financial support from the department, which continues to this day. I believe this has been a mutually helpful collaboration, as the stories and music helped to communicate the spirit of the state.

About the time we started producing the show, Tony Judge came on the scene. Tony had years of experience in radio and in producing, and helped greatly with suggestions on how to go about the mechanics of assembling a 55 minute show with a one minute break in the middle. I still have the first papers which record our struggles to accurately record minutes and seconds of the chosen parts of recordings.

We worked out all the details for Mark McGinley to record the show; Bruce Bowers to digitally edit the show; contract wording for all the performers and sponsors, Phil Anich to be station liaison, make copies and mail to various radio stations.

We eventually hired people to help with the content editing and timing. Filling that role at various times were Betty Ferris, Don Pavel, Jim Newman, and Rowan Nelson-Ferris. I took care of the bookkeeping, contracts with sponsors and performers, and the catalogue of shows. Warren had the gargantuan and relentless job of designing the show, listening to and overseeing every detail, and writing and recording the voiceovers that pulled it all together, and helping to find sponsors.

7. Talk about the "role" of your cottage and BTC.

Our cottage, next to our home on Lake Superior, has been a summer residence for many Big Top people for over 25 years. While Warren Nelson & Betty Ferris were creating *Riding the Wind* in 1985, they were also building their log home in the Town of Washburn. Rains brought flooding to the clay basement where they were also attempting to live temporarily, so we offered the cottage to them and their three year old daughter, Medora. For several more years, Betty's parents, Les and Oma Ferris, stayed there for the summer, usually hosting the Nelson-Ferris family for nightly dinners.

From that time through the present, the cottage has been the summer home of Chautauqua performers, particularly Severin Behnen when he started school in California in 2001, and returned here for summers at the Big Top. Other performers who have been my guests include: Carmel Quinn, Jimmy Martin, Drew Jansen, Garrison Keillor, Rich Dwarsky, Gary Raynor, Linda and Robin Williams, Greg Brown, Truly Remarkable Loon, Phoebe Legere, Ruth MacKenzie, Eric Peltoniemi, Jeffrey Willkomm, Randy Sabien, Michael Stanwood, Monica May, Tom Gilshannon, Felix Knox, Weymouth Bowen, Phillip Hamilton, Cal Aultman, Mary Lou Williams, Sue Spencer, Bruce Bowers and a host of others.

8. Challenges of sustaining the tent all during your leadership.

I continue to believe that the major challenge for BTC leadership has always been to design, build and sustain the base and structure of the organization, aiming for a positive bottom line without losing the magic that is so essential and so nebulous.

9. What was the hardest part or parts of your job?

The challenges of raising enough money. Hiring all the staff needed for summer crews and year round administration, some board meetings and then trying to find time to communicate adequately with all of them.

10. Favorite moments off the top of your head, all years.

- Being back stage and knowing I was fulfilling an important role, the coordination of all aspects of what Big Top Chautauqua is.
- Watching happy audience faces from behind the curtain, knowing some of the people who had big heart aches in their lives, and had their spirits lifted for at least a brief time
- The joy of being part of the many moments when live performance blends with audience appreciation. Because our venue is so intimate, the front row only a few feet from the stage, and the back row only about 130 feet away, audience response is immediately felt by the performer who then gives even more back to the listeners. As audience and performer "feed" each other, there is often an explosion of enthusiasm and excitement.
- Warren calling me to say, "Well, I booked Carmel Quinn as you've been asking, and she's staying at your house." (The beginning of a truly special friendship.)
- Greeting entertainers and audience members who had become acquaintances and friends in previous summers.
- Warren singing "Godsend," accompanied on guitar by the song's composer / Warren's hero, Mason Williams.

11. Favorite shows...all years.

The heart of our whole operation, and what made it so unique, has been our "house shows", the original historical musicals about the area, most created by Warren and Betty, some by Warren alone, all with Warren's wonderful songs played by the fantastic musicians who came here to play those songs on the Big Top Stage and on tour, and then were able to move and live in this area. It's hard to choose a favorite, but I guess mine would be *On the Velvet*. I love all the great music, dance surprise and goofy humor in *Riverpants*. Because it is such an excellent diary of life on the Apostle Islands, *Keeper of the Light* should show regularly. And the end song of every house show.

Favorite outside performers include: Arlo Guthrie. Carmel Quinn, Jimmy Martin, Nitty Gritty Dirt Band when Jimmy Ibbotson was with them, Tommy Emmanuel, Gayle LaJoye, Judy Collins, Chad Mitchell Trio, Natalie MacMaster and Donnell Leahy, Mason Williams with Warren Nelson & The Blue Canvas Orchestra Band, The Smothers Brothers, Cherryholms, Different Drums of Ireland, Leahy, The Kingston Trio, Garrison Keillor's stories.

One annual show I was particularly proud of was "Pie and Politics; Tomorrow Tonight." It was a show free to the community with lecture and discussion, always about an issue of land use and the importance of protecting the environment.

12. What do you think was lost from the innocent early days?

A kind of pure excitement and camaraderie, a happy atmosphere with performers, crew, local people all working together for a common goal, with no obvious undercurrents of discontent.

13. What was found over the years as BTC became established?

A respect for the unique artistic excellence of our shows and for what this organization means to the area and to the state, and admiration for sustaining it all. An acknowledgement of the importance of "The Arts" to the spirit and economy of a place.

14. What has BTC meant to the Chequamegon Bay Area?

BTC has had a great economic affect on this area, bringing in at least $1million / year directly, and well over $3.9 million indirectly. Over 25,000 people come to our shows each summer They use area lodging, restaurants, grocery stores, gift shops, gas stations, etc. Our touring shows and *Tent Show Radio* bring this area to the attention of people in other cities and states; and those people often make their way up here to see what is going on under the big blue tent, and to experience the beautiful Lake Superior area for themselves.

In addition to the economic benefits is the equally important fact that the original songs and illuminated stories translate the spirit of this northern community, recognize and appreciate the various cultures that are the foundations, and help promote the message that we need to be good stewards of the land and water.

15. *If you were to explain what Chautauqua is (or what it was earlier) to someone who had never heard of it, what would you say?*

I would say that it is a magical experience and a magical place where all kinds of people can gather on a summer night in the woods of northern Wisconsin and enjoy great entertainment in an intimate setting under a blue canvas tent.

16. *Talk about your decision to retire.*

When I told the Board in 2005 that I planned to retire from the executive director position in thirteen months, my intention was to remain with the organization and continue as show coordinator, and whatever else might be helpful to a new director. All of us recognized that fund raising for BTC needed a big boost and that was not my area of expertise. I felt that BTC might follow the examples of most universities and other non-profits where the head executive is also the leading person for fund raising. It also seemed that the timing was right: our financial condition was very stable, we had gained positive recognition throughout the state and region, we had developed a successful formula for how to run "this dang deal" (as Warren called it); and I would be around to help ease the transition. It seemed to me that we should look for an experienced and dynamic fund raising leader whose position would be strengthened by also being the Executive Director.

The Board recognized that significantly more money would be needed for the position, as I had always donated most of my service; and they indicated willingness to be more aggressive in fund raising to get this off the ground.

Certainly a larger salary would be needed to attract the most experienced prospects. The Board decided to make my "retirement" a fund raising event. It was a magnificent party. Many important government officials along with friends and family; I was humbled by the nice things that were said about me. When the time comes for me to leave this earth, I will not need a funeral. I have had the celebration of my life when I could appreciate it.

However, it was confusing to some people when I showed up the next summer, still with my clipboard.

17. What do you miss about BTC now that you have retired from active duty?

I miss being part of the inside of the operation as it was.

I fear that in the future, BTC may change the direction of what was our original focus and core: original shows about the area and region performed by wonderfully talented local musicians. Those shows have helped to foster community and spirit; they have helped many local people to better understand and appreciate where they live. They have helped local people and visitors to appreciate and want to care for this precious and unique space, the land and water and air and all life that is sustained here.

18. What don't you miss?

Hundreds of sleepless nights trying to figure out how we were going to raise the money needed to keep going, and how to find time to attend to everything. Attitudes of a few. The responsibility of the tent when a violent storm rages through.

One thing I "miss and don't miss" is going to the tent every night in the summer. Sometimes it was hard to push myself up there, particularly by the end of the season when we were all exhausted. But always when I turned onto the grounds and saw the tent I was exhilarated and ready for another night.

Carolyn Sneed

*"I'm the one that got us in this mess—and you're gonna
get us out of it."*
                    Warren to Carolyn on May 13, 1997.

Carolyn stepped into the dream of Big Top Chautauqua
by knowing the magic needed a business sense, an
organization, and a platform for the players. She understood
the dream from the start and without hesitation came
aboard.

I always thought of Chautauqua as a big ship, a passenger
liner, loading every night and sailing for spirit. Through all
the years Carolyn and I stood the pilothouse, hands on the
wheel, ready to ride whatever weather arose. On the good
ship Big Top Chautauqua. Just a little tent show by the Big
Lake.

FOR CAROLYN

August 1986.
The lights are on late past midnight in the tuck-a-way house
on Bodin Road.
Carolyn Sneed is up counting ticket stubs
and stacks of checks and credit card slips,
summing the night of the show packed away,
the kitchen table a slate for chalking the score.
It was old-fashioned shoebox accounting
at Chautauqua's start, careful but computerless,
pencilled in by hand, paper clipped and manila-folder filed.

October 1992
The lights are on late past midnight in the tuck-a-way house
On Bodin Road.
Carolyn Sneed is up preparing the final annual budget
sheets for the Board meeting tomorrow afternoon.

I'm down at Northland Lodge throwing
for muskies.
I'll drive up tomorrow amazed
To see the tent all unrolled in
pieces of paper.

July 1999
The lights are on late past midnight in the tuck-a-way house
On Bodin Road,
Carolyn Sneed is at her computer
after the show typing up new pages of script
for tomorrow's rehearsal.
Night after night after night after
day after day after day after day
she keeps her eyes on the prize,
seeing
all is sung, all is done.

August 2008
The lights are on way past midnight in the tuck-a way house
On Bodin Road.
Carolyn is prioritizing bills that are stacking up
for Woody to pay. To her clipboard
she clips a list of a dozen questions Warren must
finally make up his mind about.

June 2011
The lights are off in the tuck-a-way house
on Bodin Road.
Carolyn is sleeping peacefully.

BIG TOP'S AMAZING LIVE CONCERT SOUND
Here's to Canvas, Mark McGinley, Andy Noyes, Andy Okey!

For the years and ears of most excellent attention at the music circus with long gratitude from the ringmaster.

Mark McGinley, Andy Noyes, Tom Blaine	1986
Mark McGinley, Andy Noyes	1986 - 1994
Mark McGinley, Andy Noyes, Andy Okey	1995 - 2002
Andy Noyes, Andy Okey	2003 - 2005
Andy Okey, Tom Fabjance	2006 - 2008
Mark McGinley, *Tent Show Radio*	1993 - 2008

Talk about being spoiled! At the tent or on the road I arrived ready for sound check, uncased my guitar and banjo backstage, and hauled my script and charts to my stage cockpit at the microphone. There was my DI (direct input) unit, electronic tuning box with cords plugged in, my wireless mic on the music stand, and usually a small pile of flat picks that I had dropped before, during or after the previous show. I've always been one to lose things. Don Pavel once described my scattering of lost flatpicks as a Hansel and Gretel trail. You could tell where I'd been. Don would keep them in storage for the many times I would walk up to him to borrow a flatpick. Lisa, our stage manager, had a drawer full of them at the stage manager's stand.

The sound setup was the same for the rest of the band and singers. Talk about being spoiled!

Along with all cords and mics, our music stands with lights and chairs were in place, set up by the stage crew. It was certainly not like the years and years I loaded sound systems and amps into the bars and theatres with the rest of the band. Before the gig it wasn't so bad, the good times just up ahead.

Afterwards, especially in bar gigs, it was a pain in the back to lift and carry the sound system out to the van around 2 a.m.

Talk about being spoiled! The huge sound system, house and monitor boards were in place for the concerts. The road shows were toil heavy for Mark, Andy and Andy. Drive a day early, haul in, set up, tear down, long long days and nights. The hardworking three musketeers that we depended on were Mark McGinley, Andy Noyes and Andy Okey. There were others filling in occasionally but M, A & A were there 98% of the time. The sound engineers are as important as the musicians. You can perform to the best of your talent, the band can be cookin' on a great night, but if the audience doesn't get the sound balanced and near perfect there is no chance for a great show. It is an extremely complicated process. One bad guitar or mic cord has to be traced through the maize, feedback dealt with and the individual performer's mic honed in. It's taken for granted by the band and the audiences. I hope I said thank you often enough.

At the tent, setup for the next night's show was always done immediately after the show that just ended. No small job night after night. It was relentless labor all through the summer.

There were many 2 and 3 a.m. endings for the crew's tasks, one reward being eating the leftovers from the stars' dinners up in the Spirit Cottage kitchen. It was always great when the guest artists' riders included rich foods, stashes of expensive wine and exotic beers. I was always first in line not having to do squat during tear down and setup. Talk about being spoiled.

The shout of "Hey Andy" raised the heads of both Andys. For the guest artists it was thus easy to remember their names. "Hey Andy." Andy Noyes handled the house sound, Andy Okey the monitor board, Mark McGinley, the *Tent Show Radio* recording along with house sound on occasion. The list of world famous artists for whom they all have run sound is astonishing. Mark, Andy and Andy have impressive resumes, their memories full of fantastic shows. Patience under pressure is a trait you look for in a soundman. All three of ours had it.

The sights I remember are: Mark in the Spirit Cottage studio with 50+ channels facing him, a much needed couch behind him; Andy Okey side stage with his display of stuffed animals; and Andy Noyes sitting on the tailgate of his pickup playing guitar before the show. Mr. Noyes has become an accomplished guitar player; I imagine many licks were found in his Chautauqua years.

Here's a side trip. One windless night after a show, Mark suggested we take to his boat and go out on Lake Superior. There wasn't ripple on the great water. Mark was cruising us along when we spied a Great Lakes freighter running up the Bay two miles off. "Let's run to it." So we did, not thinking that the wake from the ship would be rolling down the Bay in the dark. Whap! We hit it. Severin, after grabbing onto the boat grabbed onto my young son. It's a memory that still scares me.

Hats off to Mark, Andy and Andy for the great years I had the professional pleasure of working the tent and traveling with them.

No small P.S.—I had the pleasure to have Tom Fabjance working the house sound during my last year with the Big Top. Tom currently sits in that chair at the tent and carries on with earsful of talent. Tom co-mixed my CD "Song In Your Hat."

TECH AND STAGE CREWS

Wanted: Tech and stage workers for northern Wisconsin summer tent venue. Three and a half months contract. Six days per week. Must be prepared to be overloaded, underpaid and hardworking. Long long long hours. Apply to www.bigtop.gettowork.

There you have it. We were amazingly lucky to find talented and dedicated summer employees during my 23 years at the tent. Carolyn did the hiring. I can't remember a single lazy crew member on the big ship Big Top. Many of those who worked with us were heading to full time careers in theatre and the mad scramble of our schedule gave them plenty of experience. For our touring we kept in touch with those who might be available in the off season to sign on. With our unique setup it helped immensely when they knew the shows, especially our lighting people.

Our stage manager's job description differed from "normal" theatres because of the great variety of shows we put on: the sit-down-and-sing-illustrated musicals in addition to concerts, lectures, plays and the guest artists who came with many demands.

Our lighting system evolved from light trees clamped on to the quarterpoles and follow spots to an intricate grid system. I remained uneducated in lighting, counting on those in the know to do their jobs. The system for Chautauqua's lighting is now set and the stage manager's duties well defined. It's important for performers to recognize the crew from the stage. Behind the scenes workers can make or break a show and the audience takes their work for granted. Our final bows always included gesturing to the crews.

I single out Noel Meyer, Barry Gawinsky, Jim Allen and Philip "Cruise" Warren for top of the Top of the lighting designers I had the fortune to work in the lights of.

As for stage manager, Lisa Sandholm was with us for five years. If I ever put the big shows up again, she will always be first call for me. I simply loved working with (for!) her.

Great people, great times. Here are the general job descriptions and names in the great parade of our tech and stage crews:

The STAGE MANAGER leads and maintains good working relationships with all stage crew, regularly communicating with the other tech directors to coordinate requirements for each show, and to be sure all is ready behind and on stage for the performers.

Anni Bowers	1986
Joni Vaughn	1987 - 1990
Pauline Tyer	1991
Jim Musil & Scott Fuller	1992
Jim Musil	1993
Bob Donahue	1994
John Teeter	1995
John Pivetz	1996
Geoff Ehrendreich	1997 - 2001
Darcy Deems	2002
Jeremy Oswald	2003
Lisa Sandholm	2004 - 2008

The LIGHTING DIRECTOR is responsible for all lighting of the stage and house, for all exterior lighting and electrical set up, equipment and supplies. A "legitimate" theatre usually has an electrician on staff; not so at the Big

Top Tent; electrical tasks usually fall to the Lighting Director. Jerry Carlson was always there to help.

Noel Meyer	1986 - 1992
Jim Allen	1993; 1998 - 2000
Barry Gawinski	1994 - 1996
Rachel Oftedahl	1997
Kenn Macur	2001 - 2003
Geoff Ehrendreich	2004
Rick Corley	2005
Brian Hatfield	2006
Philip "Cruise" Warren	2007, 2008

The VISUALS DIRECTOR is a position unique to our tent show because back projected images on a huge screen are vital along with the music/acting on stage in performance of our original, illustrated musical shows. In addition, visuals showed sponsor credits and coming shows.

Betty Ferris and the Big Screen

Star of the big screen as I've told of throughout this book, Betty Ferris is a performer extraordinaire in her hidden projection nest behind the stage. I give her added thanks here for all the last minute calls I made for shows in the tent and on on tour. I give her thanks again for her creative talents in researching and putting together the glorious parades of old photos sent out over the songs. From the old slideshow days to the laptopping digital buttons, it was often a mad scramble, a jazz of its own sort to bring it all to performance. Outside of our big original shows, it was always a delight to take to the cities and towns we performed in a portrait of their own past and present. Carry on Ferris!

STAGE HANDS AND ASSISTANTS are also required. Every year Carolyn called the theatre directors at the high schools in Ashland, Washburn and Bayfield to ask whether there were any students who were passionate about theatre and would work really hard for really little money. Most years we hired one of those students to perform our most menial tasks in exchange for their being around the stage. It was a great interaction with the schools and often led to that student progressing to more responsible duties in subsequent years.

Fulfilling the roles of assistants and stage hands over the years were: Michael Valliant, Jim Musil, Nathan Bitzer, Michael Fazzino, Bob Donahue, Naomi Galloway, Justin Roth, Rachel Oftedahl, Geoff Ehrendreich, Mark Gostomski David Hymans, Timothy Vener, Ian Grunfeld, Jacob Wolf, Michael Ouckama, Paul Klitzke, Teresa Young, Vaughn Draughon, Darci Deems, Lisa Sandholm Rowan McMullin, Noah Siegler, Jacob Cogger, Rick Corley, Sara Nemec, Graham Terry, Emily Chesley, Tim Chaney, Kris Berge, Orion Jackson, Stephanie Brown, Linda Eschke.

COSTUMES were managed by Kirsten Pedersen.

HOSPITALITY was provided by Marcia Trelstad.

The HOUSE MANAGER role is also an important position unique to the Big Top, in that it requires an individual to manage and coordinate the volunteers needed to keep customers happy, and also to be in charge of tickets and money and transporting all kinds of information and goods from the BTC office in Washburn to the Tent at Mt. Ashwabay.

Carolyn Sneed	1986 - 1994
Geoff Ehrendreich	1995
Herb Lindsay	1996
Christopher Gruhl	1997
Jim Lien	1998, 1999
Kate Fynn	2000
Josiah Lamb	2001
Emily Miller	2002
Ernie Bliss	2003
Ernie & Myra Bliss	2004 - 2006
Lew Miller	2007, 2008

THE OFFICE STAFF

The Big Top's workload certainly was lightened for a time after Old Last Night but soon the planning and working began for the season to come with budgets, publicity, fundraising and booking on the table. Big Top Chautauqua resembles an iceberg. The peak you can see is just the tip of the iceberg, the summer showing of shows, but the work it takes to get it ready is the unseen bulk underneath.

Over time, our year-round staff grew. Carolyn and I discussed each job and reviewed applications or suggested people we knew that would ably fill the positions. She did the hiring. I never had much contact with the day-to-day operations. Carolyn overlooked all and we agreed from the start that we should trust all workers to do their jobs without us hanging over their shoulders during the work days. Each position had a job description outlining the tasks that were needed in order for the ship to sail. Staff meetings helped with planning. Do what you do, get it done, have some fun in your job, handle the stress, pass the test.

I hoped the office staff could remember always that they were main cogs in the wheel, and the tent standing was a show of their work.

> To Therene Gazdik and Phil Anich
>
> It is my intent to thank from the tent
> All who worked behind the scenes
> But to big Phil and Therene
> A toast and a tip of the time from me
> To these two who
> Were alway there where
> What was needed
> In the push and hurry
> In the day and night scurry
> Was all done on the run
> To raise the canvas show
> In the summer's fun and light

Bill "Woody" Woodword

One of our most important positions is that of bookkeeper, and we have been fortunate to have Bill Woodward in that role. I've asked Carolyn to talk about him here:

I can't think of anything that was more helpful during my years at the helm of BTC, than the coming aboard of Bill Woodward as our bookkeeper. I remember interviewing Woody in 1997, over coffee, at a window table at Sandie's Restaurant in Washburn. John Rucks had helped me some years earlier, and then we had a few other bookkeeping assistants over the years; but we needed someone who had the necessary skills and who would plan to be in the chair for years to come. Once again I had advertised the position. When Woody expressed interest in adding the Big Top to the list of his businesses I hoped he would be "the one"; and he was (still is / lucky for BTC). He had a great store of bookkeeping / accounting knowledge and all the skills, as well as being an all around great guy.

Every year one of my favorite tasks was finding a large calendar to hang over Woody's desk—always with a theme of one of his favorite pastimes: fishing or golf. Thank you, Woody, for the years we looked at numbers together.

Terry Meyer
May 2011

Dear Terry,

How's that big chair feel? What are the odds that two natives of Fairmont, Minnesota would become partners in programming for Big Top Chautauqua? It was great for me when we brought you over in 2002 because it freed me to do more writing and dreaming. Just booking the tent is a full time job but as you know there are always another thousand things to do to be ready for the parade beginning third week of June. Sometimes I miss the booking, talking to agents from all over the U.S. Is Paul Lohr still at it in Nashville? If so, say hello from me and tell him I'm still looking for antique wooden fishing decoys to add to his collection.

What I don't miss is the waiting by the phone. I appreciate you taking that on so successfully. Pick a date for the so and so big timer to play the tent, make an offer, they call back, you call back, they need to talk to the artist, you call back, they call back, they need to change the date, you just booked somebody else on that date, will this date work,

OK let's do it, what's so and so's lowest fee? I know we're at the end of the world, I know it's way out of the way, maybe we can route them with another date at another theatre, OK, they need a warmup act, how many rooms do they need, what do they eat before the show, when will they load in, what time is sound check? Some equation I worked out over the years for Chautauqua's seasons, how do you like that big chair?

Chautauqua is lucky lucky to have you. I heard over the phone lines while I was booking here and you were booking in Door County that agents liked you. Helps doesn't it? I do remember being impressed when I talked to you in Fairmont that the work of your life would be in show business. By the way, thanks again for all the concerts you brought us over to play when you managed the Door Community Auditorium. I loved that theatre. What was it? 8, 10 years we played there? I loved hanging out in Door County.

I hope things are going smoothly. Patience is something I wish I could have had a little more of but the pressure of raising money for what has become a huge operation was enormous and relentless along with the booking, writing and performing. It all looks so easy, doesn't it, when the season is booked, the tent is up and full and the audiences are happy.

My best memory with you is in the time of the *State Fair Chautauqua*. I recall that afternoon we met with the fair staff in St. Paul. The easel pages turned and turned with ideas of how we would do it. I got to sit back for once and watch. You handled it expertly. It was apparent the state fair folks were having a bit of fun with it. We were bringing a music circus to town!

I'm grateful for the years working with you Terry. I'm knowing the big dream hat is in good hands.
Love, WPN

OFFICE STAFF 1986 - 2008

Artistic Director/Manager
    Warren Nelson   1986 - 2008

Executive Director
    Carolyn Sneed (&/or asst. manager)   1986 - 2006
    Katherine Beeksma   2007

Executive Team_   2008
    Terry Meyer: Executive Director, Program Director
    Therene Gazdik: General Manager, Event Director

Co-Artistic Director
    Sally Kessler   1986 - 1988
Theatrical Director
    Sally Kessler   1989 - 1991

Program Director
    Terry Meyer   2002 - 2007

Operations Manager
    Phil Anich   1995-2008

Development
    Teresa Wagner   1991
    Janet Blixt   1993
    John Gustafson   1995 - 1997
    Michelle Gustomski   1998, 1999
    Mark Frankart   2001 - 2006
    Paula Bigboy   2007, 2008

Publicity and/or Marketing
    Don Albrecht   1986
    Todd Kessler   1987 - 1988
    Phil Anich   1989-1994; 1996, 1997, 2006
    Nori Newago   1995
    Naomi Shapiro, Ray Smith   1997
    Nicole Wilde   1998, 1999
    Dawn Rivard   2000
    Wendy Miller   2001
    Gwen Keith   2002, 2003
    Michael Mencel   2004 - 2005
    Jamey Penney Ritter   2007, 2008

Publicist / Photography
    Don Albrecht   1986 - 1995
    Norm Regnier   1996 - 1997

Box Office Manager
    Bridget River-Smith   1994
    Lisa Pavel   1995
    Theresa Lindsay   1996
    Bonnie Gregoire   1997 - 2002
    Sara Wroblewski   2003 - 2004
    Paul Frechette   2005 - 2008

Big Top Shop Managers
    Hank Cole & Lois Albrecht   1989 - 1993
    Lois Albrecht & Wendy Adams 1994
    Therene Gazdik & Teresa Wagner 1995
    Therene Gazdik   1996 - 2008

Customer Service Manager
    Therene Gazdik   1987 - 2006

Bookkeeping
    John Rucks   1992 - 1995
    Gordon Watters   1996
    Wm. Woodward, Nicole Soden 1997
    Wm. Woodward   1998 - 2008

THE VOLUNTEERS

If it wasn't for you where would I be?
All tuned up with no place to go
As it is lucky me
Get to go do a show here
Five summer nights a week
Stand on the stage get to see you

If it wasn't for you brave volunteers
We simply couldn't do this
We wouldn't be here
Thanks for sellin' tickets and T-shirts
CD's and ushering the crowd
Up at the tent get to see you
wn

I've made mention of Chautauqua's volunteers throughout my memorywars but it can't be said enough–BTC couldn't exist without them. I've made many new friends over the years in the ranks of the volunteers. They number in the hundreds. Our gratitude was immeasurable. "Help! We need somebody! Help! Not just anybody! He-e-l-l-l-p!"

The famous acts were easy to find help for. I was always the most grateful for those who worked our house shows. Many of them had seen the shows dozens of times. The award for the ultimate volunteer of all-time is Kathy Moore. Kathy became indispensable taking on phone calling, scheduling, ticket selling, gate watching. She was there every night. I got to know her from my Patsy's Bar years. You want side trip stories, talk to her. On second thought, maybe not.

Other stalwarts were Essie Marzolf, and Lou Welton who were firmly in charge of their patrons. Mark and Elaine Frankert gave extraordinary gifts of time. Lois Albrecht and Hank Cole handled the Big Top Shop for five years; they sold merchandise and designed the "Hank built" storage units for outdoor-damp-or-dry conditions. Lew and Marlyce Miller started as volunteers and later moved to staff positions. And here's to George Eggers, king of the camera and heavy lifting.

As long as Big Top Chautauqua shall stand, the volunteers will be hub of the wheel, keeping the summers rolling along.

And now, the Attendance Award for our most important partner—the Audience! The ticket envelope please! And the winners are: Joe and Char Lambert! - Ron and Ann Matta! - Don and Kay Putnam! Those of you blessed Chautauqua Goers who have attended year after year after year are awarded Honorable Mention. You know who you are!

BTC BOARD OF DIRECTORS

One thing you might not know about being a member of the Board of Directors of a non-profit theatre, is that when you sign up for a term you become personally financially responsible for the organization's assets and liabilities. This simply means that if the organization ever sinks and fails financially, board members are liable for the bills. This meant that this million dollar outfit was trusted to the running hands and mind of Warren Nelson and in the good sense and diligence of Carolyn Sneed. We carried all the insurance we could obtain to cover all possibilities. We knew what got us to where we were and what would push us forward. Proof is in the history of how we succeeded.

We always found folks eager to be on the Board. The shining light of what we had become interested prospective members. Budget time came to a head at every annual meeting in January. The early years were easier. What's up Warren? What's up Carolyn? What are we doing next summer and how are we going to pay for it. "People are going to come. Don't worry," I'd say. "Acts of God" were part of our development plan. It proved more than once through fire and high winds to be true.

It was sometimes a test of my patience to deal with board members who had no experience at all in show business. Much explaining was necessary. Frightful numbers were crunched. Faith, faith, faith is what I preached over and over and over. It paid off.

To all the Board members over the years, I raise a toast to your volunteer time served, to your efforts, to your faith in us. Ballyhoo.

PARTNERS
Jerry and Carol Carlson

We were great partners. Jerry and I said that to each other often. Since Jerry and Carol live on the hill, the Big Top is a tent put up in their backyard. Jerry has run the Mt. Ashwabay ski hill for who knows how long. I know he knows. The site is perfect for a Chautauqua—private, a parking lot, flat ground to pitch a big top on, a bar, protection from wind provided by the steep ski slope. From the first tent raising day in 1986, Jerry was a canvas man with handy guy knowledge that was needed regularly in the entire operation. He and Carol kept the grounds. Jerry was king of the hill on his tractor. Carol planted the beautiful perennial flower garden in front of the T-Bar, decorating the evenings.

Speaking of the T-Bar and the concessions, it is Jerry and Carol's business and they do it well. They got to know the in and outs, the ups and downs of handling a show night like we did. Both of us got better at smooth-running our operations. I think of how complicated the food service is, not knowing the numbers of folks coming to the show. Advance ticket sales certainly is an indicator but who knows?

Perhaps the most important memorywar of mine here is Jerry's parking lot and weather history of Chautauqua. Every night Jerry counted the number of cars at intermission and took the temperature. He'd say, "323 cars tonight and the temperature is 78." He could guess the attendance by the number of cars. "You can figure on average two and a half people per car, Warren." "Yeah, Jerry, two and a half people per car and the half is not a pretty sight."

I write of the tent in past tense, but Jerry and Carol (lucky for Chautauqua) are still there. I have nothing but great memories of working with both of them. I miss seeing them six summer nights a week and hanging out in the T-Bar after the shows. So it went, so it goes.

Tony Judge

Around 9 p.m. one night in 1991 I took a call from Chicago from a man who introduced himself as Tony Judge. Board member Eric Kramer had told Tony about Chautauqua. It wasn't long over the phone before he proposed to lead the fund-raising for a Big Top tour with corporate sponsorship. He got right to it, which is my style. At the time he was Development Director for the Chicago public radio station WEBZ. Carolyn sent him stuff and soon Tony called to tell me we had an appointment with Wisconsin Bell in downtown Milwaukee to present a sponsorship. We met for the first time in the middle of the street, shook hands and two minutes later were sitting across the table from Carla Buttenhoff of Wisconsin Bell. Tony and I were an instant grant-winning song and dance team. A four city 1992 tour came of it, the first touring for Big Top Chautauqua as an outfit.

Tony opened a lot of doors during the many years he was involved with us. For the first several years he was Executive Producer of Tent Show Radio, leading the fundraising and giving much needed advice to me, the novice radio host. In Chicago I met a good pal of his, a good pal to the wide world, Studs Terkel. Studs was at his desk at the station when Tony and I walked in, the stub of a fat cigar in his mouth. He suggested we leave immediately for the local pub down the street for a bump. There are well over a hundred top five hours of my life and this was one of them: sitting on a barstool with Studs Terkel talking baseball and Chicago in a frumpy little neighborhood bar. Some of the talk was of his wife, Ida, who was born in Ashland. A thrill, an honor, a keepsake of an afternoon.

Every year I'd ask Tony if Studs would consider coming up to speak at the tent but, alas, no luck. During one of Jack, Phil and my appearances in Chicago promoting Chautauqua, Tony arranged for us to go to Studs and Ida's house to sing for them. Tony said he knew Studs would love my songs.

If you're somehow unfamiliar with Studs Terkel (that would be shame on you), know that he, beside's being one of America's great radio hosts, is a popular author of books of the stories of working people, of uncommon common folk, the gist of America. Studs knew the art of the interview, how to get souls to the tongue. All his life Studs had "conversations with America."

We sang a dozen songs, Studs telling stories in between. I saw that Studs was really listening...listening...he heard the words. Ida especially enjoyed "Ore Dock Pockets," an Ashland song story. Just before we departed, Studs shook my hand and said to me, "Warren, we haven't had such a time in our living room since the Almanac Singers played here in the early fifties." The members of The Almanac Singers included Woody Guthrie and the young Pete Seeger. Thanks Studs. Thanks Tony.

Don Albrecht

As a historian working out of moments frozen in photographs, I've been looking at the photographs of Don Albrecht in Chautauqua's story through the years and am grateful Don was there from the first tent on to give us museum portraits of how, when and who made it happen. He's still shooting the incoming crowds before *Riding The Wind* to project pictures during the end song. Elsewhere I've told of his other occupations with us.

I was honored Don asked me to write the Forward for his book BAYFIELD Lake Superior.

Here's a snippet from it:

> *I have admired his eye on the prize of the people and this place for a good while. Don's talent as an artist is to find and freeze the big picture in a small frame. Isn't that what we call the glimpse of a day? He is a short story writer in his photographs: There is one soul around which the new moment stands and sets itself. Gifts are earned as well as given to all of us, and it's our time and place that Don has sequenced.*

Mark "Pete" Alvin Nelson 1959-2008

I miss him everyday. He was my brother. He passed from colon cancer in February 2008 in Duluth where he was well known in the folk and bluegrass music circles. He, of course, knew BTC from hour one. He pumped pews, pushed poles, distributed promo materials, attended shows whenever possible and gave an ear to me whenever I needed to talk outside the circle of my work here. Gave great advice too on booking. It was Pete who introduced the music of Bela Fleck and The Flecktones to me. Pete played banjo at Chautauqua with us all through the 22 years he was alive. Highlights for him were playing with John Hartford on stage, jamming with Bill Monroe in the beer tent and becoming acquainted with Bela Fleck. "Pick it clean!" Bela signed in an autograph. Pete worked hard at the banjo craft and picked it clean.

When he was 15 I gave him a Gibson banjo my mom had bought me, one that I had carried and played for 12 years. He became an outstanding picker and frailer. He knew my songs better than I did. We both began buying too many banjos and guitars as most musicians do. When he bought what he described as "my perfect banjo" he surprised my son, Rowan, by giving the Gibson to him. Will The Circle Be Unbroken? Rowan picks it clean.

He left behind his wife Karen, a fiddler. He was on his way to being the greatest dad ever when he died. His son Eli was four. Someday I'll play him a tape of his dad in the band on the Chautauqua stage, picking it clean.

Song

*"My voice leaves my throat,
as if a large bird startled my name,
And the flock of small songs that is me,
Rose from the grove to praise this amazing air."*
wn

SONG

No the words and music don't come easy,
Somehow they always come just in time,
Up and down my thinking
It's hard to make everyday rhyme.
　　from "Afraid Of My Own Songs"

Sometimes they do come easy. A frequent question to me is "What comes first, the words or the music?" The answer, of course—the contract! Partly true in light of the commissioned shows with their deadlines but true song has true heart and however it arrives it is a gift.

How To Write A Song

God whistles and I sit up.
The song writing class I can't do. How to explain.
Well, I like to have a baseball game on the radio in the next room.
Well, start paddling with the guitar in the rolling rivers of melody.
Fool around.
Carry the canoe of song one portage at a time.
A manual typewriter is best, the rhythm knocks there.
How many have I just throated out the window and
given to the wind?
Memory begs later.
Have a tape recorder ready.
Just start and trust your own voice.
When the high note breaks the window, you've begun.
Lyrics come in invisible as spores, you breathe in and out.
Inspire. Lick the page.
If the seed takes, the verses will grow.
All choruses need a hook and you are the shepherd.
Make sure only the day hears it first. Otherwise it's jinxed.
Wrangle the thing around.
Watch for the smile or squinch when you bring it to someone.
Save the first draft.
If it stays in the toes of your shoes, you've got something to walk with.
Sing it three days and if it still holds water, it's a keeper.
Don't call me, I have no idea.

I've written over 500 songs since summer 1963. I've tossed equally that many out the window into the air, just singing spontaneously to the moon. Some of those I wish to God I'd remembered. Some I thought I would surely but they flew away.

The impulse to write songs found me gradually landing a career in show business. That and nervously having no fear of getting up in front of people and making a scene of myself. I give you now a few stories of how some of my songs have come in.

Whiskey Before Breakfast

This song is frequently requested and is the oldest of those I've sung at the tent. In Denver in the early 1970s my partner, Michael Kotik, and I were invited by Mason Williams to a recording session for his album *Fresh Fish*. They began the session with an instrumental, "Whiskey Before Breakfast," an Irish fiddle tune. My soul was drunk with joy. Michael and I took the tune home in our heads and immediately sat down to play. We remembered it, sort of. Mostly. We played it all night.

I couldn't sleep with the melody dancing in my head. The first words "Fiddlestick fiddletune, the October pennymoon" fit the rhythm and stood me up. I finished the lyric in an hour. I think that was the first of my being inspired by a traditional melody to write lyrics over the tune.

There's a line in it that has always confused listeners who have loved my adaptation: "The wind and a sweep over crumbs of the wood cake." The image to me was the dry crumbled leaves in the woods being blown around, I guess the Earth being a cake of some sort. Why I haven't changed it in the last 40 years is beyond me. I'd get questions from people who listened to the Lost Nation album where it was first recorded, asking about the lyric. That phrase is almost as bad as Jimmy Webb leaving his cake out in the rain and wondering why it took so long to bake it and never having the recipe again. I should probably rewrite but I'm stuck like a boot in the clay with it.

Fiddlestick fiddletune the October pennymoon
The wind and a sweep over crumbs of the woodcake
Pumpkin's in the pie and the goose goes high
Thistle thistle pennywhistle play a jig quick

There's a dance at the town hall later on tonight
There's a band from the big city come to play for money
Have you ever heard them play you ought to hear them play
They got a banjo a flute and a fiddle in the middle

There is whiskey in the jar and there's beer in the keg
It's looks like rain no work tomorrow anyway
A chance to wear your suit and your new brown shoes
The ladies will be waiting for a man who can dance

I'll be by to pick you up we'll take the motorcar
We ought-a leave soon be in town a little early
Have dinner at the hotel before the dance
Take a bath get a shave and a shoe shine

Autumn Fancy

My most requested song, it was written for the show *Dance of the Seasons* in 1984. I was driving with my friend Katy Rumsfeld up Highway 13 just past the Sioux River Bridge. It was a clear October morning in full autumn color, a little wind, the sun's brush painting the day. The big hill seen driving north (the South side of Mt. Ashwabay) stood gloriously in maple red. Katy proclaimed "It looks like a fox's coat." Watch for that hill next October.

The lake hills turn the color of a fox's coat
Easy in the breeze the leaves go float
When the birch burn yellow and the maple red
And the apples are ripe up overhead
When the fall is falling all around
Get your wood up quick winter coming to town
The way the Indian summer lays on the Bay
This fine October day

Blue on the Big Lake blue in the sky
Blue down the river of the time gone by
Green come a summer to a golden end
Yellow is the eye over Earth my friend

September winds are a sailor's charm
The new moon's up in the old moon's arms
Up the little rivers go the trout to spawn
You can see your breath rise in the dawn
Come early frost the summer people go
Back to our old selves broke and slow
It's the harvest moon we dance around
When the garden's in the jar

Come gray November the month of gales
Superior sings her shipwreck tales
In the waves that beat and pound the shore
Light your home fires now and close the door
When the geese are honking high in a vee
And the boat slips are naked as a popple tree
By Thanksgiving Day and the herring run
Be done with all you've started

North wind at the window stand and stare
Daylight dwindles the brown Earth bare
Big Lake be still freeze first on the Bay
Whoever's here now is here to stay
Go deep to sleep one cold clear night
Wake to a new world all winter white
Those who love the cold can lick the ice and toast the Solstice

Down To The Dock

The photo history of Bayfield's maritime heydey is exceptional and well organized by the Bayfield Heritage Association. For *Riding The Wind*, we needed a portrait of the great parade of ships, boats, barges, in sail, steam and diesel, that called at the Port of Bayfield or called it home. The photos were all in the archives, including captions of owners and schedules. They are hypnotic. They cry out for the wind to again fill the sails, for passengers to step up the plank and embark on those beautiful old wooden passenger ships, for fishermen to come in with barrels of lake trout and whitefish, for barges to tow in log rafts, for pleasure cruises on boats large and small to launch on the Sunday lake.

Three days I waited for this song to come in, to come ashore. It wasn't happening. I was inspired but blocked. And so, getting away from my desk, I bought a six-pack of Leinies at Patsy's Bar and went to the Washburn West End dock and finished the six-pack and the song.

Get down to the dock to see what's about
See who's coming in and who's going out
Appear on the pier for the floating parade
Take the lake air now all promenade
A stream of dreamers down on the strand
Lovers alone where the waves greet the land
Stare at the water place your face to the wind
Walk all the way to the end with your friends
Sittin so pretty on the hill the Harbor City
Port of Bayfield Lake Superior Gateway to the Islands

Standing on the landing in the steamboat days
Dressed in your best steamer take you away
Are you traveling on the Asia or the good Manistee
The Peerless is due in from Sault Sainte Marie
Those grand regal portly proud magnificent boats

So splendid and pompous those palaces float
Boarding by day or by light of the moon
Soon you'll be strolling the royal saloon

At Booth's Dock waiting for the India
At Vaughn's Dock waiting for the Iroquois

Ahoy there a packet liner bringing in mail
A schooner with all the wind she wants at full sail
The mackinaws are tilting and lying ashore
Out to the nets go the fish boats once more
Excursion vessels launches and yachts
Coast Guard cutters tied at the docks
Outboards inboards trolling for fun
Tugboats pushin' in the hot summer sun

Anything that floats anytime of day
You can see from the wharf cruisin' the Bay

Always the men standin' around
It's a wonder any work gets done in this town
Always something happening down at the slips
Shoot the cool breeze gawk at the ships
Someday I promise when my ship comes in
I'll push off this post you may not see me again
I'll take to the blue open water someday
Pack up my troubles sail them away

Ore Dock Pockets

This song was written for Ashland's musical *Whistle Comin' In*. I used it again in *30th Star*. It seemed a bit long so the last verse hasn't been sung since 1987 at the Civic Center in Ashland. The Soo Line steam locomotive used to sit on Highway 2 next to the ore dock; they'd been together so long;

I wished they'd left it there, it was a marriage. The ore dock yet standing is one of four that once welcomed the big boats over the water. Kiss it goodbye; it's coming down. Insurance risk you know. Shame shame, Ashland won't look the same.

My name is William Williams born in Cornwall
Been a miner since I was eight
I worked Hell's Gate in New York Harbor
Before coming to the Norrie Mine
I worked the whole Gogebic Range
From Ironwood Hurley to Mellen
It's a midnight tale in the first day's light
How we sent the Bessemer rock off to Ashland

It was old Nat Moore stumbled on the ore
Started the rush and the wild speculation
It was known before but the time had come
Iron was king Cleveland mills were roaring for the ore
Work your way up down in the hole
Take a little out timber as you go
Stand aside the Captain cries come a tram car by
Two trammers to the bucket and up

Shine a light down the shaft of those days
When the hematite paid when we were all wearing the candle
You'll see me there too with my sisters in the crew lower us
There's diggin to do a thousand feet down
In the drift and shaft down the tunnel come a blast
Through a new wall at the Ashland Mine
In the snow in the Colby open pit in the mud in the clay
Can't say I like it

Ore made iron iron made steel steel made a nation
How did Ashland feel
When iron made Ashland a queen of the lakes
To the Great Lake freighters that came here to take
From the four ore docks each a quarter mile long
The raw red rock been railroaded on
Three Chicago-Northwestern one a Soo Line song
From the ore dock pockets come and get it

1885 year the Lake Shore Road arrived
We built the first of the four docks
On the ice in the winter cold
Heave Ho raise it the boss says double time
First ore train come up from the Range
July fourteen twenty cars on the shove
Up the trestle approach up the grade
Switch engine put 'em in place for dumpin' up above

I was an ore dock puncher
Punchin' rock in the ore dock pockets for Chicago Northwestern
I was an ore trimmer level out the stone load
Way down in the ship's hold
I remember way back to the Whaleback's day
The Pigboats stirrin' up mud in the Bay
I can tell just when the Soo Locks grew
And the new bulk freighters come easin' on into their landin'

In the railroad days engine crew Soo Line Dock 1916
Makin' up shoves in the ore yards back and forth and back
From the dock to the stockpiles
Orange ore dust on your boots in your hair
In the bars in your house on your paycheck everywhere
Eighty years cars wheeling by to the last load out August 1965

Now the Soo Line dock lays quiet in the bones of its heyday
And the steam locomotive number 2-10-0 sits cold in her cage
Nothing to do but stand and stare
At the two big ghosts just standing there
The railroad watch is all unwound
On the time we loaded the big boats over the water

Decoration Day

Written for *Old Minnesota: Song of the North Star*. The song came to me while walking in the Fort Snelling National Cemetery. My grandmother always called Memorial Day Decoration Day. I like the old name. Everytime we performed this song I would ask for a raise of hands of all those in the audience who were veterans. Then I would ask them to please stand. All proudly but humbly stood up immediately. The audience would spontaneously applaud. I received a letter after one of the shows from a veteran in his eighties who said in 60 years since he served no one had ever publicly thanked him. Thank you.

In the sad but lifted air we follow the parade
Soldiers leaving the home town ground
Buttoned spit-shined off to the war
A sad and lifted air we sing true and too sad to say
For some the home is coming
For some the going goes one way

Look long as there is a sight and wave and wave and wave
The train pulls out from the depot the camera makes us brave
The bus turns from the driveway the plane flies from the field
For some the home is coming
For some the going goes one way

And the flower speaks for the short sweet hour
We all have been given
And the weeping sweeps the sorrow to keep it from tomorrow
The band plays here comes the parade
The bouquets laid today fresh on the graves
At the beautiful end of May on Decoration Day

Mississippi Flyway

This song I first wrote for a rally in Ashland when there were plans to fill in a part of the Fish Creek Slough to widen Highway 2. I used it in *Wild River*. We continued to sing it in many of the *Best Of The Big Top* performances. Just before the end of the song the band vamped and I'd ask for bird calls from the audience. The crowd whistled, hooted, quacked and throated calls. There was always a blue ribbon call.

> *Dawn on the watertop the fog is burning away*
> *The egg is broken open on a brand new day*
> *On the Mississippi Flyway   Mississippi Flyway*
>
> *Here's to the all the critters who croak or stroke*
> *Who paddle or swim who nest or rest*
> *Who fly by high overhead*
> *On the Mississippi Flyway   Mississippi Flyway*
>
> *Spring is on the wing in the backwater sloughs*
> *From the coast of Mexico and the Louisiana Bayous*
> *Up the Mississippi Flyway   Mississippi Flyway*

Over to Old LaPointe

If there's one song of mine that is bound for folklore, that may someday become a "traditional" tune, this is it. I'm hoping a hundred years from now the composer will be listed as "anonymous," which would be the greatest legacy for me. For 16 years I sang it every Fourth of July after the parade at LaPointe's celebration in front of the museum on the site of John Jacob Astor's trading post. I would always stop singing on the chorus and let the crowd in the grass sing it to the Madeline Island air. They all knew it.

Over to Old LaPointe rowing to old LaPointe
Summer is here we'll have our share
Ferry carry us over there
We miss the boat back we don't care
We'll dance with the ghosts of old New France
On the Island on the Rock on the shores of Old LaPointe

An Ojibwa town it was up and down a famous little port
Village in the shade of an old fur trade
Then a new found summer resort
Once you visit Madeline and come to know her well
She'll tell you tales of Nebraska Row
And the Vaudeville man Al Harvieux
In the windsled over the ice we go to Madeline

Let's not forget Gram Johnson they called her the Island Queen
Or Thomas Stahl hauling behind his two-dog team
Leo Capser left behind a museum it was his dream
The name of Captain Angus floats
With old Ed Valley who built the boats
Raise the mast of the Island past on Madeline

The Chippewa know it's Holy Ground spirits are in the air
On his journey to the other world Chief Buffalo left from there
Protestant and Catholic missions rang their mission bells
Heaven thought that hell had come
When Astor brought his rotgut rum
God and the Devil are still havin' fun on Madeline

Nothing to do but visit and fish and play on the Big Bay sands
Nothing to do will do for me that's what I come here for
And when I leave when I push off
Won't you give me the Madeline yell
Kemo Keimo Daro-o Mahe Mahi Marumski
Poodle won't you knit cap Polly won't you Keimeo Madeline

The Beer Belly Polka

Just for fun, from *30th Star*. I was driving back from Milwaukee with Chris Engfer and we stopped for lunch at a watering hole near Oshkosh. Severin and I had finished this song for the show. Two guys, I'd say in their thirties, were playing pool. They were carrying two of the largest beer bellies I have ever seen. Oshkosh! By Gosh! Look at'em! I asked them if they would let me photograph their bellies for a show I was writing. I told them the picture would be projected in front of thousands of people. They not only enthusiastically agreed but, as I was focusing the shot, they each lifted up their T-shirts for the grand view of these Wisconsin monstrosities.

Where did Antigo? I don't give a Beaver Dam
I'm a cheesehead Brewer Packer Bucky Badger fan
Anyone from Wis-con-sin We will always cheer
Leinies Leinies that's our beer pass another one over here

On my Harley on my Harley roar for Pardeeville
Dance the old Beer Belly Polka bratwurst on the grill
Roll your dough at the Casino try your one-armed luck
Have you ever fished for, fought and caught a muskie?
Did you get your buck?

Friday try the fish fry Saturday elbows on the bar
Lurch to church on Sunday forgive our weekend Wiscon-sins
Later watch the Packers win then take a little snooze
Turn the channel just in time to see the Vikings lose

Oh beautiful for spacious skies for cows big pasture eyes
That follow me that milky way whenever I drive by
How now Brown Swiss Jersey Guernsey
Milking Shorthorn Holstein she's the queen
Alice I will marry you in Dairyland if you will just say cheese

Yo Ho Buffalo

Driving west in 1991 to Denver, we stopped to stay a night at The State Game Lodge in Custer, South Dakota. It was the first time my kids, Medora and Rowan, had seen the Badlands. Custer State Park has a major herd of Buffalo; it was the herd filmed in *Dances With Wolves*. We had just had our first sight of the big herd. As I was driving, I heard my children in the backseat singing a phrase that went "Yo ho buffalo, my name is Yo ho buffalo." "I can steal that." I mentally taped a memo on the bulletin board of my mind. The song has become one of my signature tunes, a favorite especially of young children. And a favorite of mine. It was used in *Earth to Wendell*, an environmental show; and is the show title of the *The Yo Ho Buffalo Hour* which we played only twice and ought to revive. The song was written to give voice to Meriwether Lewis of the Lewis & Clark Expedition.

Into the western wind up the Missouri Jefferson sent us to the ocean
This side of the Great Divide
The short grass was black with backs of the buffalo

Some say sixty million ran in the middle country
With gangs of wolves and coyotes following the grizzlies
Yo Ho Buffalo my name is Yo Ho Buffalo

Now the buffalo chews its cud wallows in the mud
Rubs its winter coat off on the willows
In the running season we heard the herds miles away
Thundering towards the river

In the book of the Sioux it is written
They have gone in the Earth to hide
Nothing will bring them out again but the people dancing
Yo Ho Buffalo my name is Yo Ho Buffalo

Now the USA is just like the buffalo got a fence around
The old home and wandering grounds
And all the green new children who want to run out West wild
To the high and unknown places to the country of imagination

Too small a percent of the wild land left
Is put aside and promised forever wilderness
Yo Ho Buffalo my name is Yo Ho Buffalo

Green room to run green room to run
Leave it to the children let 'em take off their shoes
Loose the uptown blues green room to run
Green room to run green room to run
Green room to run
Yo ho buffalo my name is yo ho buffalo

Set of Keys

I've told you of Felix Knox, who played the porter Daddy
Joe in the railroad show *On The Velvet*. The phrase "set of
keys" came out of the black community in the high flying
days of passenger travel on the great trains of yore, especially
relating to the Pullman sleeper cars. When you landed a job
on the railroad, you got your "set of keys"

The Civil War is over 1865
Man named George goes to Georgia his idea come alive
He says you were a genteel servant in the plantation South
You're free now where you goin? You'll be livin hand to mouth
He said come work for me on the Palace Sleeping Cars
Be a porter my name is Pullman

Well my Daddy was a slave in some ways still am I
The big difference is I get to wave goodbye
Now I got my set of keys got my set of keys
Porter on the Pullman Palace Sleeper got my set of keys

They put a car on the sidetrack they put me in the car
Taught me how to fold and make a bed how to tend the bar
There was two pages alone on how to serve a beer
How to fold a pillowcase the towels go here
Noise in the night is taboo never shout
Never knock on a berth shake the curtains from without
Got my set of keys got my set of keys
Porter on the Pullman sleeper got my set of keys

Hey there George my name ain't George
This car's too hot this car's too cold
This car's just right I want another room instead
Oh Porter someone's been sleeping in my bed
Porter come here, sire Porter stay there
Porter open the window and give us more air

I can read a train for tips fat, soft or slow
We call this a boxcar the Conductor Big-O
Call the engineer hogshead the fireman greaseball
Conductors paid twice for doing half the work we do
All in all though I'm happy to be most polite
As the Pullman Palace Sleeper goes streaking through the night

They keep my wages low so I go go for you
I live by my tips on this trip you just holler
If you need something sir, I'll come right away
Leave a silver dollar in my big tip tray
Porter on the Pullman Palace Sleeper
Got my set of keys

This train is pullin' out on its run once more
There will be a paper in the morning at your door
I buy the polish to shine your shoes
I buy my uniform I pay my dues
To the Brotherhood of Sleeping Car Porters
Makes me a man thank you Mr. Randolph

Dreamboat Steamboat Heydays

Illustrated with projected photos of beautiful old steamboats that once plied The St. Croix River, this traveling song was written for *Wild River*. Inspired by the style of Captain John Hartford.

Up and down the river up and down the river
Runnin' the St. Croix trade
Up and down the river up and down the river
In the dreamboat steamboat heydays

Once upon this shallow shifting waterway
In the clang banging racket of a time long gone
In the flush old rushing northern steamboat days
The St. Croix was a main traveled road
Though nothing will ever compare with the Mississippi parade
Once it was payday in the St. Croix trade
All the way up to St. Croix Falls
All the way down to the Prescott levee

She's layin at the Stillwater levee
Apply for freight or passage on shore
Keep this ticket in sight at table and return at the gangway
Yes sir yes ma'am you can now step on board
Excursion bound for Red Wing cabin passage to Dubuque
Are you down for the day to St. Paul
Flags a flyin' bands a playin' jackstaff's on the mark
Paddlewheeler kickin up her heels in Lake St. Croix

When the ice goes out in April look downriver
Any hour now you'll hear that whistle blow and blast
She's run past the catfish bar at Afton
She's crossing now and due in here at noon
She's just a big barge with a wedding cake on top
They say three trips down you're hooked forever
You'll never stop pinin' for the feel of the wheel
What goes up must come down and stop at every river town
Along the St. Croix way back when

All the steamboats, men and days are history
All gone downriver to the mystery below
There are two boats you should know of on the St. Croix
Both built in the Osceola boatyards
The little packet G B Knapp ran here for twenty years
With the old man himself his soul turning in the gears
Two longs three shorts of the whistle
It's the Nellie Kent comin' in to carry you

When I die don't take me to heaven on a steamboat
There's no snags or sandbars up there
I wanna go full steam toward Hell's landing
Just to see if we can get there on time
Let the Devil take a ride on a steamboat
He'll sweeten up with his finger on the wheel
When the red haws on the islands hang over the river in the fall
And the moon lays it's silver on the shoals

New Barn Floor

This fiddle square dance tune honors the great story of Wisconsin farmers and their neighborliness in gathering for a barn raising. Written for *30th Star.*

Bow to your partner who married the farm with you
Swing your children into the light of the spring planting moon
The spring planting moon

Bow to the plowboy and the ox who broke the sod
All hands pray for the summer rain better say your grace to God
Say your grace to God

The wheat lays neat in windrows on the ground
Tie the knots and bundle now circle the county 'round
Circle the county 'round

All the men left where'd they go?
Followed the threshers down the road
Followed the brand new threshing machine
J I Case made in Racine
Made in Racine

Now we'll dance the harvest dance the harvest
Dance the harvest home
Thresh the wheat jar the garden pick and store the corn
Call all the neighbors over who came the spring before
To raise the barn beam wall and rafters lift and hinge the door
Now let's dance the harvest home on the new barn floor

Enough tears to water the year Mama she lost a child
Papa slap hard boots on the oak Mama swingin' wild
Mama she's swingin' dancin' wild

Mama took to the fields when Papa went to the war
And every night for him we'd light a candle at the door
A candle at the door

I stood the best I could in his boots though I was still a boy
Then one day at the end of the fence we saw a soldier's joy
Papa step home to a soldier's joy

We danced all night we kicked the harvest moon
Papa said work those dance boots polish these slivers smooth
Shine the barn floor smooth

The threshers come again one fall with another new machine
A traction engine belt to the wheel this one run by steam
This one run by steam

Gone the cradle and flair gone the power pushed by steam
Come another new day on the old farm
With the tractor and gasoline
The tractor and gasoline

Gents shed your tools ladies lay down the yarn
Come Saturday night in your Sunday best
There's a fiddler in the barn
A fiddler in the barn

Let The Summer Go

Written the day of an *Old Last Night* to the audience with
good wishes.

Oh the monarch is up on the butterfly
Migrating back to old Mexico
Clouds of their colors flickering by
Wings in the wind are a-whispering

How do I say so long to you
So long it may be before we two
See each other again on the common ground
I wish you well in all you do

Oh oh oh let the summer go
Oh oh oh it's time for the autumn show

Sailors now take your boats from the sea
Gardeners dry your leaves to tea
Lovers button up and hurry inside
Swimmers now come to the shore

I'm gonna miss you what else can I say?
If I could only think of some clever way
But never a word have I heard that can sing
Of the goodness you bring on to me

Carpenters sharpen and pack up your tools
Children now step yourselves back into school
Bumblebees I don't know just what you do
Black bears soon you'll be asleep in the snow

Oh how I hate to see you drive away
So far you must travel to rise the next day
Think of me often call when you can
Or write me a letter in longhand

Somewhere Under My Car Seat

Here was hoping they'd laugh. For a middle-of-the-week evening at the end of the summer, when the population of tourists had gone home, I always took to "Well, the tent is still up; let's put on a show." And so I put together *Show For A Slow Night.* "Show for a, show for a, show for a slow night. What you got to show for a show for a slow night?"

As I got in my car to head to rehearsal, I tried to find a place in my big 1990 Buick LeSabre to sit down so I could drive. When I opened the door things fell out. Nothing new. Before I could even think of vacuuming, I thought a shovel might be handy. One autumn, the IRS sent me notice my taxes weren't paid. I was going to draft a letter letting them know that somehow my last year's 1099 return got stuck down between the car seats. You know the tune to this. Judy Garland sang it so beautifully in *Wizard Of Oz.* So sing along.

I swear I put it in the mail
You know I'd never lie to the IRS
I know I had it in my hand
I drove it into town oh wait unless it fell down

Somewhere under my car seat way down low
Careful when you stick your hand down there
Things there are staring to grow

Somewhere under my car seat old bananas go to die
Some people do keep their car clean why oh why can't I?

There's combs and cough drops cans and pens
And empty bottles, matches and a post card
There must be almost 3 bucks in nickles dimes and pennies
It's down there you'll find me

Somewhere under my carseat Old bananas go to die
Some people do keep their cars clean
Why then oh why can't I?

Bound For Old Ashland

Ashland in the shallow waters of Chequamegon Bay became the major commercial port hereabouts in the 1880s with the discovery of iron ore in the Gogebic Range. Four ore docks were built along with coal docks, lumber docks and mills and merchandise platforms. Rails brought the ore to Ashland; the great freighters carried it to the roaring furnaces of Cleveland, Toledo and other Lake Erie ports. Ships were built and designed for their cargo.

I had read notice in a small paragraph of the hobo jungle camps in Ashland and was aiming a song at the story. Someone gave me the name of Herbert "Chuck" Wilson telling me he was the man who knew all of it. I called.

A raspy voice answered. I asked him about the camps. He was ready to talk. I began taking notes over the phone asking exactly where the railroad hobo camps were. He paused, "Railroad hoboes, they were the other side of town from me. I'm talking about sailor bums." This being a thing I had never heard of, I didn't understand. "Sailor bums, coming up like birds in the spring to work the shipping lanes. They camped under the ore docks on the East End. There was Toledo Whitey, Sausage Dutch, the King in his beat-up Cadillac, and a camp full of other sailor riff raff. When they ran out of money for whiskey, the king would send some of the crew down to the Ashland docks. At that time, crews on the lake freighters were hired right from the docks. Ashland sailor bums could make a whole crew. They were wheelsmen, dock hands, cooks, firemen, etc." "When can I come over?" "How about tomorrow, I'm retired."

Betty and I, with camera and tape recorder in hand, met Chuck at ten o'clock the next morning. His wife welcomed us. Chuck was sitting in his easy chair. He had the look of a man with heart trouble, didn't look well, red-faced but sallow at the same time. From word one Chuck Herbert was one of the friendliest humans we had ever met. And as it was soon apparent, one of the best, if the not thee best, storytellers we had ever met.

"I haven't got long on this earth so we better get started." We explained our project; he introduced his boyhood in Ashland, working for his father who hauled coal by horse and wagon from the coal dock to homes and businesses. Chuck told stories for three hours. We were mesmerized, hypnotized, and I went home to the prize of the song, the voices of sailor bums singing under the ore docks.

> *Meet you down St. Clair Street the one we used to know*
> *Drink one down to the long shore town*
> *In the wake of the lake trade here not long ago*
>
> *Was a time what a time season 1892*
> *Half the trade was Ashland locking through the Soo*
> *The tonnage shipped from here, now dock this in your mind*
> *Twice all other ports on the Upper Lake combined*
> *Was a day what a payday in this harbor*
> *A forest of masts along shore*
> *The lake dollar, full sail, upbound*
> *On the great water highway Superior*
>
> *Bound for old Ashland in a bygone day*
> *A vagrant sailor's fancy now bears me away*
> *We'll dance down the docks that once stood the shore*
> *We'll go before the captain and the mast once more*
> *Bound for old Bay City we'll whistle comin' in*
> *Have our fun tonight there on the old East End*
> *Meet you down St. Clair Street the one we used to know*
> *Drink one down to the long shore town*
> *In the wake of the lake trade here not long ago*

Carloads of pig iron on the pig iron dock
From the Blast Furnace west end on the hill
Boilers and parts for the mines and mills
From the Parish Plant out at Parishville
Quarryman size and cut your brownstone
We're running out to Houghton Point to load
The stone all piled up at Ashland
Mr. Prentice says is already sold

Waney board cork pine for Liverpool
That's me there hands on the pole
My mates on the deck of the Grimsby
Come on down boys and hoist 'em in the hole
That's me now master on the Hilton
Sailing for John Schroeder's Company
Outbound from Ashland for Chicago
Three days on these freshwater seas

Tell me mate how long before this coal is all unloaded
Captain says we're due down below
Reiss dock number two foreman Mr. Miller
Says fifty-six hours till you go
I wouldn't work that mantrap ore dock number one
Once I punched ore there all day
Now I'm standing watch on the Morely all night
Let go the lines we're sailing away

One ticket please to the flush old times
Round trip passage to the past
Here's to the dreamers of the steamboat age
To the prosperity we all thought would last
I'd sooner board a schooner face the lake wind again
Say hello to the long shoremen
A young tar off to new Wisconsin
And new lake port Ashland

I can still see Weed's white front drugstore
It was a landmark to guide us all in
Starboard to the Central Dock
Where we put off the passengers then

I can still hear the whistle talk
Music of the lake trade's band
Mill to men to slip to ship
Ship to ship to shore
Whistle tell us where to land.

Take It ToThe Lake

There have been rumors over the years of dipping into the freshwaters of Lake Superior and transporting millions of gallons by pipeline or truck to water-starved parts of the country. "Keep your buckets out of this world jewel," is the prayer of this song. Written for the end of the show, *Take It To The Lake.*

Lay yourself out on the old lake bed
Just a stone's throw away from the waves
Peace comes like water to the shores of your soul
Take it to the lake, lay it on the water
Take it to the lake

Now the North Shore is more like a dinosaur
The North Coast is the wild coast hey where can you land
I love to wade in the shallows of the South Shore sands
In the lee of the Islands where the light is so sweet

The desert states south got their mouths wide open
Thirsty for the freshwater here so abundantly
Keep their golf courses green and their brown cities growing
Want to mess with the flow that goes east to the sea

You can't drink oil and you can't swallow silver
Will gold hold water for the good of this Earth
We all know they're coming with their facts and their figures
Waving their money What is it worth?

The little towns all sprinkled on the slopes of the shoreline
Who owe their existence to the ice of the past
Should watch like a father and guard like a mother
Be brother and sister let the miracle last

Give the old fisherman who's lived his whole life here
His final wish on his last sailing day
A shroud made of birch on his head put a whitecap
The lake was his church send him floating away

BIRTH OF THE FISHTAR A One Act

Cast: Carolyn Sneed (C)
       Warren "Anglin' Wayne" Nelson (W)

*The drama takes place over a phone call from a
kitchen to a lake. Sun rises stage East spotlighting older
guy drifting in a boat, throwing musky lure on Lost
Land Lake.*

Cell phone rings older guy in boat answers.

W: Hey

C: Hello, where are you?

Silence except for loon calling.

C: Where are you?

W: What, are you writin' a book?

C: I hope you're not fishing, the show is three weeks
away, (*pause*) I think I hear waves lapping.

Silence except for waves lapping.

C: Let me hear the guitar.

W: I just got an idea for a song

C: Where are you?

W: I'm off Christy Point...nothing is biting

C: Oh, Warren

W: I'm really getting good ideas...got my notebook

C: Call me when you get home

W: *(thinking)* Wow, if I could attach this rod and reel to a guitar.... John Gray could do it...the reel goes inside the sounding board and the rod eye-hooked up along the neck..I could fish and play guitar at the same time...Carolyn would never know...a Fishtar!

Two weeks later, Anglin' Wayne in boat, cell phone rings.

C: Hello, where are you?

W: *Strums Fishtar*...I'm working up a new song

Waves lapping against boat, sun going down stage West.

SERMON–"DOWN AT PATSY'S BAR"

I am honored to have met so many folks over the years who have taken my work to heart and let me know so. I have a longtime great friend from afar that I see at most once a year at the tent. He is a huge Chautauqua fan; he is Rabbi Alan Bennett of San Francisco.

He wrote me a letter dated October 10, 2005. "I first learned about Patsy's Bar and was so moved by the song that I used it as a basis for my Rosh Hashanah sermon, the most important sermon that I will deliver all year." Of all my songs, he chose "Down At Patsy's Bar."

From Alan's sermon:

> One of the things I do on my summer vacation in the North Woods is to go to a sort of magical place created about twenty years ago by a fellow named Warren Nelson. Warren Nelson's specialty is writing about local things, places and people. One such place was the inspiration for my sermon tonight. I found it a little ironic that on the one night a year that Jews all over the world begin a one day fast, refraining from food and drink and other pleasures of the flesh, I should be talking about a place as opposite from that as it is possible to be. But this is what blew me away, folks. It was Warren Nelson's song called "Down At Patsy's Bar" that rang the bell for me.
>
> In the song about Patsy's Bar, Warren sings about all the locals who come to the bar, most of them every day. And I'm sure none of them give it a second thought. It's where they go, even if they don't drink. Warren mentions them each and all by name, because by doing so he indicates that every patron of the bar counts, that each one is important in his or her right, and that they are all worth mentioning and remembering, whatever their idiosyncrasies, their special talents or traits, or even their unremarkable sameness.
>
> Patsy's Bar is where people know one another, and where they share their same Midwestern values that are transmitted from generation to generation more by deed

than word, but which are unmistakable and solid throughout the community.

The refrain in Warren's song goes like this: "Do we even know who and where we are? We are human seekers peekin' through the glass down at Patsy's Bar. Do we even know who and where we are? We are neighbors, friends, strangers to the end down at Patsy's Bar."

I have never heard anything that resonated so clearly and loudly than the simple words of this refrain. "We are human seekers." What are we seeking? We are seeking the sense of community that shares its values together, we may not understand what is involved in being an intimately involved member of such a community. It means being able to be counted on in an emergency. It means caring enough about the survival of the community and its values and institutions that you spend a lot of time not only doing those things that build community but also reaching out to those people who ought to be part of the community, but who either don't know about it, don't care about it, or don't understand how important that sense of community can be to them.

Yet we are often strangers in our own community, or at least we often feel that way. But in reality we are often friends and, with a little transformation or reorientation, we could grow those friendships, we could realize that we have friends or are friends in ways we haven't realized. When all the shouting is done, we will realize that we are neighbors to the end, landsman, and more closely connected than we have ever imagined.

I dedicate this to Patsy Avery. Was a time Friday nights at Patsy's Bar we were run over by our young children who had their own hour there to get to know one another. Not to mention it was our hall for gossip, fun and Chautauqua news. The Patsy's Bar story doesn't end there.

I was sent a photo from a St. Louis surgeon I had met a year earlier. The photo was taken while he was performing surgery on a man, three nurses around him. In the foreground of the photo was the Live At Patsy's CD cover. His caption read: "Toe tappin' in St. Louis. We were all enjoying the CD...well, all except that one guy."

DOWN AT PATSY'S BAR

When I die don't put me in the ground
Put my ashes in the ashtray and drive me around
Drive me around this old town that slowly drove me crazy

Stop at Patsy's Bar first sprinkle some on a bar stool
Where I sat in my infinite wisdom most every afternoon

Throw some more on the floor where my brain cells went to die
Raise a glass to my name at my last big bye bye

Do we even know who and where we are
We are human seekers peekin' through the glass down at Patsy's Bar
Do we even know who and where we are
We are strangers friends neighbors to the end down at Patsy's Bar

Florence comes in at four o'clock
Sits same place with her can of pop
Electric Al and Chris and Sue are there
Homer's in and out what's he down to now

Mike comes in after work to see his Ma
That's Patsy herself if you don't know
Kathy's drivin' around and around where and why nobody knows

Candy says Jimmy's comin' home for Northern New Years
Sons of Bunyan meeting
Jimmy my son he the King of Fun
He drinks like a tuna he the big Kahuna

Patsy's Bar's for sale 30 years she stood here through thick and fun
All good things come to an end maybe the old lady's done

Do we even know who and where we are
We are human seekers peekin' through the glass down at Patsy's Bar
Do we even know who and where we are

We are strangers friends neighbors to the end down at Patsy's Bar
Okee dokee here comes Andy Okey
And McGinley fresh from the stable
We're laughin' at Ralph's old jokes again
Holman here's over there at the table

I'm here first again today and Kirsten is tendin' to my thirst
Remember don't talk politics or sports
When the bar's full throttle on the bottle

Hey Patsy put it on my tab one more and I gotta go
One more and I gotta go one more and I gotta go
Patsy pourin' margaritas beer all kinds of wine and things that fizz
Remember even before you're born Patsy knows who your daddy is

Do we even know who and where we are
We are human seekers peekin' through the glass down at Patsy's Bar
Do we even know who and where we are
We are strangers friends neighbors to the end down at Patsy's Bar

In 1978 Burnside booked a Lost Nation gig
At Archie's Supper Club in Washburn
We hurried up Highway 13 the greenway

To Washburn Wisconsin where I had never been before
Tell me what kind of goof in this goofy world
Would paint their bar orange?

I stopped in for a burger and a Walter's on tap
Soon after we all moved up 25 years have passed
I look back at those 25 years boy I've really gone far
I moved my seat by my two feet to the other end of the bar

Do we even know who and where we are
We are human seekers peekin' through the glass down at Patsy's Bar
Do we even know who and where we are
We are strangers friends neighbors to the end down at Patsy's Bar

Guest
Performers

The Carnegie Hall of Tent Shows
Claudia Schmidt

THE ROAR OF THE CROWD,
THE SMELL OF THE BAND

In this daily age, over-stimulated from every media horn with recorded music, it is live performance that holds life up to the minute. There is a bend in the road in live music, a journey of two hours or so that piles everybody in attendance in the same vehicle for the ride to who knows where.

The perfection of digital recordings spoils the ear, though I've certainly sought it in the studio making new albums. No one wants to put down a mistake that's frozen for all time. But life's rarely that perfect.

I love to be front and center of musicians who make music right in front of my eyes and ears. It seems more of a miracle. And I love most the spontaneous combustion of a group of singers and musicians rolling on one wheel in front of a crowd. There is more of a lift in live music. It often comes near to perfection. It often derails a little or a lot. It's live, ladies and gentlemen, interaction between breathing, playing, singing human beings and there's no going back.

As for recordings, I guess I join with Neil Young and many others who think the analogue good old 33-rpm LP's have a warmer sound, a closer relay. Yes, yes, I'm an analogue man. It seems every time you buy a new player a newer device comes to replace it. Edisons to 78's to 45's to 33's to 8 tracks to cassettes to CD's to DAT's to MP3's and iPods. What's next? Who's going to able to play this stuff in a hundred years? (A live musician will play for you.) Hold on to your devices. They'll bring antique prices not too long from now. From the list, I have players that will play all except for the old Edison cylinders. It is true certainly that ear phoning yourself along during the day keeps up spirit. It's the memory of really getting to know a song and the love of a singer or group that is in your camp. Later, seeing a group play your favorite songs live is the ultimate.

There's just too much out there for me. I find myself about-facing and re-listening to the old groups and songs that hit once and stuck. Shame on me for listening to so few of the new fabulous artists that come rising with each new generation. But that's my way to prevent overload and blowing my circuits.

I once was told there are only two kinds of music, good and bad. That is a proverb that has opened me up to listening to any and everything with an open ear. As an old folkie, I resisted the Beatles when they changed the music world. So it went for me for rock 'n rollers and the new sounds of the last thirty years. I missed a lot but there's time to catch up! I listen for songs one a time that are singing and saying what I would sing and say if I could. I'm lucky as a songwriter that I can sing and say what I would.

What does all this have to do with Big Top Chautauqua? The Big Top is a rare, rare venue that exudes warmth presenting live music. The cotton canvas softens the sound. There is no bounce from the back walls. It's as if the performers were in your living room. Not every tent show works. Vinyl is terrible for sound. It's plastic.

Big Top Chautauqua, best venue in the history of the Universe? I vote so. Give me canvas or give me death!

Bill Holm

Bill was one of my favorite all-time characters, a poet, writer and teacher from Minneota, Minnesota. I met Bill early in the 1980s while I was performing with Lost Nation at an old-fashioned Thresher's Bee in Butterfield. He was a great thinker, reader and ragtime piano player. He was an enormous man, a cherub-faced Icelandic giant of the kindest most sensible strong opinionated temperament.

I booked Bill to play the tent 1990. The morning of his appearance he called from northern Minnesota from his uncle's cabin on an island and asked how long a drive it would be from near Bemidji, where he was, to Bayfield. It was a little before ten. "How far are you from Duluth?" I asked. Bill thought two to three hours. "Better plan on at least five hours then," I said. "OK, look forward to seeing you." "You, too, Bill."

Bill called back about a quarter to eleven. "Warren, how far is it again from Duluth?" "Two hours Bill, at least." "OK, I better get going."

Bill called back about one, a little crooked brightness in his voice. "Warren, I'm still here at my uncle's cabin. He'll boat me across the lake and I'll be on my way." "Great, Bill" I took another look at my watch.

Bill called back about two-thirty. I could smell bourbon and coffee over the phone. "Warren, we haven't left yet but I'm packin' up." "You better get started, Bill, you're barely gonna make it." "How long of a show do you want?" "Two sets Bill. We start at 8:15. I got the piano all tuned up for you." "An upright?" "No, Bill, it's a small funky grand and it ought to do you right." "Thanks, Warren."

Bill called back about 4:00. "Warren, we're gettin' ready to boat on over. My uncle's got a plane and he's going to fly me there. Where's the nearest airport?" "Ashland, Bill. It's about

35 minutes from the tent. I'll come pick you up. Call me right before you take off." "OK, Warren."

Bill called back about five. I wasn't exactly furious, but I was thinking about an alternative show, at least to start the evening. "Warren, we're almost in the boat. My uncle says it'll take us two and a half hours to get there, so that's seven thirty, plenty of time." Bill called back about a quarter to six, pretty looped. "Warren, we had a little trouble getting the plane ready, what should I do?"

"Take off, Bill, get your ass over here." "OK, Warren."

Well, here's what happened.

I told them they better land at the LaPointe airport. Since there was no way to communicate by telephone when they were in the air, I told Bill to have his uncle dip, dive and buzz the tent before landing on Madeline Island. I called Tommy Nelson and asked him to be on call to go to the airport and pick up Bill and deliver him to the LaPointe marina where Captain Dave Nixon, a friend of mine, would speed him by boat to Port Superior where I would have a car waiting to run him up the hill. They buzzed the tent; I called Tommy and Captain Dave. Our stage manager waited at the dock.

The bell rang for the audience to enter the tent. Still, no Bill. As I prepared to go on and do who knows what, a very red-faced smiling Bill Holm walked into the back of the tent with books and papers in hand.

"Good evening Ladies and Gentlemen, Big Top Chautauqua is proud to welcome a friend of mine, a great poet, writer and storyteller, Bill Holm." It was a helluva show. Never seen him in better form. I miss Bill. He has crossed over.

Bill Monroe

I booked Bill Monroe and the Bluegrass Boys in 1994. He had broken his hip in the spring feeding pigs on his farm. Paul Lohr, his agent in Nashville, called me and told me that Bill would be back out on the road again in time and not to worry. At Bill's age, 82, my grandma broke her hip and went to the nursing home; Bill, after a short time, got back on the bus.

The long awaited Saturday came and the bus rolled to the Chautauqua stop. Bill stepped out first. My heart was doing mandolin back-beats under the melody of seeing Bill Monroe in person approaching our big blue tent.

By studying up, I knew that Bill and his brother Charlie got their start in the 1930s traveling with their own bluegrass tent show. To raise the dust of interest, they also played a baseball game in the afternoon against a local team for money. You had to be able to play both music and baseball to be in Bill's band. Perfect for me. A doubleheader– a game and a show. Bill told me later he played third base. Of course, the hot corner fit his style.

Bill, in his perfect white hat and silver suit with the Jesus pin on the lapel, looked up at the flags flying on the centerpoles, at the sidewalls (he saw it all) and asked "Where's the guy runs this place?" I knew that voice so well by his records and the radio. "That'd be me, Mr. Monroe."

He grabbed my hand. Holding my hand he led me through the open folded canvas backstage flap and we walked in. Bill Monroe was holding my hand as he pulled me up the stairs to the stage. Bill Monroe. Bill Monroe. I swallowed that delight.

It was a beautiful summer afternoon, an easy breeze waving the poplar and maple leaves in the long woods near the sweet hang of canvas. The blue of the sky and tent matched hues. I always loved being in the tent with 950 empty seats– the padded church pews front and center, and back to rows of the antique folding theater seats and the bleachers up against the back wall. Bill Monroe, staring out, was still holding my hand and squeezed it, not saying a word while a smile wrinkled up his wide face. Bill Monroe was seeing a canvas show tent, I'm guessing for the first in a long long time. The stage was ours until Bill stepped on it and took it.

When I booked Bill, it was for one 55-minute set to close our one-day mini bluegrass festival. His agent had said that's all he can play. I said fine. Opening the show was Stoney Lonesome featuring Kate MacKenzie. Bill was still holding my hand. He said sharply in his Kentucky pitch, "Show me around." We walked through the aisles and then headed to the concessions tent.

If I remember right it was a little after 5 o'clock; Stoney Lonesome had finished their soundcheck. In the corner of the concessions tent were four or five pickers jamming. My brother Pete was there on banjo with Kevin, John, and Kate of Stoney Lonesome. Maybe eight showgoers were sitting at the picnic tables. As everywhere in the bluegrass world, there is jamming before and after shows.

Now out of the blue Bill Monroe and I ambled towards the pickers while his band was setting up. My brother turned his head and I'll never drop the memory of the mile-wide grin on his face. They brought the tune they were playing to a standard shave-and-a-haircut ending.

The folks at the picnic tables all moved up, hot dogs in hand. There's the man. The father of Bluegrass. Bill asked without hesitation, "Anybody got a mandolin?" A mandolin was quickly handed to Bill. We were all in awe of ourselves for being there.

Bill looked out beyond us as if we were an audience of ten thousand and declared in his tenor drawl, "It was nineteen-hundred and thirty-nine when I first played the Grand Old Opry. I played 'The Muleskinner Blues' and I got three encores. Boys, let's do 'The Muleskinner Blues' in A." (Bill's to play only one set later you remember.) Bill, with my brother on banjo and the others on guitar and fiddle, jumped in, Kate and I leaning as close to Bill as was polite. He called out songs for well over half an hour, taking his solos, calling up solos. We were there.

My brother and I often declared this was our favorite day and night at the Big Top. Years later my brother would still declare, "Oh yeah, I played with Bill Monroe for a while."

Later of course, with the tent packed, Bill came out with The Bluegrass Boys to hoots and whistles. We had received permission to record him for *Tent Show Radio* as long as we paid the standard radio royalty. I loved it. It's the only time we did. Bill wanted a real radio intro for his show. Standing together just in back of the curtain before I intro'd him, he said to me, "Yeah...we'll do that 'Watermelon Man' and then you bring me out." It was his old radio theme on WSM, Nashville.

At the end of the first set, he announced from the stage, to the delight and surprise of us all, that he would return and play another. Don Pavel was standing with me at the back of the tent. We were stunned. He turned to me and said, "Miles Davis and Bill Monroe are the same guy."

Backstage afterwards, one of the Bluegrass Boys thanked me for the evening and told me that in the past two years or so Bill's performances had been understandably uneven, but tonight the old Bill was back. At 82 Bill stood our stage, still carrying that high lonesome sound vocally and on the mandolin.

I shook the Bluegrass Boy's hand and said, "This is a night the angels came down." "Yes sir," he said and stepped into the bus.

The Chad Mitchell Trio

In winter 2006, I read in the Minneapolis paper that the Chad Mitchell Trio was playing Orchestra Hall in a reunion concert; also on the bill, was The Kingston Trio. It sold out. I was ecstatic to hear the trio was singing together again and wondered if this was a one and out or were they back? It was what I would call the original trio but in fact Joe Frazier replaced a member before they hit the big time. Chad Mitchell. Mike Kobluk. Joe Frazier.

How to find their agent? I knew Allan Shaw, founder of Rediscover Music, whom I met at our 1987 concert of the Kingston Trio; he would know how I should proceed. Allan gave me Chad Mitchell's home number. I called Chad and gave him my old folkie spiel, naming albums and songs, the changing parade of trio members. He could hear I was in the know, a super fan. The idea piqued him since their concert in Minneapolis had sold out and was well received. "I'll call Mike and Joe and see if they're interested. Call me in a few days."

"Yes, we'd love to do it." (Another notch in my campaign to meet my heroes.) We talked several times soon after, making arrangements for lodging, rehearsals and the show. The word spread and fans of the Trio came out of the woodwork. I wasn't surprised but didn't know that Jerry Phillips of the Rittenhouse in Bayfield was a fan. He told me dinner was on him for the Trio and he helped arrange rehearsal space in the old Rebecca Hall in Bayfield.

They arrived three nights before the concert and I found them having dinner at Maggie's. I invaded. It was another head and heart shaker for me, introducing myself and being invited to join them for dinner. I felt like I had known them for 40 years, indeed I had by records and TV.

They asked me if I had a favorite song of theirs I would like to hear. I chose "Hello Susan Brown," a rather obscure song they had recorded. They looked at each other and laughed. It was not on their songlist but the next morning at rehearsal in Rebecca Hall they sang the cobwebs off it. Rebecca Hall is remodeled now but I loved its old musty look and smell, kitchen in the back, ribbons, medals and photos on the wall of The Daughters of Rebecca, Benevolent Society of old Bayfield.

I walked in as they were singing and stayed for the two hour rehearsal. The concert, I could see, would be all the classic material I knew so well, exactly what we wanted to hear; those of us who were fans and still are. I was imagining all their history, recording, touring, rehearsing. They had obviously honed their rehearsal skills. It was almost all business. It was lighthearted, serious, friendly, and in tune. Their attention to detail both in the singing and figuring out intros to songs, cues to the flow of the show, was a wake-up call to how we could better run rehearsals.

After soundcheck, I arranged to interview them for *Tent Show Radio*. I was comfortable, having a list of questions that I hoped led sensibly from one subject to another. The time began to jump with surprising turns. I remember one story well. They were the first group offered the Bob Dylan song, "Blowin' In The Wind," to record for single release. Dylan had just written it like a day before. The Trio was unbelievably excited, recognizing the simple power of the song. Their manager, nameless to my memory, talked them out of it, or ordered them out of it, saying it would never sell with the word cannonball in it, and how many people must die. So it was offered next to Peter, Paul and Mary who recorded it and instantly watched it climb to number one on the charts, essentially launching their career. There was pain in the shaking of their heads and a little bite of anger in this story during the interview. Who can double blame them? They would have had the megahit they never quite found.

What has always set the Chad Mitchell Trio apart is not only the strength of their musicality, their perfect vocal blend, powerful or tender as needed, but a body of work, that along with the wide range of songs with common folk music themes, featured outspoken songs on current political and social subjects and events. They were the best. They still are.

Their rendition of the song, "The John Birch Society," poked at Joe McCarthy style Commie hunters and right wing extremism. They debuted the newest version on our stage. "The George Bush Society." It was Dave Obey's idea, longtime Wisconsin Representative. While I was having dinner with Dave in Wausau, we were talking about the trio and he suddenly said, "How about The George Bush Society?" He sent his rewrite to Chad and me; they worked it up with a few changes of their own. It rocked the house. The single is available online at the trio's website.

Today in these flammable times it's great to see the Trio back out there for those of us who step forward with the left foot, a step that calls and begs for honesty, humanity first, and a healthy environment.

Two extraordinary musicians accompanied the trio: Paul Prestopino, on banjo and guitar (he was Peter, Paul and Mary's accompanist); and David Anders on guitar. Paul and

David played with them back in the good old days following Roger McGuinn who left to form the Byrds in the 60s.

The tent was full of fans who knew all the songs. A minute before I introduced the concert, a man approached me saying he came up from Miami to see the show. He was wonderfully surprised at the chance to hear the trio again. His tickets were ten rows back on the side and when I spied two empty seats in the second row, I motioned him up. He was Alan Jacobson.

Something fabulous came out of Alan's trip to the tent. After the rare evening, a group of us went with the trio to the Northern Edge, a bar outside Bayfield, to celebrate. We found ourselves out in the hall in a circle, jawboning into the wee hours. The punch line is that a plan emerged to film and record a new DVD of the trio live. The idea included a return to Chautauqua with a film crew, invite Tom Paxton along, and get it done.

The following summer they returned. The DVD was filmed in our tent and in a theatre in Spokane, Washington, their home ground. Entitled *Then and Now*, it's a 3-DVD/Book Combo including film and recordings from the 60s, and the 80s during a reunion concert with John Denver and 2007 performances at the Big Top and in Spokane.

We were and are proud to have been the spark. I consider it high privilege to have gotten to know them and be considered a friend. They sound better than ever. See and hear for yourself. www.chadmitchelltrio.com.

Doc Watson

During the off-season in my booking years, I'd keep a notebook of performers I wanted at the tent. On the A list was Doc Watson, the guitar player's guitar player in acoustic music.

Over the winter of 1996 I heard through an agent that Doc was traveling in the summer and doing shows. I put in an offer. I knew of Doc from the early 1960s during what he refers to as the years of "the folk scare." I think the first album of Doc's that I bought was the double LP *Live at Carnegie Hall*, recorded with his son Merle. Merle's playing was impeccable, in the style of his dad's. The apple doesn't fall far from the tree. When Merle was killed in a tractor accident on his Missouri farm, the music world lost decades of a great father-son duo. There's tenderness in Doc's voice that I believe must come from the pain of losing his son.

I lined up the date and called Terry Meyer to let her know. Terry at the time was the Executive Director of the Door Community Auditorium in Fish Creek, Wisconsin. We coordinated bookings whenever possible to share the cost of the famous ones making their way out of the way to way up here at the end of the concert trail. Terry hosted him on a Friday night in Fish Creek and I booked him for two shows the next day and night. How to get Doc here was the question as Door County is six driving hours away. We asked and received a generous gift from a local businessman to fly over and pick Doc up at the Sturgeon Bay airport.

I don't know what type of plane it was, looked like a Lear jet to me, or a turbo prop, whatever that is. All I knew was it had wings and a pilot and would bullet us to Sturgeon Bay in forty-five minutes. When I say us, I mean Jack Gunderson, Don Pavel, my son Rowan Nelson-Ferris and yours truly.

Jack, Don and I had been playing many of Doc's songs over the years in the Lost Nation String Band. I first introduced Doc's recordings to Don, who not only learned the licks, but found his singing fit the tunes. "Peach Pickin' Time In Georgia," "Deep River Blues," "Old Camp Meetin' Time," "The Black Berry Rag" and Doc's signature piece, "The Black Mountain Rag," were at the top of our repertoire.

On a Saturday morning in July we boarded at the Ashland airport. As far as I was concerned we were going over to pick up Elvis. As we taxied in I could see Doc standing outside the terminal in the sunlight with his guitar case. Guitarist Jack Lawrence who is a flat-picker extraordinaire in his own right accompanied him. We all introduced ourselves. Doc from his first word enlightened the morning. Doc's aura is immediate. Don and I could only look at each other with Buddha smiles. We felt a kindness and calm. Here was man in his late 70s on the road. After an evening concert he was up and awake and trusting whomever to carry his soul.

It's something to meet a man in person whose voice and face you've known so well. It's something more to find what you thought was true was truer. Greatness with humility has a high grace.

Even though Doc has been totally blind since the first year of his life, we unrolled a red carpet out for him. I believe he thought a small Cessna or such was coming to carry him. Jack led him up the steps. The engines were humming and Doc broke into a grin at the sound. He took a seat at the back of the plane and before we took off he was asking the Captain about the plane, showing a surprising knowledge of aeronautics. I was thinking he was thinking, "If only I could fly this thing."

This great man that I was welcoming to the tent was born Arthel Lane Watson on March 2, 1923, in Deep Gap, North Carolina. According to his own story he got the name Doc while performing on the radio. The host asked him about his unusual name and someone in the crowd yelled "Doc," referring to Doctor Watson, Sherlock Holmes' sidekick.

Of the thirty-six hours Doc was in Bayfield, I spent twenty-eight hours with him. Afternoon sound checks of the famous ones were always my favorite hour of the concert days. We arrived at the tent a little after noon and the smooth, clean, rapid-fire of Doc's flatpicking filled the empty tent. There are many great pickers playing today including busses full of young players but there are no shortcuts to the time it takes to become a master musician. The longer the wine or whiskey has been in the bottle, the smoother, more delicate the taste. What time and knowledge there is in Doc's hands.

Don and I stood the back of the tent during the matinee holding those Buddha smiles. I went alone to dinner with Doc at Port Superior. Where was the tape recorder? He talked about his boyhood in Deep Gap, learning the guitar while playing with family and neighbors. I asked him who his favorite guitar player was. "Merle Travis" he said with no hesitation. He told me he named his son after Merle. I remembered that Merle Travis and he had played on the *Circle Be Unbroken* album the Nitty Gritty Dirt Band put together in 1977. The subject of the album led him to talking of Earl Scruggs, Mother Maybelle Carter, Roy Acuff and Jimmy Martin, all of whom the Dirt Band recorded. He told me of his home in North Carolina, a state I'd never been to. There was never an awkward minute with Doc. He is the real deal when it comes to openhearted human beings.

The evening show was packed. He walked to his chair on stage saying, "howdy folks" to the crowd and telling us he wasn't giving a formal performance– it would be like we were all invited over to his house while he played in the living room. Doc and Jack passed solos seamlessly. He came back for an encore to a standing ovation, the audience applauding extra long in appreciation.

I rode with Doc and Jack to the Duluth airport the following morning, another three hours sitting with Doc's stories.

I brought him back a few years later, this time he traveled with David Holt who played guitar and frailed the five string. The concert, of course, was astounding. After the show as our crew and David were packing up, I found myself alone with Doc in the canvas dressing room. He began to talk of his son, Merle. They had played together professionally for 15 years before the tragedy. His head down, he let it all out, his voice falling in pain. He talked of his wife Rosalie whom he had married "once and forever."

I recognized the honor of sitting alone with Doc Watson backstage. It was as if he were watching a movie of the shadow side of his life. He went silent for a spell. "You know Warren, in World War II, I volunteered, I wanted to have a job, however small, in the war effort. Sorting nuts and bolts, answering phones, anything. They refused me." "Doc, you've brought soul and joy to millions and I think there is nothing more important than music to move the American spirit along." Silence.

David came to get Doc and they walked to the van back of the tent and drove into the night. As for Backstage Big Top, no hour has ever touched me more.

The Good Doctor

Doc Watson in his chair on the Chautauqua stage
Licks up and down the neck of his guitar
While he welcomes us.
"Jack, let's start with The Blackberry Rag."
Running blind the man's hands finger without a cane
Into the trail of melody.
Every audience eye is on his hands
Unrolling silk,
The flat-pick angled by his soul.
We are all alone with Doc.
I close my eyes to go with him.
Outside the tent
In the summer grove
Birds go silent hearing
The call.
wn

Earl Scruggs

Earl Scruggs and Bill Monroe, who both played the tent, are the two greatest legends of bluegrass music. Bill with his Bluegrass Boys first defined the group sound of bluegrass with his high lonesome sound. Earl, who was a player in Bill's band, originated the three-finger picking style on the five-string banjo. The fast, driving sound is known as Scruggs picking. All banjo players owe Earl.

Earl was 79 when he played for us the first time. I was wondering how an old man could keep his famous fingers flying up and down the neck. His band, fronted by his son Randy, sang a couple numbers and then to thunderous applause Randy introduced Earl. "Ladies and gentlemen, let's bring him out. Please welcome my dad." Earl walked slowly to the mic, a North Carolina smile on his face. We were ready! 1 2 3 and Earl took off. You'd think the speed of his picking would involve his whole body but it's all in his fingers. Not a wasted motion. He rarely looks at the neck. His thumb and two fingers run like a rabbit being chased. He also picked a tune on the guitar.

Louise, his wife, was first to walk in the tent when they arrived. I approached to welcome her and introduce myself. Without saying hello she looked at me and asked, "Where's the one who's got the check?" "Carolyn Sneed has the check, I'll go find her." Now that's old time show business.

Earl left Bill Monroe's band in the late forties with Lester Flatt, singer and guitar player. Flatt and Scruggs quickly rose to the top of the bluegrass world rivaling Monroe in popularity. During the fifties, bluegrass music was all a southern phenomenon. It was the rise of folk music that brought it into the American mainstream. For Flatt and Scruggs the *Beverly Hillbillies* TV show jumped their name into the lights. "Come and listen to a story 'bout a man named Jed..." The tune that changed banjo master Bela Fleck's life. Bela went out and bought a banjo, learned the Hillbillies' song and the rest is a string of Grammys.

Then came the movie *Bonnie and Clyde*. Earl's composition and signature tune was great escape music for the two outlaws, that tune being "The Foggy Mountain Breakdown."

He played both in his set at the tent, closing the night with "Foggy Mountain." I don't remember Earl saying one word the entire evening. He didn't have to. The audience grinned the whole night, strangers looking at each other with a nod–Yes! Yes!

He has a star on the Hollywood Walk of Fame; he's won two Grammys, including a Lifetime Achievement Award. He was awarded a National Medal of Honor. In September 2003 he was saluted at Turner Field before an Atlanta Braves baseball game as 239 banjo players gathered around him playing "Foggy Mountain Breakdown." He returned to us two years later, not having slowed a bit. After the show I'm sure everybody did what I did– rolled the window down and drove home to the speed of Bonnie and Clyde, looking in the rear view mirror for flashing red lights.

Garrison Keillor

As for dressing rooms, there are two of them backstage canvased by used sidewalls. There's a mirror, table and a chair if you're lucky. Old time vaudeville closets, tent show green rooms, mirror-lit nervous bins for the show-makers. In the dressing room I often felt like I was an old-time hoofer, who had just arrived fresh off the train, in from a vaudeville theatre, hurrying to iron my show clothes I had pulled fresh out of the trunk.

When Garrison arrived and the band was setting up, he'd say his hellos to us as we welcomed him back. Friendly man. The soundcheck over, Garrison would sit a bit catching up on the news from Carolyn and me and then about an hour from the show he'd hole up in his dressing room. He came out when he was good and ready.

There is a star's dressing room in the Spirit Cottage, complete with couch and shower. I loved Garrison Keillor's refusal to use the fancy-pants Spirit Cottage dressing room. He always took the tented one, backstage stage right. Now that's class.

I don't believe anyone ever recognized the rare air of a real American tent show any more than Garrison. It fit him like butter on sweet corn. I first met him on the phone. He called from New York and after a short talk I had to ask how much would it take to get him here? "You tell me." I started low and he immediately said yes.

He was always generous in his fee. For the incredible shows he put on the boards for us, for more than one summer he brought us a profit sorely needed. A gift. He always agreed to two shows. The Sunday matinees lay open-walled to the high summer afternoons, the night shows full of different material. They were Sunday services of jokes, songs and stories as only Garrison delivers.

I drove to pick him up at the Ashland airport the first time, delighted to finally meet him in person. I immediately presented him with a Sons Of Bunyan pin, the treasured award the Sons receive on joining the brotherhood. Sons of Bunyan? Founded in a below zero night in 1985 at my home, the Sioux River Songfarm, the Sons, our all male fraternity, celebrate winter every third weekend in January, standing all night in the snow, smoking cigars, sipping strong medicine from long-necked bottles, passing resolutions that are never remembered, eating chili at dawn after a night of reveling. Garrison, though I didn't know it, on our van ride to the tent was filing away the Sons. Some time later I received a postcard from Garrison from Memphis with a postscript to give the SOBs his best.

About a year later Garrison's new book came out—*The Book of Guys*. The first paragraph tells of a guy winning a poker game and a membership in a club known as The Sons Of Bernie. It was a January night when he drove his truck deep into the woods around River Falls, Wisconsin, to go to the Sons annual campfire. There was boozing and lifting of song into the pines as the Sons circled the fire. The temperature was thirty below, the snow waist high, the Milky Way and the moon showing through the all-night revelry.

The Sons of Bernie ate chile out of cans and complained about women in self pity in the wee hours. At six o'clock in the morning, the Sons drove to their homes to recuperate. As for the Sons of Bunyan, all the above accurately describes our annual fires except the chile was always homemade by Patsy Avery and we didn't drive home afterward. Our meetings were always on Friday nights and after a day of recuperating we celebrated the Northern New Years' Eve at Patsy's Bar with noisemakers, dancing and the frivolity of renewed friendship.

Hmmm. At least I thought he could have used The Sons Of Bunyan. I told the High Bun of the book and he said in a royal proclamation, "We're honored."

At the tent Garrison liked short intros. What was I to say to welcome him? I simply said in one of my intros, "Garrison Keillor is our Mark Twain." He is. Every year he brought a different cast of singers and band. He was a guaranteed sellout. We were guaranteed an afternoon and night full of laughter and stories.

It was the ultimate honor for us to host his private celebration of the 25th anniversary of his radio show *Prairie Home Companion*. He told the audience, "I was thinking of where I would like to celebrate the anniversary. I decided there is no better place than Big Top Chautauqua."

It could have been at the Fitzgerald Theatre in St. Paul, Town Hall in New York, The Royal Palladium in London; anywhere in the world it would have been enthusiastically welcomed. He chose "The Carnegie Hall of Tent Shows."

Glenn Yarbrough

So here we are, my brother Mark "Pete" Nelson and I standing in the pews watching Glenn Yarbrough's soundcheck in the late afternoon of another gorgeous northern Wisconsin day, sidewalls open to the greenery. So here we are introducing ourselves, sitting and talking to Glen.

Meeting someone who has meant so much to your career and music opens itself first with the voice, a voice you've listened to innumerable times on LP's. It's warmth to hear, especially with Glenn who such has an incredible tenor solo voice that fronted The Limelighters' sound beginning in the 1960s. The original Limelighters included Alex Hassilev on banjo and Lou Gottlieb on standup bass. Alex was fluent in several languages and played the old Pete Seeger 5-string style which is akin to frailing. Lou was a one-of-a-kind musicologist, humorist and arranger. I wish to high humor I could have been in the same room with Lou once in my life. I encourage you to look back and listen to their records if you've never heard them.

Our tent was Glenn's first stop on a new tour. Traveling with Glenn was Dick Foley, a founding member of The Brothers Four, yet another of the groups I was inspired by. They started in 1957 and three years later released "Greenfields," their major hit.

I had seen Glenn at the University of North Dakota in 1965 in concert and after the concert I stood in line for an autograph and a quick word. I passed him the sheet music to one of my songs for him to check out, he said he would look at it. The song I chose out of my song bag sucked. It was called "Yesterday, Tomorrow and Today." It was a three-verse-and-a-chorus abomination full of trite lyrics and the melody ran like maple syrup. Oh, well. I mentioned Rod McKuen, whose songs I really liked. Glenn said Rod was his neighbor in Hollywood and he would show the song to Rod. Rod wrote me a letter thanking me for the comments on his songs. McKuen's poems are mostly sappy but his songs are solid. The spring after I flew to Los Angeles to see Rod perform at the Troubadour, a legendary folk club that hosted and still presents top shelf folk singers and comedians.

Backstage Big Top after the soundcheck I had the chance to sit with Glenn and light into questions on his career during and after the Limelighters. He left the group at their peak, bought a sailboat and sailed the world for years before launching a solo career. He had looked over our brochure and asked about my story. He could tell I'd been around. I let loose the basics and then handed him a couple of my CD's, one of which was *Keeper Of The Light*. It didn't connect with me that a sailor would light up at the mention of a lighthouse.

Glenn went off to dinner and when he arrived back for the show he came straight at me and said, "I want to talk to you about a years-old dream of mine, a project I've wanted to make happen. My plane doesn't leave until late tomorrow afternoon, how about breakfast?"

"My pleasure."

After introducing the concert, I stood in the wings for a bit shaking my head in disbelief that the voice was here with us. At that time my habit was to walk outside to the tent back to the blues (the bleachers, remember?), and sit in the last row with that grand view of the tent, the crowd and the stage. It was a wonderful concert; Glenn ending it with his solo hit "Baby The Rain Must Fall."

I chose the Pier Restaurant in Bayfield for breakfast, hoping that old corner table closest to the lake would be open. It was. Big round booth table. There was room for the stories that were about to be laid out. We met there at ten and the fun began.

Glen started with telling me he had listened to the CD's, especially *Keeper of The Light*. As a sailor, he'd always loved lighthouses and imagined the lives of the keepers and their families living on the water, throwing a light. "In fact," Glenn continued, "I've built a new house on an island in Mexico and its feature is a lighthouse tower where I sit to gather myself. You should come down and see it. Stay awhile." "Wow! You know I'd love to." "But to get to the dream, I'm looking for a writer to write the script. It's the story of a man sitting solo day after day in the tower, living at the light, dramatically telling his observations of his life and the world. I'd play the keeper, a part I know I was made for. Do you have the time to write it for me? I'm offering the job to you."

A sickly, dreaded feeling arose in my gut immediately. It was 2004 and I was dead heat into writing my Minnesota show for the sesquicentennial. I knew there was no way I could say yes. I had to say no to Glenn Yarbrough and to a project I'd die to be able to do on a subject I know so well. I'm thinking here's a national chance. Red flags were waving all along the main street of my inner parade. Had I finally learned the meaning of the word no? Yes.

"Glenn, I can't do it. Only because of my new show. I will always regret this. Maybe someday." Glenn nodded. I was honored, I told him, that he liked my music and thought me worthy of taking to the playwright's task of his lighthouse show.

Breakfast arrived and I began questions about the Limelighters and every famous folk singer and group that came to mind. Phil Ochs. The Chad Mitchell Trio (whom I hadn't yet met), Erik Darling, Ian and Sylvia, Bob Gibson, his opinion of The Kingston Trio. What were the major recording companies like to work with? How much creative control did you have? It was all inside news to me, he knew everybody.

He answered my wondering about why he left the Limelighters. "Money was the first reason, missing money, shady accounting. Incompatibility with Alex and impatience with the relentless touring. After Lou died, Alex and I had a long legal fight over ownership of the name Limelighters. I gave up. It wasn't worth it in the end." I remembered hearing a quote from some famous rocker, "The music business is full of greed, lies, ego, slime and conniving– and that's the good part."

For nearly three hours I had such a morning glory full of stories to remember. Glenn and I shook hands and fare-thee-welled. He again extended the invitation to come stay at his place in Mexico. I, of course, answered, "I'd love to."

I'm wondering now if he ever got the show written and performed and if maybe, just maybe, the invitation would still be open. My "no" is one of the great missed opportunities of my life. I'm looking for Glenn Yarbrough's address.

Greg Brown

I first heard Greg at The Blue Whale Coffee House on the campus of the University of Wisconsin–Green Bay. Lost Nation was the warm-up band. He gave me his album *Iowa Waltz*; I heard a dozen songs I wished I'd written.

Greg's voice sounds like it's coming up from under the bridge. He has the dark snarl of truth. It's a voice that matches his songs or is it his songs match his voice? As far as I can hear he is one of America's truest songwriters and it was a pleasure to bring him back to the Big Top year after year after year after year. Of all our guest artists, Greg has played the tent more than any. The son of a preacher man, poet, tattler of secret loves and hiding places, he tattoos his songs on the audience.

If you were to walk blind into the tent before a show, you'd know it was a Greg Brown concert by the scent of patchouli oil. Take a look around and you'd see tracks of Birkenstocks, Subarus and Volvos loaded with kayaks, canoes and bicycles. His warmup for the show was a few throws of his fly rod in the backlot grass, and a quick swig of something made in Kentucky. He ambled to his chair on stage. With the tasty licks of Bo Ramsey on guitar, the tent was his tabernacle.

Where is that song he wrote for Carolyn?

Stage Lines

My CD comes with my money back guarantee: Buy it and if you don't like it, try and get your money back!.

Man, when God put a mouth on your face, He forgot to back it up and couple it to your brain. (Daddy Joe talking to Traveler in the railroad show *On The Velvet*)

OK everybody, before the show begins, remember you're up north now; it's time to check for ticks on the person seated next to you. Don't want no Lyme's Disease. Doesn't have to be your spouse. A stranger is more fun.

If you don't like this show, I'll mow your lawn with my teeth.

John Hartford

Song for the Riverman

He was a banjo pickin' fiddler he was more'n a little screwy
He was born to the River Mississippi in St. Louie
Where the river makes a bow the boats in tow
He started paddle-wheelin' music in the flow

I come to get to see him on the Cincinnati levee
In 1988 at Tall Stacks all the old
Steamboat captains shook his hand
And the stories turn about like a wheel

John John Missouri man stole upriver and away he ran
Banjo fiddle and guitar in hand
Clip clop cloggin' on the plywood
Word movies wound around his strings
You know who it is when he sings
He's gone downriver he was one of a kind still
Gentle On My Mind"

The Delta Queen backin' out for a trip upriver
Overnight excursion to Pittsburgh
John stopped his song in the middle of a verse
And he said to the crowd won't you listen to her

There's no sweeter music made
Than a steamboat whistlin' in the summer fog
In the O-Hi-O River trade
She soon disappeared in the starlit night

John rolled his derby and bowed
Then he turned again to his banjer and the mic
And he come back in on the very same word
Of the song he was singin' 'bout the steamboat days

About the ports of call and Captain Way
And the deckhands and the pilothouse
And "hangin' out by the old cookstove
With the `Steamboat Whistle Blues'"   wn

I want to tell you first hand, close ear to it, my lucky history to come to know (a long time ago) the music and riversoul of the late, great, incredibly talented and wonderfully goofy singer/songwriter...fiddler...guitar player and banjoist...storyteller and historian...John Hartford. I first laid ears on him on the *Smothers Brothers Comedy Hour* on TV and heard "Gentle On My Mind" on the radio. Then I bought the records.

I played his songs for years with musical partners in the Lost Nation String Band in the corners of every northern Wisconsin bar from here to closing time. To book him and watch him and listen to him perform at Big Top Chautauqua, under the big canvas tent, was perfect. It was a boatman's setting for a John Hartford performance, the big tent the sail, the music the wind. The first time he came solo. John's bus pulled up, he walked out in his black vest, pockets full of 3 x 5 cards. He was always taking notes on cards for new songs, jokes, stories, of places and people he met. I was aboard John's bus an hour once as John read randomly from those cards. As he walked towards the tent his signature derby was tilted on his head as crooked as the licks he plays. That was July 30, 1994.

I guess the thumb and fingers of one hand will add up to how many times I saw him live, though my first try goes away back to 1968, when as a college student with an office in a booking agency in Minneapolis, I tried to book a midwest tour featuring John and a comedian ventriloquist (black man with a white doll). The tour didn't happen but I still have the giant poster sent me, "John Hartford is Gentle On Your Mind." Yes, he still is. I can remember exactly where I was when I first heard his mega-hit, "Gentle On My Mind" recorded by Glen Campbell. Glen, whose *Goodtime Hour* was the Smothers Bros' summer replacement, featured John sitting beside him every show picking and singing a song or two. Ooowee..who writes lyrics like that? Nobody I know. John Hartford gave my songwriting soul the go of anything goes.

In 1988 I finally met him in Cincinnati at Tall Stacks, the steamboat rally where as a licensed pilot and riverman and famous guy, he was known by everyone, the headline performer on the levee. Shortly after he began to play, the *Delta Queen*, one of John's favorite boats, blew her whistle and backed out for an overnight excursion to Pittsburgh. John stopped in the middle of a song and said to us all. "Listen...there is no sound in the world making more beautiful music than that." We sat there a good while, thousands of us, watching and listening until her whistle disappeared up river in the Ohio River darkness. John came back in with the very next word of the song he was singing.

On his last visit here Betty Ferris projected pictures from his book, *Steamboat In A Cornfield,* on the big screen while he picked and sang, kick-dancing on the plywood, floating out in the back-history-waters of his storytelling.

Funny. It was a teacher of his named Miss Ferris that set his steamboat soul wheeling. He was a Mark Twain of river lore, having earned his pilot license. He worked a time at the wheel.

I never could sit during a performance of such a man as he was to me. I'd sit on the backrow bleachers and have the audience in view to the spotlight, get up and walk the grass out back, looking through the folded sidewall, circling the tent and jigging a step in pure joy. His attitude was so wonderfully unique. I cherish a photo taken of John and me in the lot.

The show being over, John came backstage and thanked me and autographed my favorite LP of his, *Morning Bugle.*

He wrote in his flourishing artistic hand– "Warren, thanks for the hospitality and your Great Tent."

He packed quickly and wondered about payment. Carolyn was on the spot with his check. I think it was for $2,500, a steal. John looked at the check and said, "I need to be paid in cash." It wasn't a lack of trust, he just wanted cash. We didn't have enough. Carolyn scrambled, bagged our ticket moneys and went to Jerry Carlson to borrow the concessions and bar money. She came back with a stack of bills, plenty of ones and more ones. For the next fifteen minutes or so we watched John, peering over the glasses at the end of his nose, counting it out to the penny on the table...one thousand sixteen, one thousand seventeen, one thousand...and so on. Whatever it took, it just gave me more time with John but it was a little wonderfully weird to see the famous man licking his counting thumb and not his fiddle.

John has pulled out from the dock of this Earth. John Cowan Hartford born Dec. 30 1937, died June 4, 2001. He was and still is at the top of my musical hero list. He loved our tent and playing on *Tent Show Radio*. We loved him.

After he passed we did a tribute show and booked his son Jamie to play a set with us and then close the show. Jamie's music is electric but he knew the lilt of his dad's songs and had the Hartford voice. Bless your memory John, music-wizard man that you were.

My favorite John Hartford story: John was playing a festival and after his set a young woman walked up to him at the stage and said, "I wish you'd play something we know so we can tell if you're any good or not."

Johnny Cash and June Carter

Guess who's comin' to town? At a spring board meeting in 1997, I closed the agenda with my usual updates on the coming summer, who's coming, what's up? Carolyn and I had a great secret we'd held until the moment.

I opened with "I've never been so excited. On the third Tuesday and Wednesday in June we are going to spend $30,000 a night. I know that's the most we've ever paid for an act but don't worry." All heads slowly turned towards me. I paused to build suspense. "Ladies and Gentlemen, Big Top Chautauqua is proud to present Johnny Cash and June Carter." I've never seen such instant wide grins of board members. There was no doubt this was a coup for the Big Top.

The setup for a show like this is a sight to see in a venue the size of ours compared to major arenas. Johnny's troupe asked for local volunteer wannabe roadies to help unload the semi. In come the amp racks, drum kit, instruments, sometimes their own sound board. In Cash's show his longtime piano player, "Earl the Pearl" Poole Ball travels with his own white grand piano. Gary Schlichting, our piano tuner, was ready when it was rolled into place. (Gary has been with us the whole time we've had our own baby not-so-grand piano.)

The sidewalls were tied up at stage left, ramp folded out, stage set. There was a huge problem on the big day. It was pouring rain. The top soaked and it was leaking over the stage.

Rain, rain go away I prayed to the tent show gods. Dreaded thought begins to rise that it is possible, if it continues, the show will be canceled. Johnny's personal manager, Lou Robbins doesn't yet say so, but the crew, looking at the water dripping on the stage near the electrical cords, amps and mics, hint. We are, of course, sold out both nights. We do not want to deal with refunds and the loss of profit. And we want to hear Johnny Cash and June Carter.

Another miracle. About an hour before the show the rain began to let up and then stopped entirely. My prayers were answered.

Tickets were $55-45-35 for this show. BTC has since made that a regular for some of the big shows. Indeed BB King tickets were more than double that amount. This may be the time to tell you what I've told locals for years about ticket prices for the big acts coming in. People will say or think–"They must be making a lot of money on these shows." Untrue. Take the Johnny Cash show. He has over a dozen people in his troupe. He has the expenses of two buses and a full-length semi plus drivers. He has 16 hotel rooms for 3 nights to pay for. He has a personal manager and agent. Usual percents are 15% for manager and 10% for agents. I would guess that he, at most, comes out with $3,000 for one night. Chautauqua's profit? If there are 800 people paying an average $45/ticket, the ticket income would be $36,000. The cost of this show was the $30,000 fee plus, probably $2,000 for hospitality and other Rider items, leaving $4,000 as "profit" for the show. However, we have calculated the year around expenses for BTC (insurance, staff, equipment, advertising, taxes, etc.) to be paid from the summer profits amount to over $10,000 / summer-show-day. That $6,000 difference must be made up in sponsorships, donations, merchandise sales, grants, etc.

To those who mentioned the ticket price to me I said– "OK, you want to see Johnny Cash live, let's say in Minneapolis. You fill up your car with gas. You reserve a hotel room in the Cities. You pay for your meals and your gas on the way home. You pay for your ticket that would be at least what you pay at BTC. Add it up. What a deal. What a once in a lifetime experience it is to see him in your own backyard."

Johnny stayed in the bus until the minute before the show started. The ten-foot walk to the backstage was roped off. June and their daughter came backstage early to hang out and talk with us.

At 8:15 I peeked out at the crowd. You could feel the energy and excitement. This was Johnny Cash come to town. I walked out for the "Good evening Wide Awake Citizens," thanked all for coming and saluted the sponsors for the help in making the show possible. I had been told I would not be introducing Johnny. His band would play a song to warm up and settle in the crowd. I told the show goers that the Johnny Cash show would start in 10 minutes, still time to run out for a beer or popcorn. How many theatres allow you to bring in food and drink?

Only our stage manager, Lisa, and Carolyn and I were allowed in the backstage area a minute before Johnny walked out of his bus. There he was. He shook my hand. I haven't washed that hand since. I welcomed him to Big Top Chautauqua. He's a railroad nut so I asked him if he had noticed my caboose in Washburn on the drive over. He said he did. "You're a lucky man to have your own caboose."

Johnny walked the steps up to the stage entrance, standing at the curtain waiting for one of his band members to bring him out. I remember walking past him, looking up and seeing the man in black standing with his hands folded ready to go on. It took my breath away, a small smile rising out of my soul. He stepped to the stage, the audience immediately standing with a long ovation.

The famous bump bumpa bump bumpa guitar intro began, Johnny with his guitar slung over his shoulder in his signature stance for a song. "I hear that train a comin', comin' round the bend..." The crowd went nuts.

John played a few songs solo and then brought out his wife June Carter, daughter of Maybelle Carter of the legendary Carter family. They sang several songs together and then Johnny introduced his band and June, leaving the stage to give her 15 minutes of the show. She told a story of knowing Elvis and sang a song she wrote about Elvis and her. Johnny came back on. Before the last song and his encore he thanked the crowd and BTC and said-"This is a beautiful area. Please bring me back." I seconded the motion to myself. Yes, how about next year and the year after and the year after.

The show was all we hoped and more. I could see up close Johnny was not feeling well but it wasn't apparent in his performance. After the encore he immediately was escorted back to his bus, disappointing a hundred fans that were waiting at the backstage tent entrance for autographs and a close-up glimpse of the great Man in Black.

The bus carrying Johnny drove off into the night and the crew wound the cables and loaded the semi.

We had miraculously been given permission to record the evenings for *Tent Show Radio*. The stipulation was that we would record multitrack, they would take the tape back to Los Angeles and choose the songs we could broadcast, mixing them in their studio. They gave us five of Johnny's songs and all of June's solo time at no royalty cost.

Carolyn and I spent a good deal of time with Johnny's manager Lou Robbins during the two days at the picnic tables in the concessions tent. Talking show business, Lou told me he had been the personal manager of the original

Kingston Trio and that he had been with Johnny for several years.

One week later, I got a call from Lou. He said the tapes were in the studio. Then he added a possibility that stood me up. If the recordings were good they would release a live album, *Johnny Cash Live At Lake Superior Big Top Chautauqua*. Imagine! I was beside myself, called Carolyn while dancing around my living room. This would put us on the world map. I awaited word from Lou.

He called back two weeks later sadly informing me that the recording was clean but Johnny's voice was not up to it. I thanked Lou for the possibility as my heart sank to the bottom. Only if.

Lou had also told me Johnny would be recording a new album in Nashville and invited me to send a song of mine for Johnny's consideration. Why oh why oh why didn't I jump on it. I finally chose a railroad tune of mine, "Night Train Lulla-Bye Bye." As I was ready to mail it off to Lou, Johnny collapsed on stage in Michigan five months after playing here. Only if. It's hard for me to even think about the missed opportunity to send the song to John. After he recovered somewhat he recorded the new album. I missed my chance to retire on a songwriter's royalty. It's painful to remember it. It's more than painful to remember it. It wasn't the first time I'd failed myself in being invited to send my songs off to Nashville. My butt is permanently bruised from kicking myself so the regret is with me for life.

I wasn't the only one around here kicking himself. Dozens of locals told me later they couldn't believe they didn't drive the ten miles to see Johnny Cash and June Carter at the Big Top.

What if? What will never be forgotten to those of us who were there is the echo of Johnny's voice at Chautauqua.

There is no doubt the Cash's enjoyed their time here. In his book *Cash: The Autobiography* Johnny gave five good paragraphs to the two days they stayed at the Chequamegon Hotel and played the Big Top. In the chapter called "The Road Again," he tells of relaxing on the porch of a beautiful hotel in Ashland, Wisconsin on the shore of Lake Superior, gazing out into the morning. He notices the house next door coming to life for the new working day, the lights coming on around eight o'clock, "by which time I'd been up almost three hours." He describes the steep pitched roof built for the snowfall, the chain link—fence and "a dog roaming back and forth along the fence, trying to find a way out, no special breed, just doggy-looking dog."

The poet in Johnny Cash is coming alive to another day. I imagine him sitting on the porch scratching notes for his book. What a life to draw from for an autobiography. He mentions he likes it when the road takes him places he's never been before. He found the people "really friendly around here." And he goes right to the subject of cheese; I guess Wisconsin remains synonymous with cheese, although he writes that Wisconsin has no more cheese than anywhere else he's been. "I like Wisconsin cheese better than the stinky stuff in Europe. Things that smell bad as if they'd been dead too long don't turn me on."

John and June apparently rate a city first by whether or not it is a "Wal-Mart town." If it's big enough, it'll be a "Wal-Mart town." They guess it is and sure enough during their stay June is seen at Ashland's Wal-Mart. Talk around town spread like flies on a picnic. I heard of the double-takes shoppers took while June wandered the store, talking to anyone who approached her. She signed an autograph for everyone who asked. "She's just like a regular person" was the word about town. Well, not quite.

The manager of the Chequamegon Hotel offered to take Johnny Cash fishing on Lake Superior. "He knows where they hide." J.C., our hero, hoped he could take him up on that but he didn't. "As usual I have to guard my resources and energies...make sure I get my afternoon nap...then I'll be able to give my audience my best." It's not unusual to find that entertainers are fishing fanatics. When B.B. King played the Big Top, he had his grandson out on the dock during the day trying to catch fresh fish. When I was invited on B.B.'s bus after the show I brought along my Fishtar to show him, encouraged by his road crew who saw it and said to me "B.B. needs one of these." B.B. told me if I sent him one he'd play it on Letterman's show. Haven't sent him one yet but like John Gray, guitar maker and partner in the invention of the Fishtar said, "He's still alive." One more thing I really oughta do. The boys in The Del McCoury's Band are fond of the hook and line and when Ronnie McCoury saw the Fishtar he said," "There's your fame and fortune." Why am I writing a book and not manufacturing Fishtars?

I'm writing a book because it makes fine hours live again and I'm at my memorywars to tell of the great times under the Big Top. There has not been a finer hour than the hour watching Johnny Cash and June Carter sing on our stage. Rest in peace Mr. and Mrs. Cash. We are beyond grateful for your two days with us.

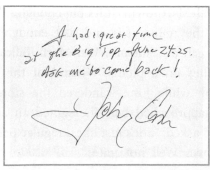

The Kingston Trio

The news overnight as I write this is that the Kingston Trio was given a Lifetime Achievement Grammy Award for their incredible history of recording, touring and changing the entire face of American music beginning in 1957. You can make that the world. It's a shame that Dave Guard and Nick Reynolds, co-founders of the group, and Dave's replacement, John Stewart, are not alive to see the day. The Trio did receive a Grammy in 1958, the first year of the awards, for Best Country and Western Act, which they never were. There was no category for folk music, so in honor of "Tom Dooley," they were presented the Grammy. They received another in 1960. The Kingston Trio is the only group ever to have four albums in the top ten at one time. Elvis and The Beatles never accomplished that.

I met the Kingston Trio on the radio and on the vinyl of their first record in the old High Fidelity days. It changed my life. I was fourteen. My high school buddies and I, like thousands of others, formed a folk group in the early sixties, wearing striped shirts, learning all their songs and stealing all the jokes and patter they spoke between songs. We gigged at FFA banquets, birthday parties, political banquets, anywhere anyone would invite us.

In many ways, my entire career is due to them. I can to this day sing along with every one of the songs they recorded. Even my discovery that I was a songwriter is due to them. I woke one adolescent morning, turned on the radio, "Tijuana Jail" was playing, I sat up in bed and instantly knew, "I'm a songwriter."

I only saw them live once in my life until Chautauqua. It was in Minneapolis during the middle sixties when John Stewart was with them. John left the group in 1967, Nick leaving not long after. Bob Shane kept the Trio going. It was past time for the folk craze. The music world was following the Beatles and the British invasion.

At the Big Top, another big dream for me came true. I booked the Trio for the tent in 1997, the fortieth anniversary of their founding. Nick Reynolds had returned to the group. George Groves had been on the road with them for years, helping keep up the sound. I booked John Stewart for a Friday show before their Saturday concert, hence calling up a reunion. It was one of the highlights of my life to be able to step to the stage and introduce them.

I was beside myself at the Duluth airport when they stepped off the plane. Nick and Bob live, in person! The drive back to Bayfield was most memorable. I immediately told them of my fanatic fanship and the influence they had on me. I know they'd been told that a million times. After reading our brochure and listening to my babbling, the conversation eased into friendship. Excuse me, I have to walk around, my soul is shaking as I write this. Be right back.

John's solo career took off after he left the Trio. He wrote "Daydream Believer," a megahit for the Monkees and John's bank account. He was one of America's all-time great songwriters in my opinion, unsung in popular music history. Before he joined the Trio, he had written the song "Molly Dee" for their album *Here We Go Again*. His father was a racehorse trainer and looked a bit down on young John's enthusiasm to become a singer/performer. John told us that back in the sixties his Dad was making six thousand a year. At one point he told John his guitar playing was driving him crazy, "Why don't you take it outside?" John sat in the car daily playing and writing songs. When his royalty check came from the Trio, it was for sixteen thousand dollars." "You can come back in the house now, son." An off the charts highlight of mine during John's second appearance at Chautauqua, piggybacked again with the Trio, was the call to join John on stage singing his song, "Anna On A Memory" with him. I had played him a tape of Lost Nation and me covering the song. "Best I ever heard," John said to me. "You're singing it with me." Excuse me; I have to take a walk. I'll be right back.

The house was sold out (a title for one of their albums) for the Trio's concert. They sounded as good as ever, performing their hit songs as well as other gems from their immense repertoire. "Oh, a tent," Bob exclaimed when he first stepped to the microphone. I was only one of hundreds that night that could sing along with everything.

I got to hang with the Kingston Trio before, during and after the show. Bob, Nick and George were in attendance at John's show Friday night. Saturday I picked up Nick from the hotel and drove him to the tent. We stopped at Patsy's Bar for one on the way. The small crowd there was amazed. There's a great photo of Nick and Patsy and me on my wall. I told Nick that when I was just starting out with my folk group, I once carried an album jacket to my barber and told him to cut my hair exactly like Nick Reynolds. The barber said to me, "He doesn't have any hair." It was kind of a flat top heinie.

I brought them back in 1988 with John for a two-show run. We staged our first 4th of July show, a matinee, a hard sell on picnic and parade day, but they packed the tent again. On the night of the 4th, Chris Engfer and I were hanging out with the trio watching the fireworks from the deck at the Pier in Bayfield. Just hanging out with my heroes, the ultimate night.

The next day I had arranged for an interview session at the Hotel Chequamegon in Nick's room. They all agreed to come and be interviewed for *Tent Show Radio*. I couldn't get the DAT recorder to work. John and I fiddled with it but, alas, I missed the hour of a lifetime. Bob Shane agreed to a telephone interview later. It's on tape and a treasure to me. Bob Shane declared he had sung "Tom Dooley" and "Scotch and Soda" 10,000 times in his career.

I kept in touch with Bob. He sent me an undistributed VHS of a pilot TV show they had made which never made it to television. They played three eligible bachelors, with Bob in the lead role as a dude that runs a ranch for a banker. During the show, out of the blue they would break into a song. Wonderfully weird, especially the scene by the pool. If you want to borrow it sometime, OK. But it must be back to me by 6 the next night.

Shortly after, Nick retired again. John kept writing, recording and touring. When Bob left the group, the originals were gone. It was sad news to know Nick and John both passed away within a month of each other in the winter of 2008.

I play their old vinyl albums more than ever. Any old Kingston Trio albums you have around and don't want, send them to me.

If you're looking for re-releases of the Trio and a huge list of other folk performers including John Stewart, check out Rediscover Music at www.rediscovermusic.com. Tell them Warren sent you. Their catalogue is overwhelming for old folk acts in addition to classic recordings of country, blues and jazz singers.

Excuse me; I have to go drive around for a while.

Mason Williams

Do you believe in what you feel, and in the love of time?
Are you the same man inside and out, do you speak your mind?
You've got to hold on to the truth now, when I throw you this line
You've got to catch up to yourself, when you get behind
                From Mason Williams' song, "Godsend"

People often ask me what my favorite song is, I guess expecting me to reach into my own songbag and pull one out. I answer easily, "Godsend," by Mason Williams.

The one someone in this book of my memorywars that I would like to assign myself to write a biography of someday is the Renaissance man, Mason Williams, although he already has written an Autobiography, the history of the cars he's owned.

He has been a great influence in my creative working life. Mason Williams is my mentor. I am incredibly fortunate to come to be a friend of Mason's, thanks to the Big Top and earlier contact with him in Colorado. To get to know a man personally who has been your hero and finding that the man more than equals his work is a true joy.

Mason is best known for his Grammy Award winning instrumental "Classical Gas." I first saw and heard Mason on the Smothers Brothers Comedy Hour; he was the head writer. He won Emmys for his work leading the show. No matter where I found myself, every Sunday night I somehow located a TV to catch the CBS series. In many ways the show changed the screen of television. The reasons for their cancellation by CBS would be ridiculous now. They aired strong controversial political opinions with satire. Along with the sketches, the hour presented performers such as Jim Morrison, Pete Seeger in his first appearance since being blacklisted in the McCarthy era, John Hartford, Glenn Campbell, Steve Martin (who performed with Mason at clubs; and Mason eventually asked Tom Smothers to hire him as a writer for the Comedy Hour), and a wide contemporary parade of others who had no other television stage to play.

I began to buy Mason's records and books. Listening to his album *Music* started most of my traveling mornings. I've played *Music* hundreds of times and to this day it has no scratches. It scratched my creative itches.

The first time I saw him perform was at Marvelous Marv's, a live music club in Denver. I'd guess the year was 1974. After the show I gave him the leather-writing satchel I had carried for ten years. It was custom made for me by an old shoemaker, road and mind worn, the closest possession of my life. Twenty years later he gave it back to me.

In 1995 I finally got to book him at the Big Top for our *Whitefish Livers' Big Bluegrass Saturday*. Cooks from Maggie's of Bayfield fried up whitefish livers for the showgoers. I loved the look of outright fear of those who had never tasted or even heard of whitefish livers as food. We converted several to the club including Mason who said, "Maybe we should also pour beer into the whitefish and sell whitefish beer bladders."

He came with an all-star band including fiddler Byron Berline, guitarist Rick Cunha, banjo man John Hickman, mandolinist Jerry Mills, drummer Hal Blaine and bassist Doug Heywood. It was another rare rare night under the canvas. I had the pleasure of singing "Godsend" with the band. Jack Gunderson sang harmony. This was Mason's bluegrassy ensemble that had regularly been playing with symphony orchestras across the country. Whatever he puts the hand of his mind to bends his way in sound. It was a front porch hoedown orchestra. Mason told our audience,

"There are only two kinds of music– love songs and chicken music. Tonight we're going to play some chicken music!"

A sidelight delight for me was driving Hal Blaine to the Duluth airport the next morning. Hal, from Hollywood, has played concerts and sessions with everybody from Frank Sinatra to the Mama's and Papa's to John Denver. In fact, he was John's drummer during all the recording and world touring in the years of John's stardom. Where was the tape recorder? I think of Hal's lifetime, having a back view of concerts and recording from his drum kits. If you still have your collection of LP's, check the credits. Hal's name is everywhere.

Mason has a comic mind that skips along all day with wonderful, odd observations and sidewinding conversation. He is a master at writing and composing in several genres. He is a master on the classical guitar. "Classical Gas" was composed in 1968. As Mason relates, "I didn't really have any big plans for it, other than to have a piece to play at parties when they passed the guitar around." "Classical Gas" is the most played instrumental in the history of radio. Think about it. He is Oregon's Music Laureate.

It was after a BCO performance in Portland, Oregon in 1995 that Mason invited me to come stay a night at his home in Eugene. He has a great room where all his stuff is filed and shelved. As a huge fan of the *Smothers Brothers' Comedy Hour*, it was a thrill for me to see the original scripts of the shows all in order. I opened the first one and noticed Mason's handwritten cue for Ed Sullivan to mention at the end of his show that a new show was coming right up on CBS. Wow!

What a hoot it was when I received a box containing 8-tracks of Music and LPs of *Of Time And Rivers Flowing* and various cassettes and CDs.

Mason returned twice to the tent. He came solo for the second performance, our Blue Canvas Orchestra was his band. Charts arrived weeks before the show. Ed Willett, Don Pavel and Severin Behnen made certain we were ready. Mason greatly appreciated and was delighted with Dr. Helmi Harrington, accordionist from Superior, WI. She drove at a moments notice from her accordion museum to perform in the show. At the rehearsals in the Spirit Cottage, I was beside myself.

In the winter before I brought him back the second time, I had mentioned his appearance to Ken Frazier, a great friend of mine and head librarian of the UW library system. I flipped out the idea that it would be grand for the University of Wisconsin's Parallel Press to print a new edition of *Them Poems*. *Them Poems* is a passel of hilarious ditties with such titles as "Them Duck Pluckers," "Them Toad Suckers," "Them Moose Goosers," "Them Beaver Cleavers." There are 20 or more. Ken printed the chapbook. I hope it's still available. Check out Mason's website: www.classicalgas.com.

Mason's last appearance at the tent was in 2008. This time he brought his longtime arranger and piano man Art Maddox along with Mark Schneider on bass and John Doan playing harp guitar. The concert was a live weaving of music into one sweet quilt of a night. Mason again invited me to sing "Godsend" on stage, this time solo, with him on guitar. The song transports me every time I sing it. I left the stage that night like a meteor just out looking around for a place to land.

Mason has mentioned lately that he is done doing shows out and about, not even his annual Christmas concert at home in Oregon. Say it ain't so, Joe. Like his "Road Song" quotes, "In good time, all good things must come to an end." I know he'll continue to write and record. At the top of his

Hollywood career he backed out and away from the LA glitz. He wrote, "Godsend" on his way out the door. He has stayed true to his genius. His gift lays out the widest and most delightful road of all creators whose paths I've followed.

For a while, Foggy Mountain Guitars was making a "Mason Williams Signature Line" of classical guitars. One was a replica of the guitar Mason wrote, "Classical Gas" on. Fabulous! Might try to get myself one of the few that got made and sold. Who knows? Maybe I'd write a piece on it to have something to play at parties when they pass the guitar around.

Dear Warren,
Traveling circuses were the roots of Zoos. Zoos happened in communities when traveling circuses went bankrupt and folded, often leaving the animals stranded. People put the animals in cages and pens at "zoos" to care for and feed them. They eventually got the idea to have people come see the animals in the cages lined around a promenade.
Big Top Chautauqua was like a zoo, except the animals were free to come and go! You and the band were in essence beneficiaries of a bankrupt circus; disguised as a traveling circus that brought the towns to you. An excellent switcheroo!

Mason Williams

Dear Mason,
Thank you. Now I know why I always bragged about Chautauqua being a National Wildlife Refuge.

Warren Nelson

The Nitty Gritty Dirt Band

It took me awhile but I finally got the Dirt Band to the tent in 2003. I'm a longtime fan. It's rare for a band to stay together as long as they have; they were formed in 1966. They recorded "Mr. Bojangles" in 1970. Guitarist/singer Jeff Hanna and drummer Jimmie Fadden have been the mainstays in the carrying on. In their first appearance Jimmy Ibbotson, a founding member, was with them. I was delighted to know John McEuen, another original had returned to the group. Bob Carpenter is keyboard man

My close connection to the band is with John, who has become a pal. John is one of the world's great multi-instrumentalists; on banjo he is a king of the strings. John came twice before I brought the band here, once with his son and the other with Jimmy Ibbotson and fiddler Vassar Clements. I followed them to another concert after they stood the Big Top, the highlight being a long van ride to a radio station to publicize the show. Time alone with performers I always wanted to meet was story time. The Dirt Band is another of the groups that fits the tent–wheels on the wagon, starlight on the ground.

MY 50 FAVORITE GUEST ARTISTS–
ALL 72 OF THEM

The Kingston Trio
The Chad Mitchell Trio
Bill Monroe and the Bluegrass Boys
Del McCoury Band
Charlie Byrd
Judy Collins
Meridel LeSeuer
The Nitty Gritty Dirt Band
Kate MacKenzie & Stoney Lonesome
Carmel Quinn
Garrison Keillor
Johnny Cash and June Carter
John Hartford
Tom Paxton
Bela Fleck and the Flecktones
Robert Bly
The Smothers Brothers
Mason Williams
Willie Nelson
Bob Gibson
Sam Bush
The Nat'l Shakespeare Company
Marie Jones' play *Gold in the Streets*
The Different Drums of Ireland
Japanese Acrobatic Dance Troupe
Tomas Kubinek
C. Willi Myles
Tommy Emmanuel
Doc Watson
Merle Haggard
Kate & Anna McGarrigle
John Stewart
Michael Kotik
Jimmy Martin
Taj Mahal
Gayle LaJoye

Greg Brown
Iris DeMent
Bill Holm
Koerner, Ray and Glover
Arlo Guthrie
Myron Floren
Riders in the Sky
Natalie MacMaster
Earl Scruggs
BB King
Don McLean
BeauSoleil avec Michael Doucet
The New Christy Minstrels
Leo Kottke
Glenn Yarbrough
Chinese Acrobats
Richie Havens
Cheney & Mills
Peter Rowan & Tony Rice
Nanci Griffith
Hot Club of Cow Town
Michael Martin Murphy
Bill Miller
Cherryholmes
Second City
Free Hot Lunch
Roy Clark
Gordon Lightfoot
John McCutcheon
Luther Allison
Leon Russell
Phoebe Legere
Michael Stanwood
Paul Schurke
John Sebastian
Corky Siegel

THE MASTERS

I hereby nominate two of all the performers or groups that played BTC in my time for the Top of the Big Top Master Entertainer Award. We've had the best of the best singers/songwriters/bands/artists. This award is for entertainers in the classic sense from the great legacy of the American stage. The criteria are: timing, great presence from the first step into the lights to the end, presenting a show that brings years of professionalism to the moment, star power, a deep connection with the audience and for the audience a sense that you are front and center in a New York theatre.

It's the moment to bestow the prize. The nominees are: Carmel Quinn and The Smothers Brothers. The envelope please, the winners are: Carmel Quinn and The Smothers Brothers.

Carmel Quinn

Carmel Quinn has played more sold-out concerts at Carnegie Hall than any other performer. She came well known from the old sod of Ireland, soon appearing and winning on *The Arthur Godfrey Talent Scout's* radio program. She became a regular on the show and moved to TV with Godfrey. She has appeared on Broadway, traveled with numerous road shows, has recorded extensively, all the while traveling the world. In 1991 she was awarded the prestigious John F. Kennedy Award for excellence in her field.

And here she was at Big Top Chautauqua, The Carnegie Hall of Tent Shows. Jimmy Martin, Carmel's piano accompanist, first suggested to Carolyn that we bring Carmel. We knew Jimmy well from his shows at the tent with Jack Gunderson and Drew Jansen.

From the moment of her arrival at the tent there was the presence of a star. I wondered how it would feel to be so well known internationally and step to the stage with expectations high in the audience. She and Carolyn hit it off immediately, as did Carmel and I. When Carmel and I stood back of the curtain ready to go on I noticed the look of stage fright on her. Ah, so I wasn't alone in netting butterflies in the minute before showtime. She looked like a little girl about to step to the front of the class and present the first speech of her life.

Then she burst into the lights, and the shine of a true master graced our stage. Along with a sweet Irish voice Carmel is comedian excelsior. Carmel quipped to the audience, "I overheard someone before the show tonight say, 'Oh look, I though she was taller. Oh, I thought she was smaller. I thought she was... I thought she was dead!' " Carmel is still out trouping to this day.

The Smothers Brothers

"How in the world did you ever get the Smothers Brothers to come to Big Top Chautauqua?" I was asked on the night of their first appearance. "You call up their agent, make an offer and wait for the word. If you want them at your backyard birthday party, make an offer!"

Tommy and Dick, real life brothers, began in the late 50's being one of the acts that brought in the folk boom. Needing an audience, most of their albums were recorded live. They quickly rose to popularity on my record player. As a young entertainer I stole their jokes and songs. They helped teach me timing, to wait for the perfect second to deliver the punch line. In 1967 *The Smothers Brothers Comedy Hour* rose to the top of the ratings on Sunday night CBS television. It was a visionary show. I've written of it in my Mason Williams chapter, Mason being the head of the table of writers.

When I got to the tent in late afternoon, they were backstage talking to our crew. "My God," I exclaimed to myself, "they look just like the Smothers Brothers." Mason Williams had called Tommy when he heard they were coming to the Big Top. It was a letter of introduction for me to the Brothers and an honor. I wouldn't call it being star struck; it was comfortable, but once again I was beside myself looking at the scene. Up in the Spirit Cottage, after having dinner with them, we sat the hour before stage call talking of old folk acts. I had dozens of questions of whatever happened to whomever and they amusedly answered all. "Whatever became of Judy Henske? Where is Biff Rose? What was Jim Morrison like when he was on your show?"

The Smothers Brothers had the classic touch of vaudeville, a new age vaudeville with intermittent swipes at the politics of the day. If you're a Democrat, The Smothers Brothers speak and sing for you. Tommy would follow a joke with "For you Republicans, I'll speak a little slower." Dressed in tuxedos, they defined "class act." One of their routines was based on an old bit performed by George Burns and Gracie Allen on vaudeville stages.

They are not performing presently, but I hope not retired for good. If so, they will be remembered in show business history as one of the all-time greatest singing comedic acts. They were here and we were there.

Afterglow

*…there must have been some magic in that old
tent top they found…for when they raised it
on the hill folks began to come around….*
Frosty the Showman

AFTERGLOW

We never charged extra for the Northern Lights in the after show afterglow. Or the pure view of the summer stars. Or for the appearance of the occasional bear that was seen before the show grazing wild strawberries in the ski slope grass. As Iris Dement spoke from the piano, "I hope they reserved a seat for the bear!" In nights with the sidewalls open, and folks in the chairs, gin and tonic in hand, I took my stance leaning against the front-side entrance side pole and watched the audience lit by stage lights and gazing to the dark back end and up at the big blue top hovering in its circus hang over all.

It was always astounding when the artists would amble to the concessions stand after the show to sign CD's and meet and greet wide-eyed show-goers. Earl Scruggs, The Del McCoury Band, Nitty Gritty Dirt Band, Judy Collins, Mason Williams, Garrison Keillor—on and on, most all did so. Or Willie Nelson after his three-hour non-stop performance waiting at the door of his gurgling bus to sign autographs, arm around fans posing for the cameras. One dude had him sign his pickup truck in permanent ink. Probably never washed his truck again. Or John Hartford walking over to a fire my brother and his pals had lit away to the wood side, his derby hat cocked in the Hartford attitude. It was unreal to be so close to the stars under and over the canvas. I never tired of it.

The night slipped away as the cars drove out under the Mt. Ashwabay portal. Therene had locked up the merchandise shelves, the food and brew crew closed shop, Carolyn finished paying off the performers, the last of the T-Bar sippers headed to their cars, the very last of us sitting at the picnic tables in the dark. And then it was only me left there most nights. I'd stare at the tent looming like a great ship tied up for the night, the Big Dipper pouring an eternity in the moment. Laugh, oh yes, to myself. Satisfied. On the way to my car in the back lot, I'd first walk around the tent, patting the canvas, oh yeah, cheek to cheek. I'd kiss it and unclasp the back entrance and stare at the emptied hold. And sit in the bleachers with the ghosts of the crowd. Or stroll the aisle to the stage and stand amazed in my workplace thinking of new jokes for tomorrow night.

Ladies and Gentlemen...Wide awake citizens...did you hear the one about...

A native of Fairmont, Minnesota, Warren Nelson has been a professional entertainer since 1967. He is a tent show man. Lake Superior Big Top Chautauqua was his idea. His awards: voted Best Folk Musician by

Himself at his lake office
photo by c engfer

Wisconsin Trails Magazine; awarded an Honorary Doctorate of Humane Letters Degree by UW-Superior; elected a Fellow of the Wisconsin Academy of Sciences, Arts and Letters; named a co-recipient of the first ever History Award of the Wisconsin Historical Society; received with Big Top Chautauqua the Governor's Award in Support of the Arts; named 2007 Minnesotan of the Year by The Minnesota Territorial Pioneers. He lives in rural Washburn, Wisconsin with his caboose and his cat.

Warren Nelson Presents
A Producing and Performing Company
www.warrennelson.com

for purchasing products wholesale or retail
Books CDs DVDs

Sioux River Song Farm
PO Box 97
Washburn, WI 54891
orders@warrennelson.com

A Warren Nelson performance is a true delight as he dips into his song and story bag for material from his show business and writing career. His unique humor and wit spill into his concerts with a stage presence he was born with and has stepped surely to over the years. He brings to the footlights a well-earned reputation as a master entertainer.

Warren Nelson
Solo or with the Nelson Outfit
private affairs, concerts, festivals

for performance or commission
please contact
Warren Nelson Presents
PO Box 66
Washburn, WI 54891
info@warrennelson.com